SCIENTIFIC DISCVERIES

THAT BUILD TESTIMONIES AND STRENGTHEN FAITH

Dan is a trusted friend. I am grateful for the events that allowed our paths to cross. We found early in our friendship that we had much in common and could have great discussions regarding both religion and science.

As you may recall, in December of 1993, NASA corrected the Hubble Telescope's vision. At that time, as Dan and I marveled at the vistas that were being opened to us, many of our discussions centered on our wondrous God and His marvelous universe. I wholeheartedly recommend this book. Reading it will be like sitting with a great friend and opening your mind to the wonders and grandeur of God.

—Kent McDonald, inventor/consultant

SCIENTIFIC DISC⚛VERIES

THAT BUILD TESTIMONIES AND STRENGTHEN FAITH

DAN NEVILLE

Horizon
Springville, Utah

ISBN 13: 978-0-88290-965-3

Published by Horizon Books, an imprint of Cedar Fort, Inc., 2373 W. 700 S., Springville, UT 84663
Distributed by Cedar Fort, Inc., www.cedarfort.com

LIBRARY OF CONGRESS CATALOGING-IN-PUBLICATION DATA
Neville, Dan, 1948-
  Scientific discoveries that build testimonies and strengthen faith / Dan
Neville.
    p. cm.
  Includes bibliographical references and index.
  ISBN 978-0-88290-965-3 (acid-free paper)
  1. Religion and science. 2. Church of Jesus Christ of Latter-day
Saints--Doctrines. 3. Mormon Church--Doctrines. I. Title.
  BX8643.R39N48 2009
  261.5'50882893--dc22
                              2009009815

Cover design by Angela D. Olsen
Cover design © 2009 by Lyle Mortimer
Edited and typeset by Melissa J. Caldwell

Printed in the United States of America
10 9 8 7 6 5 4 3 2 1
Printed on acid-free paper

To Janine, the love of my life;
and to my amazing children, who have made life a remarkable adventure;
and finally, to my good friend Kent, who has a heart of gold.

Contents

Introduction

M any years ago, I began to have an interest in physics and cosmology. In my free time at home and while I traveled around the country on business and occasionally to Europe, I spent much of my travel-related airplane and hotel time studying aspects of physics as it pertains to the nature of the universe, its origin, structure, and space-time relationships. As I did so, I was enthralled. I became aware of both a universe and, more important, of a God that are amazing—far more amazing than I ever imagined.

Through the study of science, scripture, and words from latter-day prophets, my eyes were opened and my understanding increased. A couple of years ago I began putting my thoughts on paper, resulting in the writing of this book. It has been a magical journey of inspiration and learning for me. I hope some of that same magic and inspiration touches everyone who reads this work.

The following verse is familiar to most of you. If you are like me, sometimes we see things we are familiar with and just skip over them. I have read, reread, and pondered this inspired poem by William Wordsworth and urge you to do the same, as it has much to do with the message of this book.

Trailing Clouds of glory do we come . . .
Our birth is but a sleep and a forgetting;
The soul that rises with us, our life's star,
Hath had elsewhere its setting,

And cometh from afar;
Not in entire forgetfulness,
And not in utter nakedness,
But trailing clouds of glory do we come
From God, who is our home.[1]

Because we lived with God prior to our birth and entrance into mortality, and because we will have an *opportunity* to live with him afterwards, learning about God ought to be a lifelong pursuit for each of us. If we will follow that course, we will grow closer to Him, receive greater understanding, and have more reverence, respect, and love for Him. Assuming that the poet Wordsworth is right, that we came from God "trailing clouds of glory," we should also be able to learn more about ourselves, our character, and our potential as our understanding of God increases.

C. S. Lewis, one of the greatest writers and religious thinkers of the 20th century, penned the following regarding God and our relationship with Him: "God wills our good, and our good is to love Him . . . and to love Him we must know Him: and if we know Him, we shall in fact fall on our faces. If we do not, that only shows that what we are trying to love is not . . . God."[2]

The more we know about God, His creations, His abilities, and His character, the more *we* will be inclined to love Him and reverence Him; and, as Lewis says, "fall on our faces," that is, prostrate ourselves before Him. If we aren't learning more about God and growing closer to Him, "what we are trying to love is not . . . God."

A couple of years ago while I was attending a church meeting, the person conducting told the group that we should *not* seek to know the mysteries. I am not totally sure what he was referring to, but I do believe that the Lord's intent is to bless us with knowledge, which includes increasing our understanding of Him and His universe. All He requires from us is an open mind and a little effort (study and prayer).

The tenth chapter of the first book in the Book of Mormon includes an account with which many are familiar. At the beginning of his journey from Jerusalem into the wilderness, the prophet Lehi had a dream of the tree of life. Following his dream he predicted the Babylonian captivity of the people in Jerusalem and tells his family of the future coming of the "mortal" Messiah. Nephi, Lehi's son, after hearing his father's words, desires to see, hear, and know these things for himself. Nephi goes on to explain how such a thing is possible, an account that I believe is pertinent to each of us.

> 17 And it came to pass after I, Nephi, having heard all the words of my father, concerning the things which he saw in a vision, and also the things which he spake by the power of the Holy Ghost, which power he received by faith on the Son of God—and the Son of God was the Messiah who should come—I, Nephi, was desirous also that I might see, and hear, and know of these things, by the power of the Holy Ghost, which is the gift of God unto all those who diligently seek him, as well in times of old. . . .
>
> 18 For he is the same yesterday, today, and forever; and the way is prepared for all men . . . if it so be that they repent and come unto him.
>
> 19 For he that diligently seeketh shall find; and *the mysteries of God shall be unfolded unto them, by the power of the Holy Ghost,* as well in these times as in times of old, and as well in times of old as *in times to come* . . . (1 Nephi 10:17–19; italics added)

We have Nephi's promise, then, that the mysteries of God shall be unfolded to a person under the following conditions:

First, one must study and listen carefully, even as Nephi did to the words of his father. Nephi tells us that one must believe that it is truly possible to *see, hear,* and *gain* knowledge by the power of the Holy Ghost. He had faith that was turned into action. We, too, must have that kind of faith!

Then, Nephi explains that God is the same forever—it doesn't matter what age we live in. All mankind will be treated equally. So we can have confidence that each of us, as we sincerely approach the Lord, can receive inspiration the same as the prophets of old.

Third, in order to prepare to receive inspiration, Nephi instructs that men must first repent and humbly seek God.

Finally, we are given the great promise: We are told that once we have repented and come unto God, that He, through the Holy Ghost, will reveal His mysteries to us as we *diligently seek* to know them.

The father of modern physics also tells us how important it is that we seek to know the mysteries of the universe. In his autobiographical notes published in 1949, Albert Einstein said: "The fairest thing we can experience is the mysterious. It is the fundamental emotion which stands at the cradle of true art and true science. He who knows it not and can no longer wonder, no longer feel amazement, is as good as dead."[3]

My hope is that all who dig into this writing will find something of God and His mysterious universe that will fill them with wonder and amazement.

The word *seek,* as used by Nephi used, is full of subtleties. It intimates that both effort and desire are required along the way. As the great Galileo Galilei said, "You cannot teach a man anything; you can only help him to find it within himself."[4]

In ancient and modern times, God has opened the eyes of His children so that they might see and understand the wonders of His creations. Enoch, Abraham, Moses, Isaiah, John the Revelator, and Joseph Smith were blessed with knowledge that is just beginning to be understood by today's scientists. We live in a remarkable era, a time when many of the mysteries of God have been and are being revealed in both science and scripture.

Most of us, if the truth be known, are probably a little intimidated by the deluge of scientific knowledge that is *now* being poured out on mankind. For the past 4,500 years (from the time of Noah), the scientific and technological knowledge available to our ancestors was largely static. In fact, in Europe, during the Dark Ages, it even diminished over time. Gradually—after the Dark Ages, during the period known as the Renaissance—discovery and learning began to play a much larger part in society. Then, approximately 150 years ago, parallel with the restoration of the gospel through the prophet Joseph Smith, a scientific and technological renaissance was triggered; a virtual avalanche of knowledge began to fill the minds of men. It started a little slowly but has picked up tremendous momentum in the past 100 years. And even now a flood of knowledge and understanding is being poured out on the inhabitants of the earth. Of course, as members of The Church of Jesus Christ of Latter-day Saints, we believe that the scientific renaissance that has spread over the earth is part of and parcel to the restoration of God's earthly kingdom. Since scientific knowledge seems to have come hand in spiritual hand with blessings such as the restoration of the priesthood, the gospel, and the establishment of God's kingdom on the earth, don't we have some responsibility to gain an understanding of science just as we do of the scriptures? I believe that is what the Lord expects. We have been commanded to learn of things both "in heaven and in the earth, and under the earth" (D&C 88:79). Great blessings attend those who follow God's counsel.

One of the reasons for the study and research that led me to this writing was because I wanted to obtain a greater understanding of our remarkable universe. As I dedicated a good portion of the past ten years to that end, I became excited about my new found understanding, so much so that there were times when I could barely contain myself. I am certain there were many occasions when my family, friends, and business associates were just being patient and polite as I enthusiastically bombarded them with the things I was learning. I am grateful to them because I found that as I voiced my thoughts and heard their comments that I received even more clarity of thought. I have found much in science that I believe correlates to scripture. By bringing physics, cosmology, and the scriptures together, my understanding of God has grown immensely in the past few years, which understanding has greatly blessed my life.

Part of the purpose of this writing is to share my enthusiasm and some of what I've learned. I believe that much of the mystery that surrounds God is being revealed in our day and that we will be richly blessed as we avail ourselves of the truth found in both science and scripture. I testify that this combination of study will help every person to better understand God and have a closer relationship with Him.

Most of the people in the world today are like the Athenians in Paul's day. On Mars hill the Athenians erected an inscription that was written to the "Unknown God." Just as in those days, many, if not most of God's earthly children have little or no understanding of Him. Through the restoration we learn that God is literally our creator and our Father, that He has a body, and that He, His Son, Jesus Christ, and the Holy Ghost are three separate beings. I believe this clarification helps those who accept it to more easily reach out and approach God. However, for many of us, that is about as far as it goes. If each of us was asked to respond to the questions "What do you know about God?" and "Would you like to get to know Him better?" the reasoning behind our individual responses would likely be different.

It is interesting to note that these questions are similar to those that

LDS missionaries routinely ask. Many who are approached by the missionaries are comfortable with their lives and simply don't care to know more. Some are afraid of what they might find; learning more may cause an uncomfortable stretching and change of lifestyle.

Sometimes learning and doing something new can be a little like jumping into a swimming pool. The anticipation of cool water is worse than the experience. Once we've taken the plunge, our bodies and minds adjust. We find "the water's great."

So, without further ado, let's jump in and have a great time as we come to know our Father in Heaven in ways we've never dreamed.

NOTES

1. William Wordsworth, "Ode: Intimations of Immortality, from Recollections of Early Childhood."
2. C. S. Lewis, *The Problem of Pain*, 46.
3. Albert Einstein, "The Mysterious," Einstein: Science and Religion, http://www.einsteinandreligion.com/mysterious.html.
4. "Galileo Galilei (1564 - 1642)," The Quotations Page, http:// www. quotationspage.com/quotes/Galileo_Galilei/.

CHAPTER 1

Science Reveals the Glory of God!

A s we look to science to gain greater understanding of our Father
in Heaven, the Great God of the Universe, it is first worthwhile to
hear from a prophet. In Alma 12:10 we find the following: "He that will
not harden his heart, to him is given the greater portion of the word,
until it is given unto him to know the *mysteries of God* until he knows
them in full" (italics added).

Alma urges his readers to not harden their hearts so they will be
given to know the mysteries of God. I think that implies keeping an
open and receptive mind. We live in a most remarkable age. From the
time of Joseph Smith until now, God has seen fit to literally flood mankind with understanding about Him and His creations. We have the
restored gospel and all that it brings, along with astounding scientific,
industrial, and economic progress that we just take for granted. If those
living anytime prior to the twentieth century could view the progress
that has been made, they simply would not believe their eyes.

As we consider God's knowledge, power, and greatness, there is a
marvelous verse in the Doctrine and Covenants that is enlightening:
"He comprehendeth all things, and all things are before him, and all
things are round about him; and he is above all things, and *in all things,*
and is through all things, and is round about all things; and all things
are by him and of him even God, forever and ever" (italics added).

I am sure that this scripture seems logical to most of us. At first
glance, we believe that all things were made by God, that He compre-
hends/understands *all things*, and that He is aware of all things all the

time. We can also fathom that God is above all things, in other words, that He has power over all things. However, I am not sure we know what the Lord meant when He said He was *in all things* and *through all things*. Does that mean that His light reaches all things or that He is *literally a part of all things* in our universe? In section 88, verses 7 and 13 we gain a little clearer understanding of this as the Lord tells us first that he is in the sun, and the light of the sun; then in 13: "[he is] the light which is in all things which giveth life to all things," and that His light provides the law by which all things are governed. That includes you, me, the stars, the earth, the moon, every creature, every organism, every atom, everything!

Now, let's tackle one last item illustrated in this scripture, that is, the magnitude of the words "all things." It is easy to superficially consider that Christ is in "all things." But to truly obtain an understanding we are going to have to dig much deeper. For example, let's consider the detail behind something as simple as a single cell.

Every cell is amazing. The intricate structure of cells is far beyond modern technical ingenuity. The simplest cell is made up of more components than the most modern jet airliners, yet these components have been miniaturized to fit into a space that is just five microns in diameter.

Let's suppose for a moment that we could build a cell. Then, what would we do? How could we find a way to bring it to life and make it function? Single-cell organisms—or even bodies as complex as those of a man—are of no use if they don't have a life-giving force in them.

Going one step further, human cells are far more complex than the simple cells we see in single-cell organisms. Vastly more complicated, they possess the ability to interact and communicate with the cells around them.

The following quote from a book by contemporary author Bill Bryson offers a much more descriptive, metaphoric depiction:

> Your cells are a country of ten thousand trillion citizens, each devoted in some intensively specific way to your overall well-being. There isn't a thing they don't do for you. They let you feel pleasure and form thoughts. They enable you to stand and stretch and caper. When you eat, they extract the nutrients, distribute the energy, and carry off the wastes—all those things you learned about in junior high school biology—but they also remember to make you hungry in the first place

and reward you with a feeling of well-being afterward so that you won't forget to eat again. They keep your hair growing, your ears waxed, and your brain quietly purring. They manage every corner of your being. They will jump to your defense the instant you are threatened. They will unhesitatingly die for you—billions of them do so daily. And not once in all your years have you thanked even one of them. So, let us take a moment now to regard them with the wonder and appreciation they deserve.[1]

As remarkable as it is, that which Bryson describes isn't even a blip on the radar screen of what God has created. Think of the earth, its design, and the endless number of creations that go with it and that live on it. All these things are before God and round about Him. He comprehends them, He made them, and He is in and through all of these things. The word *amazing* doesn't even begin to touch it. God has designed and created trillions of stars each containing solar systems with planets that likely have, have had, or will have life on them.

In the next chapter, scriptures will be quoted referencing the prophet Enoch, who said that there were millions of earths like ours. In that same chapter, we will show that God told Moses so many earthlike planets exist that they were innumerable to man. Today, some scientists believe that there may be as many as one billion trillion (1,000,000,000,000,000,000,000,000) habitable planets in our visible universe.[2]

As recently as April 6, 2005, National Geographic reported on a new study of planetary systems outside our solar system. That article indicated that recently there has been a theoretical boost to the search for extraterrestrial life. A group of researchers in England claim that half of the systems could harbor habitable, earth-like planets. Then, in a magazine called *Astronomy,* we find another quote referring to the same study: "Based on detailed computer simulations, British astronomers have found that half of the 130-plus [recently discovered] stars with known planets have habitable zones in which earthlike planets could orbit long enough for life to appear."[3] It is heartening to see that science is beginning to uncover knowledge that coincides with that found in the scriptures.

In the past 100 years, science has turned the world upside down. There have been so many mind boggling discoveries that it would be impossible to mention them all. However, for the sake of increasing our knowledge of God, it is appropriate to discuss a few of these.

Our lives have been made both better and worse by science. We have the printing press, microwaves, automobiles, airplanes, television, computers, washing machines—and we could go on listing inventions that bless our lives. Of course, we could list things that have also made our lives worse, like mechanized warfare, atomic weapons, and pornography being delivered into our homes at the stroke of a computer key or the push of a TV remote button.

From a religious standpoint, through the centuries most religions and religious people have been overly and unduly concerned about the damage that science does to their faith. By keeping their populations in darkness, religions have both been made rich and been given power to wield great control over their adherents. Because of the fear of losing this control and because in some cases people genuinely believed that science might damage their faith, these churches persecuted scientists, including men such as Copernicus, Galileo, and Leonardo da Vinci.

Why is it that, for a full nineteen centuries, religions have been threatened by science? Can it be that the primary reason, as a young Joseph Smith learned, is that none of them have the complete truth, that over the centuries much of it has been lost? Rather than teaching the truth, they teach for doctrines the commandments of men, "having a form of Godliness but denying the power thereof." This revelation is the foundation of The Church of Jesus Christ of Latter-day Saints as taken directly from Joseph Smith's first vision, a vision brought about by a single sincere prayer when he asked God which of all the *sects* was right.

God is the author of *all* truth! That being the case, shouldn't His doctrine mesh with science? That thought immediately raises questions even in the minds of many members of the LDS church. They ask, "What about things like evolution and carbon dating?"

If we aren't careful, we will fall into the same illiterate and uninspired trap. It is important to note: when science is correct, it will mesh and correlate with God and His correct, untainted doctrine. We must never fear the truth. When doctrines or hypotheses coming from either religionists or scientists are true, then they are from God.

As was said earlier, in the past hundred years the inventions and discoveries of science have turned the world upside down and inside out. Many of these discoveries have helped us obtain a grander perspective of God. An instructive example of this statement comes from the famed contemporary physicist Stephen Hawking. Hawking has written a number of articles and books to help the average person better understand the universe. Much of the following, relating to the universe, is taken from Hawking's book *A Brief History of Time*:

- Our Galaxy, the Milky Way, has about 100 billion stars in it.

- The universe is made up of clusters of galaxies like our Milky Way; and the universe contains roughly 100 billion of these galaxies (each with 100 billion stars).

- When we multiply 100 billion stars by 100 billion galaxies we find that there is something like ten billion trillion (10,000,000, 000,000,000,000,000) stars populating the universe.

- We have seen galaxies through the Hubble Telescope so distant that it has taken 14 billion years for their light to reach us. Because the universe has been expanding for the past 14 billion years, some of these galaxies are now 30 to 40 billion light years from us.

Astounding! It is almost more than we can comprehend. We finally get to take a peek at a distant portion of the universe, and what we see actually occurred 14 billion years ago. It makes one wonder what those galaxies look like now. When we consider this in terms of time as we experience it, God has certainly been at this for a long while.

What do the scriptures have to say about these cosmological discoveries? As will be shown in greater detail in the next chapter, God told Moses that "there is no end to my works" (Moses 1:38). And in Moses 1:35 God says they are "innumerable unto man." Enoch was shown and told the same thing as Moses: "And were it possible that man could number the particles of the earth, yea, millions of earths like this, it would not be a beginning to the number of thy creations" (Moses 7:30). Both the scriptures and science are in agreement. The universe is incredibly big!

Written in the mid eighteen hundreds, an inspired and beloved poem from William W. Phelps is found as a song in the LDS hymnbook. Titled *If You Could Hie to Kolob*, it beautifully puts the above data into gospel perspective.

If you could hie to Kolob in the twinkling of an eye,
And then continue onward with that same speed to fly,
Do you think that you could ever, through all eternity
Find out the generation where Gods began to be?
Or see the grand beginning, where space did not extend?
Or view the last creation, where Gods and matter end?
Me-thinks the Spirit whispers, "No man has found 'pure space,'
Nor seen the out-side curtains, where nothing has a place."
The works of God continue, And worlds and lives abound;
Improvement and progression Have one eternal round.
There is no end to matter; There is no end to space;
There is no end to spirit; There is no end to race.

What makes this hymn/poem even more remarkable is that it was written early in the nineteenth century, over 150 years ago.

Until recently the world of science thought that our galaxy *was* the universe. The Milky Way is so massive (100 billion stars) that even with the giant telescopes of the day, no one could see the end of it or detect anything beyond it. Then in 1929, an astronomer by the name of Edwin Hubble made an astounding discovery. He was able to prove that outside of our galaxy there are other galaxies—and not just a few. Today we know that there are at least 100 billion galaxies in addition to our Milky Way each holding in its grasp in the neighborhood of 100 to 400 billion stars.

Here are a few pictures of stars, nebulae and galaxies that we are now able to hone in on due to recent technological advances. These vivid photos were taken with the Hubble telescope.

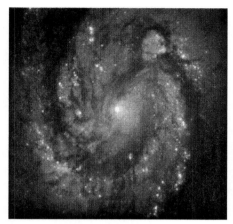

Spiral Galaxy M100

Light echo illuminates dust around the supergiant star U838

Spiral Galaxy similar to our Milky Way, NCC 1300

The heart of the Whirlpool Galaxy

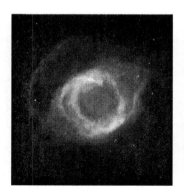

The Helix Nebula: A gaseous envelope expelled by a dying star

Sombrero Galaxy, M104, NGC 4594

Crab Nebula: A dead star celestial havoc

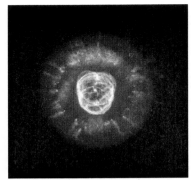

The Eskimo Nebula NGC 2392

Ancient galaxies from Hubble Ultra Deep Image, 13.5 billion light years away

Star birth clouds in M16: Stellar eggs emerge from molecular cloud

Hubble observes infant stars in nearby galaxy

Interacting Galaxies NGC2207 and IC2163

Wow! Remarkable and beautiful, isn't it? Think of it: there are 100 billion different Galaxies like this situated throughout the universe and each of them rules over 100 billion or more stars.

In the New Testament we find the Apostle John quoting Jesus Christ, saying, "In my Father's house are many mansions: if it were not so, I would have told you. I go to prepare a place for you" (John 14:2). How much God must love His children to provide all these incredible mansions for them!

By what power and by whom did God create all of that which we have been considering? We already know from scripture that it was done by Christ. But by what *power* was Christ able to do this?

It was through the priesthood, the power to act in God's behalf. Abraham told us a little about this priesthood. He said: "It came down from the fathers, from the beginning of time, yea, even from the beginning, or before the foundation of the earth, down to the present time . . . unto me" (Abraham 1:3).

This is the same priesthood that, when honored by mere mortals, makes it possible for mankind to share in all that God has. The Savior said: "He that receiveth me receiveth my Father; And he that receiveth my Father receiveth my Father's kingdom; therefore all that my Father hath shall be given unto him. And this is according to the oath and covenant which belongeth to the priesthood. Therefore, all those who receive the priesthood, receive this oath and covenant of my Father, which he cannot break, neither can it be moved" (D&C 84:37–40).

In addition to the universe or world we live in, there are many other different kinds of worlds and universes, of which scientists are just beginning to become aware. As a testament to this, we find that over 170 years ago Christ revealed this concept of other worlds/universes through the Prophet Joseph Smith. In a revelation known as "the Olive Leaf," Christ states: "There are many kingdoms; for *there is no space in the which there is no kingdom*; . . . either a greater or a lesser kingdom. And unto every kingdom is given a law; and unto every law there are certain bounds . . . and conditions" (D&C 88:37–38; italics added).

What can we surmise from the statement "there is no space in which there is no kingdom"? What does it mean? Further on in this writing we will consider the works of Einstein as well as many of the great scientists that came after him. In examining their findings we will come to learn that physicists and cosmologists are aware of "kingdoms" that many of us have never considered. Is it possible that even the fabric of space all around us and even beyond our universe is filled with other kingdoms that are governed by other laws? Through the study of the sub microscopic world that physicists call quantum mechanics, one learns that "even in the most quiescent setting imaginable, such as an empty region of space . . . there is a tremendous amount of activity. And this activity gets increasingly agitated on ever smaller distance and time scales."[4] Ultramicroscopic examination of space and time describes a kingdom or universe that functions by laws that are completely foreign to the laws of the universe we think we live in. This small universe makes the notions of left and right, back and forth, up and down, and even before and after (time) meaningless.

The subatomic "quantum" realm is different from anything ever imagined. Electrons, for instance, can move from the orbit in one atom to another without visiting the space in between. Crazy things happen in the quantum world. For instance, according to Heisenberg's uncertainty principle, an electron must be at once regarded as being everywhere and nowhere. Again, in the book by Bill Bryson titled *A Short History of Nearly Everything*, he states on page 145: "Things on a small scale behave nothing like things on a large scale."[5]

Now, what does all of this mean to us? It suggests, as God tells us in D&C 88, that wherever there is space there is a kingdom; it also means that the universe we live in is governed by laws that are definitely different than those of the universe of the very small (quantum theory). It is worth repeating: At the level of the very small, another world exists that is governed by different laws than the world we live in. This ultramicroscopic world lends tangible proof to the Lord's statement through Joseph Smith that there is no space in which there is no kingdom. What we have in the past considered empty space is not "empty." God knows each world and kingdom, large and small, and rules over them.

We live in a "multiverse," not a universe; a multiverse is made up of many universes or kingdoms. Some of them may be invisible and all around us. Others could be just too far away, or too small or refined to see (D&C 131:7).

We can take this concept of a multiverse much further. Over the years, the frontiers of physics have gradually expanded to incorporate ever more abstract concepts such as Columbus's idea of a "round earth," invisible electromagnetic fields, Einstein's "time is relative" to each individual, the wacky world of quantum physics, curved space, and black holes. During the past several years, the concept of a multiverse has joined this list. It is grounded in well-tested theories such as relativity and quantum mechanics. Many scientists today believe there are multiple types of parallel universes. It is not unthinkable that in addition to our universe with its hundred billion galaxies, there might be other universes—parallel universes to ours outside of our space.

As was stated earlier in Doctrine and Covenants 88:13, the Lord tells us that the "laws" for the governing of these different kingdoms comes from God, *who is in the midst of all things.* We discussed verse 41 earlier; now let's add verse 42:

> 41 He comprehendeth all things, and all things are before him, and all things are round about him; and he is above all things, and in all things, and is through all things, and is round about all things; and all things are by him, and of him, even God, forever and ever.
> 42 And again , verily I say unto you, he hath given a law unto all things, by which they move in their times and seasons;

How fascinating it is to see that the scriptures bear witness to the truths that physicists are now discovering. Everywhere that there is space, there is also a world, a universe (or as the Lord calls it, a *kingdom*) that is governed by laws that come from God. God knows everything, sees everything, and has created everything. And God has shared all that He has with His beloved Son, Jesus Christ, and even covenants that He will share it all with us (D&C 84:38).

So, again, science and religion agree that there are many universes or kingdoms, each being governed by different laws.

For now, let's get back to the universe with which we are familiar. Recently, scientists have discovered that the galaxies in the universe are all expanding away from each other. However, it is interesting to note that they are not moving through space; rather space itself is *stretching and pulling* the galaxies further and further apart. When scientists refer to the *vacuum* of space, they often describe it as the "fabric of space." As a side note, physicists believe that when the "Big Bang" occurred that this space fabric somehow stretched *faster* than the speed of light taking the matter that makes up the universe with it. This will be covered in much more detail later in this book. At that time we will also consider scriptural references relating to the stretching of the universe at the time of creation.

NOTES

1. Bill Bryson, *A Short History of Nearly Everything* (New York: Broadway Books, 2003), 372.
2. Max Tegmark, "Parallel Universes," *Scientific American,* May 2003, 42.
3. Robert Adler, *Astronomy*, April 4, 2005.
4. Brian Greene, *The Elegant Universe* (New York: Vintage Books, 2000), 119.
5. Bill Bryson *A Short History of Nearly Everything*, 145.

CHAPTER 2

God, a Scriptural Perspective

As we consider modern and ancient scripture in our effort to learn about God, let's first look in Genesis and the Book of Moses. Both books state that man is created in the image of God.

> And I, God, created man in mine own image, in the image of mine Only Begotten created I him; male and female created I them. (Moses 2:27)

Wow, we were created to look like God and Christ! Does that mean that they are just like we are? Of course it doesn't. We are mortal and very limited in our cognitive powers. God is eternal and His intelligence is beyond our wildest imaginings. However, being created in God's image means that to some degree we physically have a resemblance to Him and posses some of His capabilities in terms of feelings, emotions, senses, and so on. Remember, in the Garden of Eden, when man fell, Adam and Eve were given knowledge of good and evil. It was this new found ability to know and choose between good and evil—to exercise agency—that made man most like God.

Generally, each person who believes in God has an innate understanding that He is not subject to the character weaknesses to which mortal man is inclined. In distant ages there have been people who believed in gods that were subject to character flaws and weaknesses (witness the gods of ancient Babylon, Greece, and Rome) such as Zeus, Jupiter, Apollo, and so on. However, today, thanks in large measure to Christ and the ancient and modern prophets, we believe in a God who, in complete purity and righteousness, has absolute power over everything and complete knowledge of all things across all times. When or if we think about it, we probably even have an inkling that God has power over and a full understanding of all activity (past, present, and future) as pertains to His universe, galaxies, stars, planets, angels, humans, animals, creatures, plants, ecosystems, elements, atoms, electrons, neutrons, spiritual beings, and intelligences.

Remarkably, God Himself said: "My works are without end . . . all things are present with me, for I know them all" (Moses 1: 4, 6).

In another scripture (D&C 88:41) in speaking of Christ, it states:

> He comprehendeth all things, and all things are before him, and all things are round about him; and he is above all things, and in all things, and is through all things, and is round about all things; and all things are by him, and of him, even God, forever and ever.

To apply a contemporary phrase, it boggles the mind to think of all the things, large and small, past, present, and future for which God has eternal knowledge and responsibility.

So, let's begin here at this point, delve a little deeper, and consider the "things" for which Christ is responsible. Let's look and see what God's and Christ's worlds and kingdoms are like.

As you read on and participate in this search to know God better, and as you independently continue to seek after Him through study and prayer, I testify to you, as did Alma, that if you will not *harden* your hearts, you will be given the greater portion of the word, until it is given you to *fully* know the mysteries of God (Alma 12:10). For each of us, it is an individual, personal search.

Comprehending God helps increase faith; and, through this comprehension, the word *worship* takes on a whole new meaning. One of the reasons missionaries are sent throughout the world is to help earth's inhabitants obtain a more correct knowledge of God. Using the Joseph Smith experience, among the first things missionaries teach is that God really is our Father, He and His son, Jesus Christ, are beings of flesh and bone, and that we really can communicate with God and worship Him through sincere prayer.

In 1828, the word *worship* was defined by Noah Webster in his American Dictionary of English Language as follows:

Worship: To adore; to pay divine honors to; to reverence with supreme respect and veneration, with bended knees daily.

So, when we worship God, we should adore Him and reverence Him with supreme respect on bended knees daily. How can we truly worship someone we don't know or understand? In order to respect, reverence, and adore, don't you think we should know quite a bit about the Being we are worshiping? God wants each of us to find Him and come to know Him! In fact, we are *commanded* to seek Him. This search can be more far-reaching than just praying for something we want. We should seek to know God, to learn all we can about Him including His character, His purposes, His plans, and His creations.

In one's search for God, what should a person do? One of the first and more obvious things we can do is that which Christ himself taught: "Search the scriptures for they testify of me" (John 5:39). And, second, since we live in an age of science and revealed truth, should we not also consider the wealth of existing knowledge about the earth and the universe as a means to more fully comprehend God?

As we begin our search for God through scripture, we immediately find the New Testament prophets, such as the Apostle Paul, providing wonderful, thought-provoking truths about God's great and marvelous plan of creation:

> **Hebrews 1:1-2** God who at sundry times and in divers manners spake in time past unto the fathers by the prophets, Hath in these last days spoken unto us by His <u>Son</u>, whom He hath appointed heir of all things, **by whom also He made the worlds**." (bold added)

Apparently God the Father appointed His heir and Son, Jesus Christ, to make the worlds. Since Christ did nothing other than that which He had seen His Father do, we can deduce that both God and Christ created worlds. How many worlds? To Moses, Christ said, "I will show the workmanship of mine hands; but not all, for my works are without end." Wow, an infinite number of works or worlds! That is hard to get our minds around!

Enoch, an antediluvian prophet, also spoke about works without end. In the book of Moses, chapter 7, verse 30, while speaking to God, Enoch says: "Were it possible that man could number . . . the millions of earths like this, it would not be a beginning to the number of thy creations." Again, *wow!* Millions of earths like ours—and that is not even a beginning to God's creations. It is worth restating: *God and Christ created works and worlds without end!* We can't even comprehend the magnitude of their creations. But just knowing this helps us gain some insight into God's power, intelligence, and glory.

Two particular latter-day scriptures testify of the same:

> **D&C 45:1** Hearken, O ye people of my church, to whom the kingdom has been given; hearken ye and give ear to him who laid the foundation of the **earth**, who made the **heavens** and all the hosts thereof, and by whom **all things** were made which live, and move, and have a being. (bold added)

> **D&C 76:23–24** For we saw him, even on the right hand of God; and we heard the voice bearing record that he is the Only Begotten of the Father—That by him, and through him, and of him, the worlds are and were created and the inhabitants thereof are begotten sons and daughters unto God.

As was previously mentioned, one of the earliest prophets to describe God's character and ability was Enoch, who lived on the earth before Noah and the great flood. In the book of Moses we read: "And it came to pass that the Lord showed unto Enoch all the inhabitants of the earth" (Moses 7:21).

It doesn't say he saw a *lot* or *most* inhabitants, it says *everyone*. With a little more study, you shall see that it wasn't just everyone living during Enoch's time, it was all people from all times.

You ask, "How can that be? How could Enoch instantly see everyone then on the earth as well as everyone throughout all time?" Remember, as we seek to know God, it is essential to have faith, maintain an open mind, and not attribute one's own mortal limitations to God.

In addition to the words of Enoch, we can learn a little more about God and Jesus Christ by looking at the experience of Moses. While atop Mount Sinai, Moses fasted for forty days resulting in some amazing revelations. It is interesting to note that the Savior had a similar experience 1500 years after Moses during a forty-day period of fasting (Matthew 4). And, as has already been mentioned, Enoch had nearly the same thing happen to him 1500 years before the time of Moses.

In first chapter of the Book of Moses we read:

1 The words of God, which he spake unto Moses at a time when Moses was caught up into an exceedingly high mountain,

2 And he saw God face to face, and he talked with him, and the glory of God was upon Moses; therefore Moses could endure his presence.

3 And God spake unto Moses, saying: Behold, I am the Lord God Almighty, and Endless is my name; for I am without beginning of days or end of years; and is this not endless?

4 And, behold, thou art my son; wherefore look, and I will show thee the workmanship of mine hands; but not all, for my works are without end, and also my words, for they never cease . . .

8 And it came to pass that Moses looked, and beheld the world upon which he was created; and **Moses beheld the world and the ends thereof, and all the children of men which are, and which were created . . .** (bold added)

Moses was privileged to see all mankind that had lived and who were then living on the earth. Amazing!

Then, the presence of God withdrew from Moses and his glory was not on Moses. Satan suddenly appeared and tried to tempt him. But Moses could tell that Satan was not even close to being the kind of person that God is.

For behold, I could not look upon God, except his glory should come upon me, and I were transfigured before him. But I can look upon thee in the natural man . . . where is thy glory, for it is darkness unto me? (Moses 1:14–15)

We learn from this account that God is such a glorious, powerful Being and is so full of light that He must protect man when man is in His presence.

Shortly after Satan's entrance, Moses calls on God and he receives strength. Whereupon he commands Satan, "In the name of the only Begotten, depart hence." Through Christ, Moses had power over Satan. And Christ is still the only way one can have power over the adversary!

After Moses dispatched Satan, he was filled with the Spirit of God; and calling on God once more, he beheld His glory and God again spoke to Moses.

27 And it came to pass, as the voice was still speaking, Moses cast his eyes and beheld the earth, yea, even all of it; and **there was not one**

particle of it which he did not behold, discerning it by the Spirit of God.

28 And he beheld also the inhabitants thereof, and **there was not a soul which he beheld not; and he discerned them by the Spirit of God;** and their numbers were great, even numberless as the sand upon the sea shore.

29 And he beheld many lands . . . (Moses 1:27-29; bold added)

Moses not only beheld every one of God's children, he also saw every particle of the earth. You may again say, "How is such a thing possible?" Have faith! God is amazing. When we think of God, we must not ascribe to Him the limitations of our mortality. He created man in His own image but greatly limited his intelligence and ability. However, because of the accounts we have from Enoch and Moses, we learn that God can *impart* great knowledge and understanding to man when He desires.

Returning to Moses account, we learn that God continued to talk to him face to face. Speaking of the earth and His creations, God said:

32 And **by the word of my power, have I created them, which is mine Only Begotten Son,** who is full of grace and truth.

33 And worlds without number have I created; and I also created them for mine own purpose; and by the Son I created them . . .

35 But only an account of this earth, and the inhabitants thereof, give I unto you. For behold, **there are many worlds that have passed away by the word of my power. And there are many that now stand, and innumerable are they unto man; but all things are numbered unto me, for they are mine and I know them.** Moses 1:32–35 (bold added)

So, what things can we learn from this vision?

1. Having the spirit of God, Moses was able to witness incredible things, things that are not possible to see without God's help.
    - Moses saw the entire earth, all of it, every particle.
    - Moses saw every person that had or would live on the earth.
    - He discerned them by the Spirit of God.
2. God told Moses that there were so many worlds like the earth that man could not put a number on all of them.
3. God knows all his creations.

- God easily views and knows all his creations, even every particle of every creation. D&C 38:7: "Mine eyes are upon you. I am in your midst and ye cannot see me."

4. God possesses astounding power and knowledge. It is so all-encompassing that it is beyond man's ability to comprehend.

In addition to Moses, the scriptures tell us that two earlier prophets were also shown God's children and His creations. Enoch testified: "And were it possible that man could number the particles of the earth, yea, millions of earths like this, it would not be a beginning to the number of thy creations" (Moses 7:30). Abraham also learned that God's creations are endless:

> And he said unto me: My son, my son (and his hand was stretched out), behold I will show you all these. And he put his hand upon mine eyes, and I saw those things which his hands had made, which were many; and they multiplied before mine eyes and I could not see the end thereof. (Abraham 3:12)

Thus, we have three ancient prophets (Moses, Abraham, and Enoch) acting as independent witnesses to God's greatness and glory. Should we not believe it?

God not only revealed his great power and intellect to Enoch, Abraham, and Moses, but on at least one occasion He showed one of them, Enoch, that He has a remarkable ability to love and also experience both joy and sorrow. God's divine character, His capacity to experience love, joy, and sorrow, is as remarkable as His cognitive ability and His great power.

If it is true that He knows us, then our faith can be strengthened with the knowledge that He loves each of us, too. When we have faith in God's love, it helps us to have a hope and a belief that we matter to Him, a hope and a belief that both lead to and are rewarded through prayer. A Father and a Son who have such amazing abilities to create and keep track of their endless creations can certainly love. God commands each of us to love Him with all our heart, soul, and mind (Matthew 22:37). Surely what He requires from us is something of which he too is capable. Imagine the love that flows from God's great heart, His great soul, and His great mind. God's love must be nearly all-consuming.

We must believe that God loves each of us, that He loves you and me, with all our faults. We must also believe that He loves all His creations (children, creatures, plants, and so forth) on countless earths and in numberless kingdoms. As revealed to Moses, He simply and boldly tells us of His eternal quest: My work . . . my glory is to bring to pass the immortality and eternal life of man (Moses 1:39).

In chapter seven of the Book of Moses, the prophet Enoch sheds some light on Jehova's emotions and character providing us with a rare and sacred glimpse into His ability to experience love and sorrow:

> 28 And it came to pass that the God of heaven looked upon . . . the people, and he wept; and Enoch bore record of it, saying: How is it that **the heavens [God] weep, and shed forth tears as the rain upon the mountains**?
>
> 29 And **Enoch said unto the Lord: How is it that thou canst weep** . . . ?
>
> 30 And were it possible that man could number the particles of the earth, yea, millions of earths like this, it would not be a beginning to the number of thy creations . . . and . . . thou are just; thou art merciful and kind forever;
>
> 31 . . . naught but peace, justice, and truth is the habitation of thy throne . . . **how is it thou canst weep**?
>
> 32 The Lord said unto Enoch: Behold these thy brethren; they are the workmanship of mine own hands . . . I created them . . . in the Garden of Eden gave I unto man his agency;
>
> 33 And unto thy brethren have I . . . given commandment, that they should love one another, and that they should choose me, their Father; but behold, they are without affection, and they hate their own blood.

Can you feel the great heart of God breaking because of the wickedness of the children whom He loves so much?

> 34 And **the fire of mine indignation** is kindled against them; and in my hot displeasure will I send in the floods upon them, for **my fierce anger** is kindled against them.
>
> 35 Behold, I am God; Man of Holiness is my name; . . . and Endless and Eternal is my name, also.
>
> 36 Wherefore, I can stretch forth mine hands and hold all the creations I have made [remember, this is millions of earths and much, much more]; and mine eye can pierce them also . . . (bold added)

As Enoch bore witness of Jehova's remarkable love, sorrow, and anger, Enoch was then allowed to experience things even as God does.

Enoch was given power to see all of the people on the earth as God sees them; then in one giant leap, Enoch, for a moment, actually knew of the great love and sorrow God has for His children:

> 41 And it came to pass that the Lord spake unto Enoch, and told Enoch all the doings of the children of men; wherefore **Enoch knew, and looked upon their wickedness, and their misery, and wept** and stretched forth his arms, and **his heart swelled wide as eternity**; and his bowels yearned; and all eternity shook. (bold added)

At that moment, Enoch *knew* for himself. Enoch *felt* what God feels. God personally loves every one of His children. He cares for each of us, is incredibly patient with us, knows of our successes, failures, hopes, sins, health, sickness; and He listens to us and answers our prayers. And, as the great Parent He is, He experiences great sorrow because of us, and on occasion even gets angry with us.

Atonement

Finally, armed with this knowledge that God knows each soul that has lived or will live on the earth, and armed with the understanding that He experiences Godly joy and Godly sorrow because of His children, we can see how it is possible that He could ask His Beloved Son, Jesus Christ, to atone for the sins of all mankind. At the time of Christ's Atonement in Gethsemane and on the cross at Golgotha, all of His abilities and senses were magnified a million times, even greater than Enoch's were when God showed him all of His children and allowed Enoch to feel divine sorrow for their wickedness. Like God, Christ possesses the ability to experience incredible love and incredible suffering, a love and suffering so great that He rightfully became the intercessor between God and men. Even though He never committed sin himself, Christ was fully able to experience the sins of every person and suffer godly sorrow for those sins.

Now that we have some idea of God's ability to love and experience the emotions of joy and sorrow (it will be vague until we experience it for ourselves as did Enoch), we need to take it one step further. If we aren't careful and if we don't take advantage of Christ's intercession and Atonement, we will be terribly and eternally sorry. The faithful prophet King Benjamin, in his old age, addressed his people as follows:

> But this much I can tell you, that if ye do not watch yourselves, and your thoughts, and your words, and your deeds, and observe the

commandments of God, and continue in the faith of what ye have heard concerning the coming of our Lord, even unto the end of your lives, ye must perish. And now, O man, remember, and perish not. (Mosiah 4:30)

King Benjamin urged his nation and our generation, through his writings, to remember Christ and to be careful in all that we think and do. He warns us that the penalty will be terrible for those that don't control themselves, do good, and apply Christ in their lives (Mosiah 3:19–27).

Christ himself affirms this: "Except ye repent, ye shall all . . . perish" (Luke 13:2).

In the Doctrine and Covenants (section 19:1–3), Christ states that at the end of the world and in the last great day of His judgment, He will judge every man according to his works and the deeds that he (man) has done. In the Book of James we similarly find: "What *doth* it profit, my brethren, though a man say he hath faith, and have not works? Can faith save him? . . . faith, if it hath not works, is dead . . . By works a man is justified, and not by faith only . . . For as the body without the spirit is dead, so faith without works is dead also." (James 2:14–26)

Then Christ goes on to say in the Doctrine and Covenants:

> And surely every man must repent or suffer . . . endless torment.
>
> For behold, I, God, have suffered these things for all, that they might not suffer if they would repent . . . (D&C 19:4, 6, 16)

These verses help us understand that God interceded and took upon himself every transgression of every person. However, if we don't take the Atonement seriously in our lives, if we don't repent of our sins in Christ's name, we will suffer just as Christ himself suffered when He paid the price for our sins. We will suffer both body and spirit and would that we might not have to drink that bitter cup.

It is enlightening to realize that God, through prophets like Enoch, Moses, and Joseph Smith, has given us some idea as to how the Atonement was accomplished. Daily we should be grateful for the great love that God and Christ have for us.

Appearing later in this book is a section on "time" as it relates to physics and to God. In order to not detract from that discussion, I will relate a little about time as it pertains to the Atonement.

First, it is important to note that scientists don't understand time very well. As far as they can tell, scientifically and mathematically the arrow of time should be able to move in either direction, forward and backward (toward the future and toward the past). Indeed, Einstein's theory of relativity suggests that time travel is possible.

Another aspect of classical physics is that, in theory, if we knew exactly how things are now—if we knew the positions and velocities of all particles making up the universe as it currently exists—we could use that information to predict how things would be at any given moment in the future as well as how they were at any given moment in the past.[1]

From a scriptural perspective, it seems science may be right. For God, the past, present, and future exist simultaneously. He sees and knows everything from beginning to end.

Now, what does all this have to do with the Atonement? Let's put on our thinking caps and work on this together. First, we believe that Christ suffered for our transgressions; and he also suffered our pains, sicknesses, infirmities, temptations, and sorrows so that He might mercifully have the knowledge He needs to succor us (help us, love us, forgive us, and so forth.) in our times of need and weakness (Alma 7:11–12; Hebrews 2:16–18; Hebrews 4:15).

So, with that in mind, how did Christ atone for our transgressions and suffer for our infirmities, if many of earth's inhabitants had not yet been born? The answer is simple: God knows all things from beginning to end. Physicists even suggest that the past, the present, and the future should all exist simultaneously. They are right! I know that it seems crazy to us, but that is the way it works for Christ and His Father, the great and eternal Gods of the universe. At the time of the Atonement, Christ was given the knowledge and experiences of every person who had ever lived, who was then living, and who would ever live upon this earth (and countless other "earths"). He suffered for the sins and infirmities of all of them (Alma 7:11–13). It is astounding, remarkable, incomprehensible, and wonderful!

How important is this? I have a grown, wonderful child who currently lives alone with a cherished six-year-old daughter. This child of mine, flesh of my flesh, blood of my blood, whom I dearly love, has suffered sorrow, sadness, loneliness, and pain which I, as a father, am intimately aware. I have done and continue to do my imperfect best to support and sustain my marvelous child. However, Christ is able to do so much more because He suffered my child's pain and sorrow not indirectly as I have, but personally and directly; He felt and lived all the pains and sorrows with my child. Because of this, Christ truly knows how to love and help when my child is in need and seeks Him. Now, it is important to remember, He did this for every one of us. He not only suffered our pains and sicknesses, but suffered for and paid the price of our sins. As you can see, Christ truly knows and loves each of us. In a sense, He has lived our lives with us. And He is pleading for us and with us that we will take advantage of His Atonement and His suffering. He stands waiting to help us. He is there, waiting to bless our lives. All we have to do is ask. It is important that we seek the Lord and His help. It is just as important that we sincerely express gratitude for the blessings we receive.

One last thought in this regard: Jesus Christ intimately knows everything about each of God's children (past, present, and future). So, at the time of the Atonement, Christ was given knowledge of the lifetime experiences of every person from beginning to end. Because of that, He was literally able to suffer for the sins of all men (D&C 19:16). However, Christ tells us that if we don't repent, *we* must suffer. He commands us to repent or we will suffer terribly, even as He has (D&C 19:15, 17–18). Hence, if we are not always working at cleaning up our lives, repenting of our transgressions, working at being better (submitting our wills to God's), we will have to suffer for our own sins, even as described by King Benjamin:

> Wo, wo unto him who knoweth that he rebelleth against God! For salvation cometh to none such except it be through repentance and faith on the Lord Jesus Christ . . . they shall be judged, every man according to his works, whether they be good, or whether they be evil. And if they be evil they are consigned to an awful view of their own guilt and abominations, which doth cause them to shrink from the presence of the Lord into a state of misery and endless torment, from whence they can no more return. (Mosiah 3:12, 24, 25)

NOTES

1. Brian Greene, *The Fabric of the Cosmos* (New York: Vintage Books, 2005), 178.

CHAPTER 3

Greater Understanding through
Science and Prophecy

In the spring of 1966, *Time* magazine ran an issue that was kind of shocking to an LDS teenager living in a little town near Cody, Wyoming. Across the cover of the magazine, splashed in big bold letters, loomed the question, "Is God Dead?"

At the time I was on the high school track team, I had a girlfriend and was finishing up my senior year. Friends, school, and sports were almost all consuming. However, I do remember something of the stir that this cover and the associated articles created in my mind and heart.

The first lines of the issue's headline article read: "Is God dead? It is a question that tantalizes both believers, who perhaps secretly fear that He is, and atheists, who possibly suspect the answer is no."[1] The article itself was poorly written and didn't have much to say, except that it reported 97 percent of those living in the U.S. believe in God to one degree or another. So, I expect that *Time* used the "Is God Dead" byline as a sensational item to help sell its magazine. However, in the forty years since then, fierce and ugly battles have raged across America in regard to the reality of God. Prayer was disallowed in public schools and at public functions long ago; the scriptural account of the creation cannot be taught in public schools. The Ten Commandments have been barred from public places. In December 2005, a federal judged dismissed the teaching of "intelligent design" as it pertains to the creation, as pseudo-science unsuitable for teaching in Pennsylvania schools.

In the last decade, bookstore shelves have been flooded with books written by scientists both defending God and by others slandering and denouncing God. A number of these works have even been bestsellers.

Debates have raged under the broad heading of "Science versus God." Most of these have focused on the differences between Darwinism and Creationism/Intelligent Design. The big question in these debates seems to be: "Can religion can stand up to the progress of science?" In that regard, Yale psychologist Paul Bloom naively wrote, "Religion and science will always clash."[2]

Of course, the purpose of this writing is to affirm that religion and science generally *don't* clash, that the truths found in each complement the other.

In November 2006, forty years after publishing the article about God being dead, *Time* published another article that described a debate they conducted between two contemporary scientists, Richard Dawkins and Francis Collins.[3] Both Dr. Collins and Professor Dawkins have written bestselling books. Dawkins's book denounces God from a scientific perspective while Collins's book defends God from the perspective of science, scripture, and contemporary thought.

For his part, Dawkins leans heavily on Darwinian theory, which was his expertise as a young scientist. He currently occupies the Charles Simonyi professorship for the public understanding of science at Oxford University. His expertise is that of an explicator of evolutionary psychology.

Francis Collins, on the other hand, has given a good portion of his life to genetics and appears to truly have dedicated himself to science for the betterment of mankind. Since 1993 he has served as the Director of the National Human Genome Research Institute. While in that position he headed a multinational, 2,400-scientist team that mapped man's genetic structure. Think of it, this team identified some 3 billion biochemical letters in our genetic blueprint. It was an astounding accomplishment, so monumental that it was honored in a White House ceremony by the President of the United States.

Time magazine did a masterful job of not taking sides in the ninety-minute debate between Dawkins and Collins held at the Time & Life Building in New York City on September 30, 2006. The questions asked seemed fair and thought-provoking. The following pages include some excerpts from that debate and some of my comments regarding points made. The debate starts out by *Time* allowing the combatants to identify their positions:

> TIME: Professor Dawkins, if one truly understands science, is God then a delusion, as your book title suggests?
>
> DAWKINS: The question of whether there exists a supernatural creator, a God, is one of the most important that we have to answer. I think that it is a scientific question. My answer is no, [there is not a supernatural creator, a God].
>
> TIME: Dr. Collins, you believe that science is compatible with Christian faith.
>
> COLLINS: Yes. God's existence is either true or not . . . I find that studying the natural world is an opportunity to observe the majesty, the elegance, the intricacy of God's creation.

Then, as the exchange heated up and turned to evolution, it went like this:

> COLLINS: By being outside of nature, God is also outside of space and time. Hence, at the moment of creation of the universe, God could have also activated evolution, with full knowledge of how it would turn out . . .
>
> DAWKINS: I think that's a tremendous cop-out. If God wanted to create life and create humans, it would be slightly odd that he should choose the extraordinarily roundabout way of waiting for 10 billion years before life got started and then waiting for another 4 billion years until you got human beings . . .
>
> COLLINS: Who are we to say that that was an odd way to do it? I don't think that it is God's purpose to make his intention absolutely obvious to us. If it suits him to be a deity that we must seek without being forced to, would it not have been sensible for him to use the mechanism of evolution without posting obvious road signs to reveal his role in creation?

As you can see, both men make good points. Professor Dawkins argues that it is a bit incredulous to think a God would waste his time by taking 14 billion years since the beginning of the universe to create man, while Dr. Collins basically comes back with, 'Who are we to decide how God should do it?' Utilizing evolution, God may have reasoned, might be the best way, as it would require man to exercise faith.

As the interview proceeded, it turned to the subject of parallel universes. During that portion of the debate, Dr. Collins raised some of the questions commonly asked and answered by LDS missionaries.

> COLLINS: "Why am I here?" "What happens after we die?" "Is there a God?"
>
> DAWKINS: To me, the right approach is to say we are profoundly ignorant of these matters. We need to work on them. But to suddenly say the answer is God—it's that that seems to me to close off the discussion.
>
> TIME: Could the answer be God?
>
> DAWKINS: There could be something incredibly grand and incomprehensible and beyond our present understanding.
>
> COLLINS: That's God.

As was mentioned, *Time* did a good job. They asked tough questions about things like the scriptural age of the earth being 6,000 years, the resurrection, the virgin birth, good vs. evil, and stem cell research. Both Dr. Collins and Professor Dawkins did their best to explain how these concepts are either at odds or harmonize with the scientific world. Aspects of the two scientists' final statements are worth reciting:

> TIME: Do the two of you have any concluding thoughts?
>
> COLLINS: I just would like to say that over more than a quarter-century as a scientist and a believer, I find absolutely nothing in conflict between agreeing with Richard [Dawkins] in practically all of his conclusions about the natural world, and also saying that I am able to accept and embrace the possibility that there are answers that science isn't able to provide about the natural world—the questions about why instead of the questions about how . . .
>
> DAWKINS: My mind is not closed . . . When we started out and we were talking about the origins of the universe and the physical constants, I provided what I thought were cogent arguments against a supernatural intelligent designer. But it does seem to me to be a worthy idea. Refutable—but nevertheless grand and big enough to be worthy of respect. I don't see Olympian gods or Jesus . . . as worthy of that grandeur. They strike me as parochial. If there is a God, it's going to be a whole lot bigger and a whole lot more incomprehensible than anything that any theologian of any religion has ever proposed.

First, it is somewhat obvious that Richard Dawkins isn't too familiar with the scriptures; or, if he is, he just ignores them. Having said that, it probably isn't appropriate for me to comment on what Professor Dawkins knows or doesn't know. So, I will leave it alone except to restate the last sentence shared by him. He said: "If there is a God, it's going to be a whole lot bigger and a whole lot more incomprehensible than anything that any theologian of any religion ever proposed." That is the exact God that I believe scripture and science together describe! He *is* a lot bigger than most have ever imagined.

Over the millennia select individuals have been tutored by God Himself. Men like Adam, Enoch, Abraham, Moses, and Joseph Smith were even given the ability to actually see, as it were, through God's eyes. The rest of us, to a great degree, have to depend on what they reported and on the external knowledge of the universe that is available to us. However, we should realize that, like the prophets, we are not left alone in our search. Perhaps the most important tenet of The Church of Jesus Christ of Latter-day Saints is that inspiration, ongoing revelation, is available to all those who seek it. In our quest to know God and understand Him, we certainly will need the scriptures, science and inspiration alike.

Because we have been given much in both the scriptures and in revealed science, I am sure that for the most part, God expects man to learn as much as he can by using these resources. Then, as one seeks Him, He will fill in the blanks as we seek out the answers and as we are ready for them.

The rest of this chapter is broken down into the following subchapters jointly dedicated to finding this remarkable, big, incomprehensible God of which Professor Dawkins spoke. I don't think you will be disappointed.

I. The Atom and More: What is the structure of the universe?
II. Creation: How did He do it?
III. Law of Opposition: What does physics have to do with this?
IV. Predestination: What does science have to say?
V. Prayer: Is it a scientific possibility?
VI. The Temple and the Universe: What is the similarity?
VII. Interstellar Travel: How does God travel about His universe?
VIII. Time: What is it scientifically—and what is it to God?
IX. God's Great Flood: Did it really happen?
X. The Ancients: Did they really live ten times as long as we do?

XI. Evolution: Is it fact or fiction?

XII. Mystery of Light: The Power of God!

XIII. Spirit World: Is there any scientific proof for such a place?

XIV. Parallel Universes: Telestial, terrestrial, celestial, & more?

XV. Entropy: A testament to God!

XVI. Earth Rolled Up Like a Scroll: Is there any Scientific Rational?

* The physics in each of the following sections builds upon the previous sections. It may be difficult to understand concepts found in individual sections if they are read out of order.

I. The Atom and More: What is the structure of the universe?

In one of the next sections we will tackle the amazing *creation* of the universe and consider the creation from both a scientific and a scriptural perspective. However, prior to taking on something so complex, it may be worthwhile to first provide a basic understanding of the building blocks of the universe. So, let's start with a basic component, the amazing *atom*. Nearly everyone understands that the matter we see around us (sun, stars, moon, earth, houses, food, books, cars, cats, dogs) is made of tiny little things called atoms.

We owe much to the citizens of ancient Greece. During a 150-year time period, around the fifth-century BC, the Greek civilization amazingly provided us with a foundation for mathematics and science. Two Greek philosophers named Leucippus and Democritus who lived at that

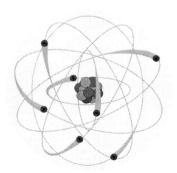

time perceptively came up with an idea that everything in the universe was made of tiny (microscopic), indestructible objects (particles). The name they gave to those particles was "atmos," or what we today know as "atoms."

Now, having said that, let's take one giant leap from ancient Greece to our day and pursue the thought that *all of the atoms that make up the entire universe* can be and once were compacted to fit into a space much smaller than the size of an atom itself. You say, "How can that be?" Trust me for a moment, and I think you will understand.

At the time just prior to the creation, or as scientists would say, "The Big Bang," the universe was actually about the size of something we call a *plank length*. That is about a millionth of a billionth of a billionth of a billionth of a centimeter. Again, you say, "You're kidding right?" When one considers the mass of the earth and the incredible mass of a single star like the sun—not to mention the billions upon billions of planets and stars—how could all this mass have been compacted together to fit into a space so much smaller than the size of a single atom?

Before we take on that question, it is first important to understand the size and makeup of the atom. Let's consider atoms in the air around us. If we were to capture a cubic centimeter of air (about the size of a sugar cube or a die from a board game) and count the atoms in that cube, it would likely contain about 90 billion, billion atoms. Think of it. In just the air that we breathe, there are so many atoms as to seem infinite in number. Then, add to that the number of atoms it takes to build an earth, a star, a galaxy, a universe. To say it is astounding is an understatement!

We find that atoms are not only very small, they are incredibly durable (just as the ancient Greeks surmised). The atoms that make up our bodies have most certainly passed through several stars and been part of millions of organisms before they became part and parcel to us. No one actually knows how many years an atom can survive; but in earth years, it is probably about 10 x 10 thirty five times. A more impressive way of saying it is, "Atoms have a life expectancy of 100 million, billion, billion, billion years." Written out, that's 100,000,000,000,000,000,000,000,0 00,000,000,000 years. With a life cycle like this, could we not say that an atom is, essentially, *eternal* in nature?

In regards to this concept of eternal matter, Joseph Smith taught: "God had materials to organize the world out of chaos—chaotic matter, which is element. . . . Element had an existence from the time He [God] had. The pure principles of elements are principles which never can be destroyed; they may be organized and re-organized, but not destroyed. They had no beginning and can have no end."[4]

This statement was written well before Joseph's death in 1844. Think of that, Joseph Smith knew something before science did. And, even better, his statement shows that science and prophesy can combine to witness the truth. As this writing moves further into science and prophesy, you will see that Joseph's words weren't just a lucky guess.

Benjamin F. Johnson wrote: "He [Joseph Smith] was the first to teach in this age 'substantialism,' the eternity of matter, that no part or particle of the great universe could become annihilated or destroyed . . ."[5]

Now, let's get back to the atom. Atoms, it was discovered early in the last century, are made of other parts:

- Atoms are a combination of *electrons, neutrons,* and *protons*
  - o Neutrons and protons are made from *quarks*
    - § Electrons and quarks are likely made from something physicists call *strings* . . .

Scientists have actually run experiments that show that an atom is essentially *empty space* with a very dense nucleus at the center. Every atom is made from three elementary particles: protons, electrons, and neutrons. Protons and neutrons are packed into the dense, central nucleus, while electrons swarm in an orbit around the outside.

The number of protons in an atom is what gives the atom its chemical identity. For instance, hydrogen has just one proton. Helium has two. Lithium has three protons, and so on. Each time a proton is added, a new element is created. Since protons have a positive charge and electrons a negative charge, there will always be an equal number of protons and electrons.

Now remember, the nucleus of an atom is made up of both protons and *neutrons*. Neutrons don't carry an electrical charge, but they do add to the mass of the nucleus; and there are usually (but not always) the same number of neutrons as protons.

Neutrons and protons are made of yet smaller building blocks called quarks. These come in a couple of different varieties or flavors (*up quarks* and *down quarks*), and the different combinations of flavors determines whether something is a proton or a neutron. All the matter in our universe is a combination of electrons and the quarks as just described.

When the ancient Greeks first came up with the idea of atoms, they were just guessing. However, physicists today have been able to experimentally detect these particles through the use of atom-smashing particle accelerators.

Finally, most scientists speculate that quarks and electrons are made of even smaller particles called strings, a billion, billion times smaller than an atom. Strings are so small that one wonders if man will ever be able to detect them. To some degree we can prove them mathematically, but that is about all.

So, here again is a theoretical composition of an atom:

o **Atoms** are a combination of electrons, neutrons, and protons
   § **Neutrons** and protons are made from quarks
      • **Electrons and quarks** are likely made from strings
         o **Strings** are the fundamental building blocks of the universe

As was stated earlier, atoms are mostly air. Well, not really air, but empty space that is filled with swarming electrons, which surround the nucleus. The nucleus of an atom (protons and neutrons combined) is very small. It is only one millionth of a billionth of the size, or rather, the volume, of an atom. This nucleus, though it is tiny, is very dense and contains virtually all of an atom's mass. If an atom was enlarged to the point where it was the size of the Salt Lake Temple, the nucleus would be smaller than a grain of sand. But, that nucleus would be *thousands of times heavier* than the temple itself. That is how dense and small the nucleus is.

Because atoms are 99.99999999999 . . . percent empty space, the world around us is largely an illusion. The negatively charged field of an electron(s), which surround an atom, repels other atoms from it. If this were not so, they could (as we imagine ghosts do) pass right through each other, unscathed. So, when you think you are touching something or walking on something or sitting on something, in reality, you are not. There is nothing there. It is an illusion created by a force-field of electrons that keeps your body from going right through the object you are touching. The electrons in the atoms that make up your body and the electrons in the objects around you are simply not going to allow you to have contact with the atoms that make up what you are touching. Electrons surround the nuclei of your body's atoms and are everywhere at once around those nuclei, thus acting as a remarkable cushion for each and every nucleus. Electrons literally form a force field around every nucleus.

One particularly strange and exciting aspect to the makeup of an atom will help explain this force-field idea. Even though there are just a few electrons surrounding each atom, these electrons can be, and are, *everywhere* and *nowhere* at once. You can never predict where an electron will be at any given moment. It is in many places simultaneously. If this concept is confusing to you, you should know that physicists have also found it confusing. The laws that govern *quantum mechanics* (the study of the very small) are very weird. Regarding this "weirdness," Einstein was once quoted as saying, "God does not play dice." Einstein found it difficult to believe that God had created such an uncertain and unknowable quantum world. However, his friend and another of the great physicists of our time, Niels Bohr, retorted with, "Nor is it our business to prescribe to God how he should run the world."

At first glance, many facets of the quantum world and our universe in general seem strange and difficult to understand. But, as was stated earlier, I believe that the more one understands about God and science, the more reasonable and understandable things become.

Now that we are armed with a better feel for the structure of an atom (it is largely empty space with a tiny nucleus at the center and a force field of electrons surrounding it), one can, in turn, understand how God was able to start out with very little mass that could be compressed into a space smaller than the size of an atom and create a universe out of it. God is an amazing chef. From his recipe for the universe came everything from almost nothing!

The key word here is *almost*. The Lord confirms this when He tells us in D&C 131, verse 7: "There is no such thing as immaterial matter . . ." Hence, we again find that revelation agrees with modern science.

Fundamental Particles

For a much more detailed look at matter and the forces that hold the universe together, you might consider the following (if it becomes too confusing, you might just move on to the next section dealing with the creation of the universe).

As indicated previously, an atom contains a nucleus made up of a densely packed ball of protons and neutrons. Nearly all the mass of the atom is centered in this nucleus. The nucleus is surrounded by a cloud of infinitely lighter electrons. The atoms are held together in this configuration by electrical forces. Since electrons are negatively charged and protons are positively charged, they create an attractive force that binds the electrons to the nucleus that contains the protons.

At one time it was believed that all matter was made up of atoms that were, in turn, made up of the indestructible subatomic particles called electrons, protons, and neutrons. However, as early as the 1930s we became aware of other particles in addition to those found in atoms. For instance, in the fifties we became aware of a ghostly particle called a *neutrino*, which is like a neutron in that it has no electric charge. Because of this feature a neutrino can pass through any object without difficulty. The sun is a big source of neutrinos. They travel at nearly the speed of light; billions of neutrinos can enter and exit our bodies every second with virtually no effect. They even pass unscathed through the earth and other planets, and then zip off into space. Neutrinos are probably the most common particles in the universe, outnumbering protons and electrons by a billion to one.

In addition to neutrinos, there exists a particle that is in all respects like an electron except that it carries a positive charge instead of a negative one. Hence it is called a *positron*. Then there is another particle called a *muon*, which is very similar to an electron except that it is much heavier (207 times as heavy). Muons can be negatively and positively charged like electrons and positrons. There is yet another particle called a *pion* which also comes in positively and negatively charged varieties. It is 273 times heavier than an electron. There is even a neutral (no charge) version of the pion.

In addition to these lighter particles, a whole group or family of particles heavier than protons and neutrons are out there. In fact, there are so many types of subatomic particles that scientists have run out of names for them, resorting to using letters and numbers to designate new ones as they are discovered.

The question is: "Why did it take so long to discover these strange particles?" It is largely because they are so elusive. For instance, a positron will simply disappear when it encounters an electron. In fact, when they come together, we suppose that the electron and positron destroy each other because they just vanish, causing a release of energy in the form of gamma-ray photons. Muons were not detected for so long because their existence is so short-lived. They decay within a few microseconds and then become electrons (if they are negatively charged) or positrons (if they are positively charged).

As scientists have studied these mysterious particles that seem to have little or no reason for existence, they have come to realize that every particle has an inverse *antiparticle*. Each antiparticle has the same mass, but the electric charge (as well as all other properties) is reversed. The positron, for example, is the antiparticle to the electron. Other antiparticles are more simply named: *antineutrinos, antiprotons, antineutrons* and so on.

All particles and antiparticles fit into two distinct categories based on the amount of mass they have. These categories are called *hadrons* and *leptons*. Heavy particles like protons and neutrons are considered hadrons, while lighter particles like electrons and neutrinos are classified as leptons.

As was discussed earlier in this section, hadrons (heavier particles like neutrons and protons) consist of combinations of fundamental particles called quarks, which come in a couple of varieties or flavors, namely *up quarks* and *down quarks*. It takes two up quarks and one down quark to make a proton and two downs and one up to make a neutron. Of course, each quark also has its opposite antiquark.

To simplify, commonplace matter is made from just four basic components:
- Up quarks
- Down quarks
- Electrons
- Neutrinos

A diagram of an atom and its constituent components might look like this:

- Atom
  - Leptons
    - Electrons
  - Hadrons
    - Neutrons
      - Quarks
    - Protons
      - Quarks

As was described previously, commonplace matter is made up of down quarks, up quarks, electrons, and neutrinos. There are actually two other families of matter besides common-place matter, however. One of these families of matter is made from:

- Strange quark
- Charm quark
- Muon
- Another variety of the neutrino

These particles are heavier than commonplace matter. They are unstable and quickly decay into particles of commonplace matter.

The third family of matter is comprised of the following:

- Top quark
- Bottom quark
- Tau
- Yet another variety of the neutrino

These particles are also unstable and decay into particles of commonplace matter.

Fundamental Forces

For some time scientists have known that there are solely four basic forces in the universe. The most common force that we are all aware of is *gravity*. Because of gravity we are stuck to the earth, the moon orbits the earth, the earth orbits the sun, and so on.

Another force that you will recognize is the *electromagnetic* force. Magnets attract one another; electricity makes it possible to run our household items (refrigerators, microwaves, televisions, and so forth). Electricity also gives us artificial light. The electromagnetic force also includes natural light from the sun and stars. So, most of the forces in the world around us that we see and with which we are familiar are a direct result of gravity and electromagnetism.

At one time scientists thought that electricity and magnetism were two separate forces. Then, in the 1800s Michael Faraday and a host of other scientists discovered a link between electricity and magnetism. Perhaps the most important outcome of the unification of these two forces was the discovery of electromagnetic waves. It was determined through this research that light and electricity are simply different forms of electromagnetic waves. After that, physicists went on to discover other forms of electromagnetic waves, including radio waves, microwaves, ultraviolet light, and x-rays.

In addition to gravity and electromagnetism, two other forces govern our universe. One is called the *strong nuclear force* and the other, the *weak nuclear force*. The strong nuclear force is the power that binds quarks (components that make up neutrons and protons) together to make hadrons, while the weak nuclear force is responsible for a form of radioactivity. This force is that which causes some nuclear particles to decay into others. For example, because of the weak nuclear force, an isolated neutron is unstable and will decay into a proton, an electron, and an antineutrino. The heavier particles (hadrons) are affected by both the strong force and the weak force, while the lighter particles (leptons) are influenced by just the weak force.

Throughout this book—and especially in the next section—I've included bits and pieces that describe aspects of quantum theory/quantum mechanics (the science of the ultra-small). It is a world that requires a completely different way of thinking about how forces work. The following is a brief overview of that world and the mechanism that was created to keep atoms (and more especially electrons) from colliding with one another.

Typically, when two negatively-charged electrons approach each other they repel and deflect away from one another, a process science calls *scattering*. The way it works is that one of the two approaching electrons will emit a particle called a photon, and the other electron will absorb it. When this happens it causes each electron to experience a little jolt that knocks the two electrons apart. The photons that exchange between *consenting electrons* are called *virtual photons*, distinguishing them from the photons that we sense as light through our eyes and brains.

Because of a theory called *quantum uncertainty*, which will be developed in much more depth in a later section, we can never know which of the colliding electrons emit the virtual photon and which will choose to receive it. It is possible to assign a range of possibilities and probabilities to each, but we can never be certain.

This theory of scattering also describes a host of other phenomenon such as emission, absorption, scattering of light by charged particles, annihilation of electrons and positrons, and much more.

The electrons or electromagnetic fields that surround a charged particle (an atom, for instance) may be perceived or envisioned as a cloud of virtual photons surrounding the object. In essence, this cloud acts as a force field, protecting the particle from other similarly charged particles.

To review, scattering is what happens when two equally charged particles approach one another on a collision course. One of the two advancing electrons will emit a virtual photon that the other particle will receive. This creates a force, a jolt that repels the two objects away from one another.

A similar scenario applies to the other natural forces. For instance, it is believed that gravitation (gravity) operates by exchanging particles known as *gravitons*.

The strong nuclear force, that binds quarks together to form protons and neutrons, operates in much the same fashion by omitting *gluons*. Gluons were also described previously as the "glue" that the strong nuclear force uses to bind together up quarks and down quarks so that protons and neutrons can exist. By itself, the strong nuclear force requires no less than eight different exchange particles to cement the neutrons and protons together. As you can see, physicists, on occasion, do use terms that make sense. Hence the term *gluon* represents the category of virtual particles that the strong nuclear force uses to glue or hold the constituent parts of protons and neutrons together.

A total of twelve exchange particles are responsible for the forces that act on the six kinds of quarks and the six kinds of leptons.

By way of review then, there exist just four forces that rule the universe:

- Electromagnetic force
- Gravitational force
- Strong Nuclear force
- Weak Nuclear force

Some physicists, interestingly enough, believe that these forces are just the manifestation of one single force. And their reasoning is sound. For instance, electricity and magnetism are linked, both being manifestations of the same force. Could it be that all of the four forces are linked and are really manifestations of the same force? Because the scriptures (Doctrine and Covenants section 88) tell us that all light, energy, and matter are literally the product of Christ, of His light, we can surmise that those scientists are correct. There is just one root force—and it comes from Christ.

In the 1960s physicists noticed and became interested in the similarities between a couple of these forces, electromagnetism and the weak nuclear force. Up front, these forces appear to be very different. The weak force has a short range and is confined to sub-atomic/sub-nuclear dimensions. In contrast, electromagnetic fields can extend tremendous distances, even across entire galaxies. On the face of it, the electromagnetic force seems to be much stronger than the weak nuclear force. However, if one views the action of the forces at the quantum level—as an exchange of virtual particles—this immediately makes the forces similar.

Let me explain. Physicists have known for many years that the range of or distance that a force can operate across is directly determined by the mass of the virtual particle emitted and received (exchanged between the two consenting objects): the bigger the mass, the shorter the exchange; the smaller the mass, the greater the distance across which the exchange may occur. For instance, a particle of light (the photon) has no mass; so, electromagnetism (light, electricity, magnetism) has an unlimited distance or range across which the exchange of virtual particles can work. As was considered previously, the weak nuclear force is the force that causes particles to break down and decay into other particles. Hence, the weak nuclear force has a short range because it exchanges virtual particles of a very high mass.

So, the forces of *electromagnetism* and the *weak nuclear force* are very similar. They are just governed differently because of the mass of the virtual particles they are exchanging. In fact, the properties of these two forces are so similar that they can be portrayed under a common mathematical structure, if they are covered with the umbrella of the Higgs field or mechanism (the Higgs field is very important to our description of the forces at work in the universe and will be described in detail in another section, as it is the Higgs field that unifies these forces).

Thus, my rationale for stating there is a single universal force coming from Christ, whereby He rules the entire universe. It is kind of like the analogy found in Tolkien's *The Lord of the Rings*: there were seven powerful rings, but just one to rule them all.

II. Creation: How did He do it?

God is the architect of the universe. It is His plan. He chose Christ, the Messiah, to implement it and to create the worlds and *almost* everything on them. Christ, receiving power from the Father, made the universe and all that is in it. Having done that, He then gave His life through great suffering as an atoning gift to all those who would believe on Him. The following is a quote from Joseph Smith that indicates God, the Father, was the Creator: "[An] Everlasting covenant was made between three personages before the organization of this earth and relates to their dispensation of things to men on the earth. These personages . . . are called God the first, the Creator; God the second, the Redeemer; and God the third, the Witness or Testator."[6]

You may have noticed that I used the word *almost* in the second line at the beginning of this section when I referred to Christ having created the worlds. There are many scriptures that testify the Father created all things through the instrumentality of His Son (see D&C 38:1–3; 76:22–24; Hebrews 1:1–3; Colossians 1:16–17; Moses 1:33; 2:1). Still, there is one aspect of the creation which God, the Father oversaw personally: "The placement of man upon the earth was a different type of creative work. And so 'when it came to placing man on earth, there was a change in Creators. That is, the Father Himself became personally involved. All things were created by the Son, use the power delegated by the Father, except man. In spirit and again in the flesh, man was created by the Father.' "[7]

Now we can better understand why Joseph Smith described God as the Creator. The creation was His idea and His plan, was done under His supervision, and He was personally involved in the creation of man and woman.

Having said that, let's move on and consider general aspects of the creation. Two distinct and separate creations are identified in the scriptures. One is the creation of the earth and all that led up to the creation of mankind. The other is the creation of the universe itself. In the book of Genesis, Moses briefly describes the events pertaining to both the creation of the universe and the earth. The marvelous language given to us by William Tyndale, who wrote or translated most of the King James Bible, is fairly straightforward: In the beginning God created the **heaven** and the earth. This is the only verse in the entire creation chapter in Genesis that pertains to the universe (heaven). All of the rest of the verses have to do with the creation of the earth, its plants, animals, and man.

In contrast, in the past seventy-five years, a lot has been written by scientists concerning the creation of the universe. Today, almost everyone has heard of the Big Bang theory. Anyone who has studied the New Testament knows the location of scriptures which state that it was by Christ that God created the universe. An often quoted creation statement is found in Hebrews, chapter 1, verse 2: "[God] hath in these last days spoken unto us by his Son, whom he hath appointed heir to all things, by whom also he made the worlds."

During the past one hundred years, creation theories have been thrown out in abundance. One of those theories describes a "Big Bang" expansion and a follow-on contraction of the universe due to overwhelming gravity. Not too long ago, scientists hypothesized that if this gravitational contraction were to occur, time would run in reverse: eggs would unscramble, we would grow from old to young, and so forth. Scientists believed that at some point in time gravity would slow the outward expansion of the universe causing all matter to be drawn together into a lump that could fit into a teaspoon. Once all matter had condensed back into such a small space, scientists believed that the Big Bang would occur all over sending the universe once again into its never ending cycle of expansion and contraction.

In addition to theories of an expanding and contracting universe, a steady state theory was proposed. Einstein and most physicists in the first thirty years of the twentieth century believed that the universe was static, unchanging, always the same, neither expanding nor contracting.

However, most recently, physicists have been able to *prove* that the universe is not in a steady state nor is it passing through endless cycles of expansion and contraction; in fact, we now know that it is expanding ever faster and faster, an expansion which will likely go on forever.

In the 1920s, a man by the name of Vesto Slipher, while taking spectrographic readings of distant stars, discovered they were moving away from us. However, his work was largely ignored. Eventually the glory discovering an expanding universe was to fall on the shoulders of

Edwin Hubble. Born about ten years after Einstein in a small town in Missouri, Hubble grew up in a suburb of Chicago. He was quite a character: handsome, fairly athletic, intelligent, a bit of a story-teller, Oxford-educated, and an astronomer. In 1919, at age thirty he began working at the Mount Wilson Observatory in southern California. In time, he went on to become the foremost astronomer of the twentieth century. When Hubble began his career as an astronomer, all of science knew of only one group of stars in our nighttime sky. At that time no one knew that we live in an independent galaxy of stars (the Milky Way) that floats in a universe of a 100 billion other galaxies. In his research, Hubble was able to take advantage of the earlier work of two individuals, Vesto Slipher and Henrietta Leavitt. Because of their groundbreaking work, Hubble went on to become quite famous. Slipher, as was mentioned, had previously figured out that stars were moving away from us, and Henrietta Leavitt determined how to measure relative distances between stars. In 1924, armed with these discoveries and having access to the best telescope on the earth (Mount Wilson Observatory), Hubble turned the world of astronomy upside down. He was able to show that scattered throughout the emptiness of space are a great many independent, island universes (galaxies) like our Milky Way.

Following this discovery, while Hubble was trying to figure out just how big our universe might be, he realized that many of the galaxies he could measure were moving away from us and from one another. But that was not all he learned. Through his calculations he was able to demonstrate that the further away the galaxies were, the *faster* they moved. Hubble proved that the universe was rapidly expanding in all directions.

This was an astounding discovery; and it quickly led to the Big Bang theory by a Belgian priest-scholar, Georges Lamaitre. Lamaitre suggested that the universe began from something as small as an atom, then exploded and expanded until it reached the great size that it is today.

It is rather remarkable that Slipher's, Leavitt's, Hubble's, and Einstein's findings as well as a host of other remarkable, cosmological discoveries all came about at the same time. One might even suggest that it was not an accident.

Here is a quote from a recent best seller titled *The Fabric of the Cosmos* by Brian Green:

[Imagine] running a film of the expanding cosmos in reverse, heading back toward the Big Bang. In reverse, everything that is now rushing apart comes together, and so, as we run the film further back, the universe gets smaller, hotter, and denser. As we close in on time zero itself, the entire observable universe is compressed to the size of the sun, then further squeezed to the size of the earth, then crushed to the size of a bowling ball, a pea, a grain of sand—smaller and smaller the universe shrinks as the film rewinds toward its initial frames. There comes a moment in this reverse-run film when the entire known universe has a size close to the Plank length—the millionth of a billionth of a billionth of a billionth of a centimeter. . . . At this moment, all the mass and energy responsible for spawning the observable universe is contained in a speck that's less than a hundredth of a billionth of a billionth of the size of a single atom.[8]

In the earliest moments of this incredibly compacted universe, the dominant force was gravity. But since gravity is a force that attracts and draws things together, what could have caused space to violently expand into the universe that we observe today? This is a question that went unanswered for most of the twentieth century. Then, in the 1980s an old idea of Einstein's was again brought to light, researched, and repackaged in a new form and called "inflationary cosmology." This discovery ironically gives credit to the concept that gravity may have been the driving force behind the expansion of the universe. You ask: "How can that be? Gravity attracts, it doesn't repel." However, physicists theorize that under just the right circumstances gravity can be a repulsive and repelling force rather than one that attracts. According to the theory of inflationary cosmology, the proper conditions existed in the early moments of the creation of the universe for gravity to become repulsive rather than attractive. For a mere one billionth of a second (a nanosecond), the tiniest fraction of a blink of an eye, the universe provided a setting for gravity to express its repulsive characteristic, and it did so with incredible force. In that extraordinarily brief moment, gravity pulled and stretched every region of space away from every other with staggeringly violent force. The gravitational energy was so massive that we now know the initial Big Bang was much, much more powerful than physicists had earlier imagined.

"During the universe's earliest moments, the size of the universe grew by a factor larger than a million trillion trillion in less than a millionth of a trillionth of a trillionth of a second."[9]

The Creation and the Law of Gravity

We can better understand how this reverse in gravity can occur by considering a bit of the history of physics research. Sir Isaac Newton, as most high school students know, discovered the universal law of gravity. As the story goes, Newton had gone to live at his country estate in an attempt to avoid the black plague that had shut down Cambridge University. One day, while Newton was walking around his estate, he saw an apple fall, triggering a sudden stroke of inspiration. He asked himself a question that would greatly change the world: *If an apple falls, does the moon also fall?* It was then that Newton realized that the same law that makes apples fall governs all objects in the universe, including the moon, planets, and stars. All things, big and small, obey the universal law of gravity.

Newton was one of the most remarkable scientists to ever live. No one scientist, except possibly Einstein, did more for science or for the improvement of life of the common man. In addition to gravity, Newton brought to light the laws of mechanics and the laws of motion.

Sir Isaac Newton, 1727

These laws became the foundation for the design of machines that harnessed steam power (like locomotives), which paved the way for the Industrial Revolution and our modern civilization. Newton's elemental laws of motion are still used in the construction of rockets, bridges, tall buildings, and just about every other modern contrivance.

According to his laws of motion, Newton believed that space and time constituted a vast, empty arena in which events could occur. His approach to gravity was that the strength of attraction between two objects depends on just two things: their mass and the distance between them. The greater the mass of objects and the closer they are together, the greater the attraction will exist between them.

Then along came Einstein with his theory of general relativity, a theory that managed to completely revamp Newton's ideas about space, time, and gravity. Mass and distance are still important to the theory of relativity; but Einstein argued that space itself played an integral part in

This picture shows space as a fabric that folds or curves around an object like the earth or the sun.

what goes on in the universe. Space and time, he came to understand are dynamic, bending, and curving in ways never before considered.

One way to better understand this is to imagine yourself sitting at home in the middle of your bed. Then, while sitting there, you take a marble and place it as much as a foot away from you. What does the marble do? It rolls toward you because of the slope of the bed created by your weight pressing on the mattress. In much the same way, Einstein learned that it isn't the mass of the earth which attracts objects to it, but the space around us that bends and causes objects to be attracted to the earth. Space is like a fabric and very much like your mattress at home, bends when mass is placed in it. The greater the mass, the more the bend there is in the fabric of space. So, the moon moves around the earth, not because of the pull of gravity, but because the earth warps the space around it, creating a push that forces the moon to move in a circle, an orbit. In this surprising new concept, gravity can be described as not being an independent force filling the universe but rather as the apparent *effect* of mass bending the fabric of space.

Yet another important factor in understanding gravity derives from the fact that when matter is heated and supplied with more energy, it will also *weigh* a bit more; it will have more mass. The energy that becomes part of a heated object is also transferred into weight. In a nutshell, something hot weighs more—it has more mass—than it does when cold.

According to Einstein, in addition to mass and distance between objects, energy and pressure also contribute to gravity. So, the strength of gravitational attraction between two objects depends on their mass, their distance of separation, and on each object's total energy that comes from heat and/or pressure! For example, when an object is heated it possesses more energy than when it is cold. A pot of boiling water certainly exhibits more energy than a frozen block of ice. The atoms in the boiling water zip here and there, while those in the frozen water are much less inclined to move about. The same can be said for other objects. We innately sense that iron, when heated, has more energy than when it is cold. Temperature, then, is one measure of how energetic the atoms are in any particular object.

It is important also to note that Einstein learned that pressure creates energy and hence increases mass and adds weight to an object. For instance, a compressed spring has increased energy and weighs more than a spring that isn't compressed. Einstein showed mathematically that the force of gravity depends on mass, distance, and energy that is created by heat *and* also by pressure.[10]

Usually pressure is positive. It provides an outward force—like a metal spring that has been compressed. However, general relativity shows that in certain situations pressure can become negative, and when it does, it becomes a force that pulls inward instead of pushing outward. When and if this happens, it causes gravity to also reverse and become a repulsive force instead of an attractive one. So, if the negative pressure in a situation is negative enough, "repulsive gravity" instead of "attractive gravity" will dominate. Repulsive gravity, then, will stretch objects apart rather than draw them together.

Now try and imagine the tremendous forces that were pent up in the compressed universe. Every part of the universe was compressed into something billions of times smaller than an atom. Conditions were just right. Inflationary cosmology suggests that this is when the Big Bang happened. The enormous pressure that was part of the compressed universe was or became negative instead of positive. At the same time, gravity became repulsive instead of attractive. These simultaneous conditions triggered the Big Bang. An outward burst of repulsive gravity was fueled by the pent up energy from the negative pressure that existed when everything was crammed together in such a small space. We don't understand all the details; they are simply beyond man's present ability to calculate. However, we do know that in the early moments of the universe, the force that stretched everything apart was ferocious. It happened in less than a nanosecond. Physicists believe that matter moved many times faster than the speed of light as it hurtled outward. The reason this was possible was because space itself stretched so fast that particles from the Big Bang were just pulled, of course, along with it. The particles themselves couldn't move through space faster than the speed of light, but the fabric of space could stretch faster than the speed of light. The particles didn't have to move within the fabric of space, they were just were part of it and simply raced along with it as space stretched out in every direction.

In a magazine called *Astronomy*, I found this great quote that makes this concept easier to understand:

> No material particle can move faster than light relative to its immediate environment. This is a consequence of Einstein's special theory of relativity. But as soon as Einstein added gravity (in context of his general theory of relativity), he realized that space itself is a dynamic quantity. In other words, space can expand somewhat like the surface of a balloon (except that space is three-dimensional, and the balloon surface is two-dimensional).
>
> Now let's imagine ants walking on the surface of a balloon. If the balloon is blown rapidly enough, the ants will be moved away from each other at a speed that exceeds their walking speed. Similarly, space itself can expand at a speed that exceeds the speed of light.
>
> In our comparison, particles of light are analogous to ants, and the expanding space resembles the inflating balloon. If space is spreading out rapidly enough (as is the case for an accelerating universe), then our galaxy could separate from a distant galaxy at a velocity that exceeds the speed of light.
>
> This is not in violation of special relativity because the two galaxies are far from each other, and there is no fundamental restriction on how fast space can expand across large scales. Relative to their immediate environments, the two galaxies might not be moving at all. Even if the ants stood still, they would be pulled away from each other at some relative speed as the balloon expanded.[11]

So, as you can see, our ever-expanding universe is not being pushed apart by an explosive force; rather, it is being stretched apart by the very fabric of space. In this circumstance, the speed of light is not a governing factor. There is no limit as to how fast space might expand.

Scientists repeatedly use a common analogy to help explain how this *stretching* might occur. Suppose we compare the expanding universe to that of a cake being baked in an oven. If you were to prepare cake batter and stir some cranberries or blueberries into the mix, the resulting concoction could be used to represent the fabric of space, with the berries representing stars and galaxies. When the batter is poured in a pan and put into an oven, the batter heats up, expands, and pulls the berries apart in all directions. The universe expands in the same way. Everything is stretching, distending, and expanding away from everything else. As the fabric of space stretches, the mix of stars and galaxies are also being stretched apart, farther and farther and faster and faster. We know that once a cake is baked, its expansion stops; however, in the case of the universe, it seems as though it will never come to an end.

Now let's take a moment and see what the scriptures have to say about this heavenly creation and expansion. Before Christ's birth, a few prophets were given inspired astronomy and physics lessons regarding the creation/expansion/*stretching* of the universe. As was discussed earlier, Enoch, Abraham, and Moses were all given firsthand views of the universe by the creator himself. It even appears that the prophets Isaiah and Enoch had some understanding of the Creation and the stretching universe, which the scientific world is just now exploring. In Isaiah chapter 42, verse 5, we find a remarkable quote from that prophet which tells us a little about the Creation and the stretching of the universe: "Thus saith God the Lord, he that created the heavens, and **stretched** them out" (emphasis added).

Enoch also knew that the expansion of the universe was a stretching rather than a pushing process. In Moses 7:30 he says the following: "And were it possible that man could number the particles of the earth, yea, millions of earths like this, it would not be a beginning to the number thy creations; and thy curtains are **stretched out** still" . . . (emphasis added)

How remarkable that both William Tyndale, who translated 80 percent of the King James version of the Bible, and Joseph Smith in his translation of Moses from the Egyptian papyrus, would use the same word *stretched* in their brief descriptions of our universe's creation. Is it possible that William Tyndale was inspired when he translated the Bible into English and that Joseph Smith was inspired when he translated the Egyptian papyrus? We, of course, believe they were.

So, here we see scripture and science in agreement. Both concur that a stretching of the universe occurred. A hundred years ago, what would have been the result if physicists had read Isaiah and Moses and had taken the stretching of the universe literally and seriously? Would physics have progressed even faster than it has? Instead of believing in a static, unchanging universe, Einstein and other physicists would likely have already accepted the reality of an expanding and stretching universe and would have more quickly pursued ideas that may have greatly advanced our knowledge of the universe.

Keeping that supposition in mind, how should we view science? Is it always right? How should we approach religion? Do the scriptures tell us everything we need to know about the universe? Should we manage our lives solely on a basis of one or the other, science or scripture? Of course not! We should first depend on what the Lord has told us through His prophets and on what God reveals to each of us personally. God is always right! At the same time, we should not be afraid of science, as it will greatly enhance our thoughts and our lives. All truth is revealed by the Holy Ghost whether it is through a prophet or someone we call a scientist. We live in a wonderful time when our Father in Heaven is revealing more to man than in any other age. In just one hundred years, our knowledge of the earth, the universe, and God has expanded exponentially. This is an age when the fullness of the Gospel has been restored and when God has inspired man and given him keys with which he may unlock many of the secrets of the universe.

Now, back to this marvelous universe that God created. Not so long ago scientists, including Einstein, believed that the universe was static and eternally the same in terms of its size, shape, form, and so on. They assumed it had always been the same and that it would always remain in its present state. Later on, Einstein called this belief the biggest blunder of his life. You and I have lived for the past thirty years with strong evidence for the Big Bang; hence, we take it for granted that the universe had a beginning. But prior to the espousal of the Big Bang theory, physicists believed that the universe had been around forever in a static state and that it wasn't expanding or contracting. Einstein claimed to have proved it. Even though his theory of general relativity told him otherwise, he couldn't bring himself to acknowledge a changing, expanding universe, much less a *creation* of the universe.

So, for some time, scientists used their theories about a static, unchanging universe as proof that the Bible had been wrong all along and that there had been no initial creation. Of course, today we have scientific proof that the universe is expanding and that there really was a beginning, a *genesis*. So, again, when it is based on true and accurate principles, science acts as a veritable testament to God and the scriptures.

It is wonderful to consider some of the wonderful truths we have learned about the Creation through science. We take so many things for granted. But what God did was so remarkable as to almost be inconceivable. Some have gone so far as to call the Creation the most wonderful gift God has given us.

The Creation and the Uncertainty Principle

There is another theory relating to the Creation that is important for us to understand, as it will provide a basis for future thought regarding the limitless capabilities of God the Father, Christ the Savior, and the Holy Ghost.

In a superbly written book called *Parallel Worlds,* author Michio Kaku refers to another book, a wacky one that has become quite popular the past few years. This second book, *The Hitchhiker's Guide to the Universe,* was written by Douglas Adams and became the source for a poorly developed film. The book's hero figures out how to travel between distant parts of the universe instantly, all without using wormholes, teleportation, hyperdrives, or dimensional portals to do it. Instead, he conceives of harnessing the quantum "uncertainty principle" to zip across vast reaches of space.

Quantum theory is based on the notion that a probability exists that *all possible events might occur no matter how wild or crazy they might be.* We should consider this thought again, as it is an important aspect of the foundation for modern physics. "Quantum theory" writes Adams "is based on the idea that there is a probability that all possible events might occur no matter how crazy or wacky they might be." That helps one understand how the hero in *Hitchhiker's Guide* was able to travel instantly around the universe. He simply was able to latch onto and turn into reality the likelihood that he could be in any part of the universe at any given point in time.

Physicist Niels Bohr, one of the all-time giants of physics, was instrumental in defining Quantum Mechanics. Bohr championed the following concept: Before one measures an electron's position there is no sense in even asking where it is. In other words, an electron does not have a definite position. There is a great likelihood that the electron, when properly examined, will be found here or there or anywhere—or even *everywhere.* The electron simply doesn't have a definite location until a measurement is done. *The act of measuring the electron somehow helps define and create reality.* Until the electron is viewed or measured, it is here, there, and possibly everywhere at the same time. Our definition of the reality of the location of the electron does not occur until it is *measured or viewed.*

In regards to this, in 1927 Werner Heisenberg postulated the following in addressing the uncertainty principle: A particle, according to quantum theory, cannot have a definite position and a definite velocity; a particle cannot have a definite spin (clockwise or counterclockwise) about more than one axis; a particle cannot simultaneously have definite attributes for things that lie on opposite sides of the uncertainty divide. In essence, what he is saying is that particles hover in quantum "limbo," in a fuzzy, mixture of all possibilities; only when a particle is measured is a definite outcome selected from an infinitely many.

If this capability didn't exist at the quantum level, our world as we know it would collapse. For instance, if atoms obeyed Newton's laws, they would disintegrate whenever they bumped into one another. What keeps two atoms locked in a stable molecular state is the fact that electrons can simultaneously be in so many places at the same time. Electrons form "electron clouds," which bind atoms together—and which then act like a force field to protect the nucleus of the atom and keep them from bumping into one another. Thus, the reason why molecules are stable and why the universe doesn't disintegrate is because electrons can be in many places at the same time.

So, the question is, if electrons can exist in parallel states, why can't the universe? As was considered earlier, at one time the universe was compacted into a space smaller than an electron. It existed in a quantum state. Because of that, quantum theory is also at the heart of the theory of the inflationary universe. That is, there is a probability that all possible events, no matter how fantastic or silly, might occur. The principles behind quantum theory lie at the heart of yet another theory of the inflationary universe. It suggests that when the Big Bang took place, there occurred a "quantum transition" in the building-block atoms to a new state in which the universe suddenly inflated by an astronomic amount. Our universe may have ballooned in size instantly out of a quantum leap. In less than the blink of an eye, the universe may have jumped to one of its many alternative states of existence.

Why God Created the Universe
No matter how the universe was created, whether by an explosion,

by repulsive gravity, a great stretching, or by a quantum leap as we have just discussed, we need to understand one remarkable fact: Christ made it all. He didn't just create the earth, our sun, and our solar system; He didn't just create the Milky Way, our home Galaxy. He made it all. The scriptures are very pointed and explicit about this. The great Book of Mormon prophet King Benjamin states: "And he shall be called Jesus Christ, the Son of God, the Father of heaven and earth, the Creator of all things from the beginning" (Mosiah 3:8).

Then, in Mosiah 4, verse 9, King Benjamin exhorts his hearers: Believe in **God**; believe that he is, and that he **created all** things, both in heaven and in earth" (emphasis added).

From physics, as was discussed previously, we have some idea as to how God may have created the universe. The next, and possibly most important, question is: "Why did He do it?"

In the Book of Psalms, David asked his famous question: "When I consider thy heavens, the work of thy fingers, the moon and the stars, which thou hast ordained; What is man, that thou art mindful of him? and the son of man, that thou visitest him?" (Psalm 8:3–4)

A basic doctrine that is taught over and over in the scriptures of many religions is that we are the children of God: "We are the offspring of God . . ." (Acts 17:28–29), and "Ye . . . are children of the most High (Psalms 82:6).

It stands to reason that if we are His children, then He is our Father. One of the tenets of a child-parent relationship is that children inherently have an opportunity to become like their parents; that is their divine destiny. The Apostle Paul said it best: "The Spirit itself beareth witness with our spirit, that we are the children of God: And if children, then heirs of God, and joint-heirs with Christ" (Romans 8:16–17).

In the New Testament we are even encouraged to become like our Eternal Father. Jesus said, "Be ye therefore perfect, even as your Father which is in heaven is perfect" (Matthew 5:48). In other words, we are commanded by Christ to obtain the character traits of our eternal parents.

If God wants us to become like him, then somehow we all become a prime part of His great plan. Over and over we find God's mission statement being used in LDS Sunday School lessons, in Priesthood and Relief Society lessons, in General Conference and Sacrament meetings. It has already been used a couple of times in this writing: "This is my work and my glory—to bring to pass the immortality and eternal life of man" (Moses 1:39).

This simple yet profound statement tells us why God created the universe, the earth, and all of the other worlds that are too countless to number (Moses 1:35). His great plan would eventually allow man to become immortal and return to live with God Himself. And through His Son, Jesus Christ, God set that plan in motion, a plan whereby man may obtain eternal life!

In *Mormon Doctrine,* Elder Bruce R. McConkie defines *eternal life* as:

> . . . the name given to the kind of life that our Eternal Father lives . . . [The word *eternal*] is one of the formal names of Deity and has been chosen by him as the particular name to identify the kind of life that he lives. He being God, the life he lives is God's life; and his name being Eternal, the kind of life he lives is eternal life. . . .
>
> Accordingly, eternal life is not a name that has reference only to the unending duration of a future life . . . it is the kind of life that God himself enjoys. Thus, those who gain eternal life . . . are sons [and daughters] of God, joint heirs with Christ, members of the Church of the Firstborn; they overcome all things, have all power, and receive the fullness of the Father. They are gods.[12]

You may recall that included in the introduction to this writing is an inspired poem by the William Wordsworth, "Ode: Intimations of Immortality." At the end of the verse, Wordsworth declares: "Trailing clouds of glory do we come from God, who is our home." From this and other inspired sources, we understand that we once lived with God. Now, He gives us an opportunity to return to His celestial home. If we are to succeed in this quest, we will have to become like Him in character. We believe that the primary reason God created the universe and the earth is so that mankind could have a place of learning and perfecting and proving, a place to become worthy to live again with God, to become like Him, and share in all that is His.

Don't for a second think that this doctrine is exclusive to the LDS Church. Many well-known ancient and modern theologians have stated that the object of our existence is to learn to become sons of God and, hence, gods ourselves:

Clement of Alexandria (AD 150 to 215): "Yea, I say, the Word of

God became a man so that you might learn from a man how to become a god . . . And the Word Himself now speaks to you plainly, putting to shame your unbelief, yes, I say, the Word of God speaks, having become man, in order that such as you may learn from men how it is even possible for man to become a god."[13]

Justin Martyr (AD 100 to 165): [In the beginning men] were made like God, free from suffering and death . . . deemed worthy of becoming gods and having power to become sons of the highest.[14]

St. Augustine (Augustine of Hippo, AD 354-430): But he himself that justifies also deifies, for by justifying he makes sons of God. "For he has given them power to become the sons of God" [John 1:12]. If then we have been made sons of god, we have also been made gods.[15]

C.S. Lewis (1898-1963): The command to be perfect is not idealistic. . . . Nor is it a command to do the impossible. He is going to make us into creatures that can obey the command. He said [in the Bible] that we were "gods" and He is going to make good His words. If we let Him—for we can prevent Him, if we choose—He will make the feeblest and filthiest of us into a god or goddess, a dazzling, radiant, immortal creature, pulsating all through with such energy and joy and wisdom and love as we cannot now imagine, a bright stainless mirror which reflects back to God perfectly (though, of course, on a smaller scale) His own boundless power and delight and goodness. The process will be long and in parts very painful, but that is what we are in for. Nothing less. He meant what He said.[16]

Joseph Smith (1805-1844): God Himself was once as we are now, and is an exalted man, and sits enthroned in yonder heavens! That is the great secret. If the veil were rent today, and the great God who holds this world in its orbit, and who upholds all worlds and all things by His power, was to make Himself visible,—I say, if you were to see Him today, you would see Him like a man in form—like yourselves in all the person, image, and very form as man; for Adam was created in the very fashion, image and likeness of God, and received instruction from and walked, talked and conversed with Him, as one man talks and communes with another . . .

Having a knowledge of God, we begin to know how to approach Him, and how to ask so as to receive an answer. When we understand the character of God, and know how to come to Him, He begins to unfold the heavens to us, and to tell us all about it.[17]

The New Testament affirms the fact that God wants us to become like Him and become gods in our own right. Second Peter 1:3–4 says: "According as his divine power hath given unto us all things that **pertain** unto life and godliness, through the knowledge of him that hath called us to glory and virtue: Whereby are given unto us exceeding great and precious promises: that by these ye might be partakers of the divine nature" (emphasis added).

One of the all-time great Christian authors C. S. Lewis affirmed the above regarding God and His plans for us: "We are a Divine work . . . something that God is making, and therefore something with which He will not be satisfied until it has a certain character."[18] He goes on to say that if we are a divine work, then, "We are bidden to 'put on Christ' to become like God."[19]

As I read C. S. Lewis's book *The Problem with Pain*, I realized that the entire work is devoted to his thoughts about what it takes on God's part and on our part for a man to become like God. It is a most remarkable book with wonderful insight. Members of The Church of Jesus Christ of Latter-day Saints have heard and read so many times the statement that God's work and glory is to bring to pass the immortality and eternal life of man, that it just rolls off us. I don't think we pause long enough to consider what it costs God and what it will cost us to get there. Again, few express it better than C.S. Lewis:

> Whether we like it or not, God intends to give us what we need, not what we now think we want. . . . To be God—to be like God and to share His goodness . . . these are the only . . . alternatives. If we will not learn to eat the only food that the universe [God] grows . . . then we must starve eternally. . . .
>
> It is natural for us to wish that God had designed for us a less glorious and less arduous destiny; but then we are wishing not for more love but for less . . . To ask that God's love should be content with us as we are is to ask that God should cease to be God: because He is what He is, His love must, in the nature of things, be impeded and repelled by certain stains in our present character, and because He already loves us, He must labor to make us loveable.[20]

It is an understatement to say that God is invested in us; and we too must decide along the way if we are going to invest in becoming like Him. Even in our premortal life we had our agency. When we as His spirit children voted for God's plan, I think we had some idea as to how difficult mortality was going to be; yet we could see the end result and were most happy about it. The Book of Job is one of the few places where we can find a description of that great pre-mortal event: "Where wast thou when I laid the foundations of the earth? Declare, if thou hast understanding . . . When the morning stars sang together, and all the sons of God shouted for joy?" (Job 38:4–7).

Joseph Smith answered this question for Job, saying: "At the first organization in heaven we were all present and saw the Savior chosen and appointed and the plan of salvation made, and we sanctioned it."[21]

Still, that was then, and this is now. We are on the firing line of mortality, not just viewing prospect of it from afar. This life is both wonderful and very tough at the same time! The earth was created so that we might progress, so that we might obtain the character qualities and attributes of God—and even become God's ourselves. Earth, as it is now, is primarily a place of suffering. Don't get me wrong, there is a lot of joy to be experienced here, and we should hang on to that. However, each of us will experience some form of hardship, deprivation, illness, as well as most other kinds of opposition.

One of the most profound messages found in scripture and history is that everyone should expect life to be difficult. Even the good suffer. In his wonderful book *The Problem with Pain*, C. S. Lewis tells us that if we are looking for a life that promises only ease, peace, joy, and happiness, what we are seeking for is a God who has *less* love, not more. Lewis proposes that God loves us so much that He created a plan that calls for pain. We therefore should be cautious and not mistake pleasure and ease as a medicine that ought to always replace pain. Otherwise, we may very well miss the best of what life has to offer.

Perhaps the biggest challenge in life is learning to embrace God and accept His will. As Lewis, again, so aptly writes:

> The proper good of a creature is to surrender itself to its Creator . . . When it does so, it is good and happy.[22]

> We are not merely imperfect creatures who must be improved: we are . . . rebels who must lay down our arms . . . [We must] render back the will which we have so long claimed for our own. . . . But, to surrender a self-will inflamed and swollen with years of usurpation is a kind of death.[23]

We who ascribe to The Church of Jesus Christ of Latter-Day Saints frequently refer to baptism as a "rebirth" and our sacrament participation as a weekly "renewal" of those baptismal covenants. This is very similar to the ideas proposed by C. S. Lewis. In essence, we, as sinful, imperfect beings, daily submit ourselves to a kind of spiritual death as we embrace the world in rebellion against God. Then we are reborn as we surrender our self-will to God. *Daily surrender* is the key. Every day each of us could improve on obedience, offer greater charity, and extend more gratitude.

Our human spirits do not seem inclined to even begin trying to surrender to God, so long as everything seems to be going well. For some reason, sin is also like this. That is, the deeper it is rooted in a person, the less that person suspects its existence. It is a masked evil . . . Human kind has the ability to rest stupidly and contentedly in sin. We should be ever grateful that we have a conscience, the light of Christ, through which God alternately whispers to us and sometimes shouts at us. When we overeat or ignore a beggar, the Lord whispers to us that we shouldn't do such things. The first time a person abuses another human being, breaks the law of chastity, or commits a murder, their conscience screams at them. During those times, they will be surrounded by spiritual darkness that is almost palpable. They will be in great pain. And this kind of pain is *good*! It causes one to seek for relief through prayer and repentance.

We have all noticed how hard it is to turn one's thoughts to God when everything is going well. We are in trouble or on the verge of trouble when we have so much or are so pleased with our lives that we find God to be an interruption.

> As St. Augustine says somewhere, [writes Lewis,] God wants to give us something, but cannot, because our hands are full—there's nowhere for Him to put it. Or as a friend of mine said, "We regard God as an airman regards his parachute; it's there for emergencies but he hopes he'll never have to use it." Now God, who has made us, knows what we are and that our happiness lies in Him. Yet we will not seek it in Him as long as He leaves us any other resort where it can even plausibly be looked for. While what we call "our own life" remains agreeable we will not surrender it to Him.[24]

Is this not the major lesson that we learn from the Book of Mormon? Throughout, God tells his people that they will prosper if they will simply obey Him. Then, when they prosper it seems like most no longer have a need for God, go on to make terrible choices, and wander off into forbidden paths. Are we not the same? Did God not give us the Book of Mormon and sentries such as C. S. Lewis to remind us of the folly of the "natural man"? It is most interesting and wonderful to see that God doesn't just give up and let us have our way when we wander. Instead, through pure love, He does all that He can to reclaim us and get us back on the path to true happiness. His efforts could be as simple as a reminder from our conscience, a loving message from a parent or spouse, or a brief exchange with a caring friend or an ecclesiastical authority. If the transgression and disobedience is so deeply ingrained that a person has no ability or intention of giving it up, then God likely will resort to more stringent and radical means.

Throughout the Book of Mormon, war-like Lamanites always posed a threat to the generally peaceful and usually righteous Nephites. There were also constant reminders that came via natural disasters such as famine and draught. And, finally if all else failed, God would mercifully inflict an extermination so that future generations wouldn't be caught in a similarly destructive cycle of wickedness.

It appears that God has created a temporal earth designed to do much of the work of dealing with our disobedience. Our marriages dissolve; we lose our jobs; and sometimes we even end up in jail. There is much that this world does to police itself. Sometimes it isn't until things get really hard—when we hit rock bottom—that we finally reach out to God.

> It is a poor thing to strike our colours to God when the ship is going down under us; a poor thing to come to Him as a last resort, to offer up 'our own' when it is no longer worth keeping. If God were proud He would hardly have us on such terms; but He is not proud, He stoops to conquer, He will have us even though we have shown that we prefer everything else to Him, and come to Him because there is 'nothing better'. . . . If God . . . would not have us till we came to Him from the purest and best motives, who could be saved?[25]

Having laid the foundation of God's perfect grace, Lewis goes on to explain what role our choices play in life's drama:

> And this illusion of self-sufficiency may be at its strongest in some very honest, kindly, and temperate people, and on such people, therefore, misfortune must fall.

Everyone will admit that choice is essentially conscious; to choose
involves knowing that you choose. . . . If the thing we like doing is, in
fact, the thing God wants us to do, yet that is not our reason for doing
it, it remains a happy coincidence. . . . The full acting out of the self's
surrender to God therefore demands pain: this action, to be perfect,
must be done from the pure will to obey, in the absence, or in the teeth,
of inclination. How impossible it is to enact the surrender of the self by
doing what we like.[26]

As I set out to write this book, I experienced similar feelings described
by C. S. Lewis when he penned *The Problem of Pain*. I too hoped that my
desire to obey a prompting had at least some place in my motives. But
now that I am thoroughly immersed in the study of physics and the writing, it has turned into more of a temptation than a service. I still hope
that the expression of this book is, in fact, in conformity with God's will:
but to claim that I am learning to surrender myself by doing what is so
attractive would be dishonest.

And so it is in all our endeavors. If we would pause for just a
moment, amidst all the commotion and noise of this world, and really
ponder our choices and actions, as they pertain to God, I think we will
correctly conclude that there is just one right act—that of "self surrender"! It is a surrender of will that has only one possible motive and is
usually unpleasant in the beginning and quite opposite to our natures.
Young men and women who go on LDS missions can tell you all about
the surrender of self. Until their missions, they are used to sleeping in
when they want. Saturdays are unstructured and full of distractions.
Evenings are usually their own (especially weekends). They stay up late,
play sports, go to movies, party, date, and so on. Before serving missions,
our young people lead lives that are, in essence, self-indulgent. When
they enter the mission field their lives change drastically. They surrender
themselves to the Lord and His regimen. It can be difficult to make the
switch. I don't think many successfully accomplish it without the Spirit
of the Lord and without a strong belief that their service is important.
The surrender of self is at first painful, but over time becomes a thing of
joy and strength.

Such an act [of surrender] may be described as a "test" of the creature's return to God. . . . A familiar example is Abraham's "trial" when
he was ordered to sacrifice Isaac. With the historicity or the morality
of that story I am not now concerned, but with the obvious question,

"If God is omniscient He must have known what Abraham would do, without any experiment; why, then, this needless torture?" But as St. Augustine points out, whatever God knew, Abraham at any rate did not know that his obedience could endure such a command until the event taught him: and the obedience which he did not know that he would choose, he cannot be said to have chosen. The reality of Abraham's obedience was the act itself.[27]

As has already been considered, God knows in advance how each of us will react. He is both aware of our individual histories and the history of earth's people from beginning to end. Why then does He allow us such pain? It is so we can gain experience, learn about ourselves and improve. Without the schooling we receive on this marvelous earth, most of us would likely never measure up. This life is extremely important.

Helping man arrive at an ultimate destination of immortality and eternal life is no easy job. It takes a God to do it, someone who possesses perfect love and perfect character. So, if you desire to become like God, remember that your greatest role will be that of *babysitting*. You will be taking on yourself the same work and glory that is God's. You will be diligently working throughout the eternities to help others obtain immortality and eternal life.

In a later chapter, the character attributes of God will be discussed. At this point in our study, it may be worthwhile to consider a few of His personal qualities found in the Book of Mormon:

> I perceive that it has been made known unto you, by the testimony of his word, that he cannot walk in crooked paths; neither doth he vary from that which he hath said; neither hath he a shadow of turning from the right to the left, or from that which is right to that which is wrong; therefore, his course is one eternal round.
>
> And he doth not dwell in unholy temples; neither can filthiness or anything which is unclean be received into the kingdom of God . . . (Alma 7:20–21)

These verses teach us that we can always, eternally count on God. He is completely and perpetually good, and He always keeps His word. In this same chapter, Alma reminds us that there is much to be learned in this life. We must be willing to submit ourselves, our appetites and passions, to God's will (verse 23). Even the Holy Ghost is an extension of God. It cannot dwell in unholy souls or temples (verse 21). If we can take to heart this one lesson, that all good character attributes and all truth come from a single divine source, we will find much peace and happiness in this life and in the next.

Now that we more fully understand the central purpose for God's creating the universe (and in our case, the earth in particular) we can resume our discussion of the science behind His Creation.

Unsolved Mysteries

Plenty of mystery still surrounds the mechanics of God's creation. Clearly it is an understatement to say that there is much that we don't know about God and His universe. Even so, scientists continue to be given glimpses and clues to help them focus their search for truth. I believe that God wants us to know more about Him and His universe and that some inspired physicists, mathematicians, and cosmologists will yet come to an understanding of more of the remarkable mechanics that cause the cosmos to tick.

At the top of the list of things scientists are seeking to discover is the unification of relativity and quantum theory. However, there are other, more contemporary mysteries such as *dark matter* and *dark energy* that have yet to be understood. In this section we will focus on these two mysteries.

Prior to considering dark matter and dark energy, it would be wise to review some basics about matter and energy. If you recall, Einstein's remarkable equation $E=mc^2$ gives us to understand that energy and matter are interchangeable. Matter can become energy and energy can become matter. In addition to being interchangeable both have many of the same characteristics. For instance, both produce gravity. Hence, the greater the mass of matter and the greater the mass of energy, the greater are their associated (and often combined) gravitational forces.

It should be noted that the word *dark,* as science applies it to dark matter and dark energy, is not something sinister. It simply means that we can't see it; we don't know what it is. It is darkness to us.

Believe it or not, 96 percent of the universe is made from something that, for lack of better understanding, we call *dark energy* and *dark matter.* Yes, you read it right. Most of the substance in the universe is something that we cannot see or understand. Only 4 percent of the universe is made up of matter and energy that is familiar to us (planets, stars, galaxies). And the problem is, we don't really have a clue as to what it is that we can't see or understand. We can guess and surmise, but that's about all.

The first notion that the cosmos isn't what we can see and measure was put forth by Fritz Zwicky in the 1930s. Zwicky, a physicist from Switzerland, was then working at the California Institute of Technology. Because of the work of Edwin Hubble, Zwicky understood that the universe was expanding uniformly. However, he also knew that galaxies aren't always isolated from one another; they often clump together in clusters. Then, within these clusters, the galaxies seem to randomly move about, unfazed by the expansion around them. In a nutshell, Zwicky could see that in addition to the expansion of the universe, where galaxies were moving away from one another there was a separate world of complicated local movements within clusters of galaxies. An example of this is our home cluster of galaxies, which includes the Andromeda galaxy and our own Milky Way. Instead of moving away from each other, they are converging at 130 kilometers per second.

As Zwicky studied the localized motions occurring within galaxy clusters, he found something quite strange. Most of these galaxies were moving zooming along at too fast a pace. At first he assumed that they were held in the clusters by the gravity produced by their visible materials. He soon realized, though, that the galaxies were traveling faster than the visible matter's gravity could sustain. In fact he observed that the clustered galaxies should have split apart and been flying away from one another. There just wasn't enough gravitational attraction from the visible matter to hold the galaxies together. Yet, there they were, bound together in clusters by some force that was entirely invisible. Puzzled by this seeming contradiction, Zwicky went to work and mathematically came to the conclusion that there existed not just a small problem but a huge one. The amount of gravitational force needed to hold the galaxies together in clusters was hundreds of times greater than the visible source of matter could sustain.

So, what invisible, gravity-producing matter was keeping the galaxies clustered together? Zwicky didn't know—and even today we don't know. This unseen material came to be known as *dark matter*. "Dark" because we can't see it; no light comes from it. Shortly thereafter, scientists realized that in addition to holding galaxies together in clusters, this dark matter was working even within the confines of our own galaxy and in *all other* galaxies. When one considers the rotation of the stars within a galaxy, it becomes apparent that these celestial bodies on the outside of the galaxy, like our sun, are moving way too fast to remain gravitationally bound to our galaxy.

The following picture of a galaxy similar in structure to our Milky Way helps one better visualize this cosmic quandary.

Because of the way the galaxy is spinning, one would think that the stars on the fringes would be thrown off into space.

Somehow, an invisible gravitational force holds the stars together, yet the gravity from the visible stars just doesn't add up to enough force. Astronomers have mapped the distribution of mass needed to hold galaxies like ours together and now realize that our galaxy and others sit in the middle of spherical blobs of dark matter that stretch far beyond the fringes of a galaxy's luminous regions. The makeup of this dark matter is one of the most baffling mysteries that scientists are working to unravel.

Physicists initially thought that the abundance of neutrinos in the universe could be one of the candidates for this dark matter. As previously discussed, neutrinos greatly outnumber other nuclear particles (neutrons, protons, electrons, and so on). However, neutrinos just don't weigh enough to create the necessary gravity. Scientists wonder if there isn't something else, something *like* a neutrino, but a particle with a mass that is much greater, more like that of a proton. Of all things, physicists call these kinds of theoretical particles *WIMPS*, a term that stands for "weakly interacting massive particles." The problem remains that no one has been able to come up with any proof for these particles; so far it has been impossible to detect them. In some unknown way they interact very weakly with standard matter. So, with nothing further to go on, today scientists believe that these WIMPS form a soup of sorts that the earth and the sun and the rest of the stars must pass through on their long journey around the Milky Way.

It is important to note that this dark matter must have been extremely important in the early formation of the universe as we know it. Without its existence, the stars, galaxies, and galaxy clusters would not have formed into the clumps we see today. Matter would have been so universally widespread that no objects of any size would have been formed. Dark matter—or something akin to it—was responsible for the clumping of matter that now forms planets, stars, galaxies, and clusters of galaxies. Without it, no life could exist anywhere.

Interestingly enough, Brigham Young may have known something about the existence of dark matter. On one occasion he said the following: "How much matter do you suppose there is between here and some of the fixed stars which we can see? Enough to frame many, very many millions of such earths as this, yet it is now so diffused, clear and pure, that we look through it and behold the stars. Yet the matter is there. Can you form any conception of this? Can you form any idea of the minuteness of matter?"[28]

The following photograph shows some of the effects of dark matter:

This large, isolated, elliptical galaxy is embedded in a cloud of 10-million-degree Celsius gas (**NASA**/CXC/ E.O'Sullivan et al). This image is not a picture of **dark** matter. Rather it is a picture of its *effects*, captured by the Chandra X-ray Observatory. It's a galaxy surrounded by a cloud of extremely hot gas. A halo of dark, invisible matter must be holding the gas in place through the strength of the matter's gravity.

As strange as dark matter is, there exists something even more mysterious, astronomers call it *dark energy*. Again, the term "dark" doesn't imply anything sinister. It is simply energy that we can't see or understand, but we know exists in abundance. In the past decade (1990s), a couple of groups of cosmologists determined that the expansion of the universe is speeding up instead of remaining constant or even slowing down, as it ought to.

In 1998 two teams of astronomers, the Supernova *Cosmology* Project and the High *Z* Supernova Search were looking for distant supernovae (using the Hubble Space Telescope) in an effort to measure the expansion rate of the universe. Factoring in gravity and time, they expected that the cosmic expansion would be slowing. This would be indicated by supernovae appearing brighter than their red-shifts would show. Instead, they found the supernovae to be *fainter* than expected. With this evidence in tow, they were able to conclude that the expansion of the universe has not been slowing due to gravity, as everyone had thought; instead, it has been accelerating. No one expected this. Somehow, a mysterious anti-gravity force is causing the galaxies to accelerate away from one another in all directions. The general term "dark energy" is what scientists came up with to describe this force.

The term "dark energy" refers to the fact that some kind of "stuff" must fill the vast reaches of mostly empty space in the cosmos in order to be able to make space accelerate as it is. In this sense, dark energy is a "field" just like an electric field or magnetic field (both part of the electromagnetic force).

The long history of dark energy was initiated in 1917 by Albert Einstein. A constant (which he called Λ) was needed in his equations of general relativity to allow for a static universe. But shortly thereafter, when Hubble made his famous discovery of the expanding universe, this constant, Λ, seeming unnatural and superfluous, was rejected, even by Einstein himself (an act that he labeled the "biggest blunder in my life").

Later, when quantum theory came to be known, it was theorized that "empty space" was full of temporary (virtual) particles continually forming and disintegrating. Physicists began to suspect that indeed the vacuum ought to have a dark form of energy, and that Einstein's Λ constant could be interpreted as vacuum energy. Using this constant, scientists found it possible to calculate the energy of empty space. The answer was so huge that astronomers dismissed it as ridiculous. The amount of energy they calculated that empty space should have is 10^{120} more energy than has actually been measured. That's the number 1 followed by 120 zeroes, a difference that scientists found, and still find, so out of line that they dismissed it as being ridiculous.

Because of that, Λ was forgotten by most astronomers for nearly seventy years. Then, the constant Λ was given new life in the 1990s in order to reconcile mathematical theory with actual observations. Nowadays, it has become fashionable to label Λ "dark energy."

Physic's theorists find it unsettling that the universe contains just enough dark energy to have allowed galaxies and other structures to form—and, coincidentally, human observers to exist. If there were a small amount or none at all, the universe would have collapsed rather than expanded during the early moments of the big bang. However, as was stated above, if dark energy matched the incredibly large proportion predicted by general relativity and quantum physics, it would have caused the universe to expand so rapidly that nothing more than a thin fog of matter and energy would fill the universe today.

In short, we seem to live in the best of all possible universes. For that reason, many physicists find all of this unsettling. They are forced to consider the likelihood that the universe wasn't just a big accident, that there is a possibility there may be some intelligent design behind it.

In order to get around those kinds of thoughts, to explain this cosmic coincidence—one that seems to stack the odds in favor of our existence—some scientists simply throw their hands up in the air and invoke what they call the *anthropic principle*. It says that the universe, as we know it, was just a big accident. The universe has the ideal amount of dark energy just *because*. We wouldn't be here to measure it if it hadn't happened that way.

No matter what the dark energy is called, a mysterious "anti-gravitational" force truly exists that is strong enough to oppose gravity and cause the galaxies and clusters of galaxies to accelerate away from one another in all directions. Scientists have come up with a plethora of possibilities for the cause of this expansion, but today they really don't know what to make of the dark energy that is causing the universe to expand at such a break-neck speed. Whatever it is, if you add up all the dark energy needed to make the universe expand as it is, it represents a mass far greater than both the combined visible matter and the *dark matter* previously discussed.

The following quote from the May 30, 2004 issue of *PhysicsWorld. com* brings the concept of dark energy into better focus:

> New evidence has confirmed that the expansion of the universe
> is accelerating under the influence of a gravitationally repulsive form

of energy that makes up two-thirds of the cosmos. It is an irony of nature that the most abundant form of energy in the universe is also the most mysterious. Since the breakthrough discovery that the cosmic expansion is accelerating, a consistent picture has emerged indicating that two-thirds of the cosmos is made of "dark energy"— some sort of gravitationally repulsive material.

The cosmic expansion, discovered in the late 1920s by Edwin Hubble, is perhaps the single most striking feature of our universe. Not only do astronomical bodies move under the gravitational influence of their neighbors, but the large-scale structure of the universe is being stretched ever larger by the cosmic expansion. A popular analogy is the motion of raisins baking in a very large cake. If we choose one particular raisin to represent our galaxy, we find that all the other raisins/galaxies are moving away from us in all directions. As a result, our universe has expanded from the hot, dense cosmic soup created in the Big Bang to the much cooler and more rarefied collection of galaxies and clusters of galaxies that we see today.[29]

Note: The May 30, 2004 issue of PhysicsWorld.com goes on to state that an even bigger mystery than dark energy itself is that it suggests the existence of a substance that is gravitationally repulsive (antigravity).

We know how much dark energy there must be out there because we know how it affects the universe's expansion. Other than that, it is a complete mystery. Here again are listed percentages of matter and energy that make up the known universe: roughly 70 percent is dark energy. Dark matter makes up about 26 percent, and the rest, 4 percent, is everything that we know and can observe (the earth, stars, galaxies, and so on).

The following diagram from NASA illustrates the rate of cosmic expansion over the past 14 billion years. The more shallow the curve the faster the rate of expansion.

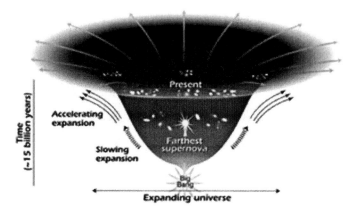

The curve changes noticeably about 7.5 billion years ago, when objects in the universe began flying apart at a faster rate. Astronomers theorize that the faster expansion rate is due to a mysterious, dark energy that is pulling galaxies apart.[30]
(Credit: NASA/STSci/Ann Field)

So, we have been speculating on two great mysteries, dark matter and dark energy, both of which have yet to be revealed scientifically. Scripturally, there may be references to these forces, one that holds the stars and galaxies together and the other that causes the universe to expand. As you will see in a later section, certain scriptures and scientific thought lead us to better understand that Christ is literally the source of all matter, energy, and force in the universe. In speaking of Christ, one scripture that will be quoted later on is Doctrine and Covenants, section 88, verse 41: "He comprehendeth all things, and all things are before him, and all things are round about him; and he is above all things, and in all things, and is through all things, and is round about all things; and all things are by him, and of him, even God, forever and ever."

As revealed in this scripture, Christ is the source of all matter and energy in the universe. He is *in all things and is through all things and round about all things*! Whatever dark matter and dark energy are, we know that they are of Christ.

One final thought derived from both the scriptures and physics may possibly provide a better clue as to where dark matter and dark energy come from. If we return to the Doctrine and Covenants, section 88, verse 37, we find some possible reference to the force and mass that fills what we call empty space, and that could be thought of as dark matter and dark energy: "There is no space in the which there is no kingdom;

and there is no kingdom in which there is no space, either a greater or a lesser kingdom."

In some ways, this sounds like a sort of riddle: "There is no space in which there is no kingdom and there is no kingdom in which there is no space." However, this verse makes a lot of sense when we contemplate the universe and all that fills it, large and small. Mankind exists in the realm of the big (the greater kingdom), yet all around us—and even filling what we think is empty space—lies a quantum world (a lesser or smaller kingdom).

As mentioned previously in this document and as will be put forth later, many scientists believe that empty space is filled with activity at the quantum level. This notion can be illustrated by zooming in and sequentially magnifying ever smaller regions of the fabric of space. The uncertainty principle tells us that *everything* is subject to quantum fluctuations. Although reasoning implies that empty space is just that, empty, quantum mechanics shows that *on average* it is empty and carries a zero gravitational field, but that its actual value undulates up and down due to quantum fluctuations.

The famous physicist John Wheeler coined the term "quantum foam" to describe the frenzy revealed by such a microscopic examination of space and time. The following is a representation of that activity as it might exist under super-magnification:

As one can see, at the first level there appears to be no activity. However, the further one drills down into the cosmic foam, the more violent and frothy the picture becomes.

The quantum foam that fills space is teeming with virtual particles. These theoretical, virtual particles, like real particles, contain energy; and they also possess negative pressure that exhibits properties exactly like those of dark energy that is causing the universe to expand

and stretch out (similar to what Einstein proposed).

About thirty years ago, a group of theoretical physicists worked out how much dark energy would be produced by all the virtual particles found in space at the quantum level. The number they came up with was so large as to at first glance be unbelievable. However, there is something called *supersymmetry* that helps the number come more in line with what is needed to produce the tremendous quantity of dark energy causing the universe to expand at an ever-increasing rate. The point is—and the reason for bringing up the concept of supersymmetry is that *both science and religion are in agreement that there is no space where there is no world or kingdom.*

Not only does this conjectured agreement between physics and religion lead us to believe that there is no space where there isn't a world of some sort (quantum or large), but both sources concur that the laws governing these worlds can be very different. Physicists are astounded—even confounded when they consider the laws that govern the quantum world. Everything is so different from the world we live in that our common sense doesn't apply. The scriptures essentially agree that distinct laws may exist for every world (kingdom): "Unto every kingdom is given a law; and unto every law there are certain bounds also and conditions" (D&C 88:38).

Then, speaking of God: "he hath given a law unto all things, by which they move" (D&C 88:42).

* Any reader wishing to access more detailed information about virtual particles and dark energy can refer to a book by Paul Davies, *Cosmic Jackpot*, pages 146 thru 150.

Final Aspect of the Creation

Is the Creation as it pertains to the earth and mankind finished? I would like to suggest that another final chapter in our planet's history is yet to be completed—specifically the aspect of the resurrection. In the King James Bible Dictionary used by The Church of Jesus Christ of Latter-day Saints, the resurrection is described in the following fashion:

> The resurrection consists in the uniting of a spirit body with a body of flesh and bones, never again to be divided. The resurrection will come to all . . . a resurrection means to become immortal. . . .
>
> One of the most fundamental doctrines taught by the Twelve was that Jesus was risen from the tomb, with his glorified, resurrected body.

I would submit that the resurrection not only pertains to mankind but also to the earth itself. The earth, like each person who ever lived on it, will likewise die and be resurrected (see D&C 88:25–26). Once our world has fulfilled the measure of its creation and we are finished with mortality, an event will transpire that will bring much purpose to those who merit it: "This earth, in its sanctified and immortal state, will be made like unto crystal and will be a Urim and Thummim to the inhabitants who dwell thereon . . . and this earth will be Christ's" (D&C 130:9).

First, what is a Urim and Thummim; and second, why would God cause the earth to become one?

Nearly all members of The Church of Jesus Christ of Latter-day Saints are aware that when Joseph Smith received the gold plates from the angel Moroni, included with them were two stones set in silver bows, fastened to a breastplate. The two stones set in silver bows in particular have been called the Urim and Thummim. Joseph Smith used them to translate the Book of Mormon just as Moroni had used the stones to translate the Book of Ether.

Those familiar with the Bible are also aware of the existence of Urim and Thummim that were in the possession of Moses and handed down from prophet to prophet (Exodus 28:30; Leviticus 8:8; Numbers 27:21; Deuteronomy 33:8; 1 Samuel 28:6; Ezra 2:63; Nehemiah 7:65). The Lord, in speaking to Moses, said: "And thou shalt put in the breast-plate of judgment the Urim and the Thummim; and they shall be upon Aaron's heart, when he goeth in before the Lord: and Aaron shall bear the judgment of the children of Israel upon his heart before the Lord continually" (Exodus 28:30).

This scripture clearly shows that Moses's brother Aaron used the Urim and Thummim extensively.

The Book of Mormon also provides a brief description of the Urim and Thummim. Ammon was asked by King Limhi if he knew of anyone who could translate an ancient text (the Book of Ether). Ammon responded:

> I can assuredly tell thee, O king, of a man that can translate the records; for he has wherewith that he can look, and translate all records that are of ancient date; and it is a gift from God. And the things are called interpreters, and no man can look in them except he be commanded, lest he should look for that he ought not and he should perish.

And whosoever is commanded to look in them, the same is called seer. (Mosiah 8:13)

In addition to this description, Elder Bruce R. McConkie's *Mormon Doctrine* offers the following:

> URIM AND THUMMIM:
>
> From time to time, as his purposes require, the Lord personally, or through the ministry of appointed angels, delivers to chosen prophets a Urim and Thummim to be used in receiving revelations and in translating ancient records from unknown tongues. With the approval of the Lord these prophets are permitted to pass these instruments on to their mortal successors.
>
> A Urim and Thummim consists of two special stones called seer stones or interpreters. The Hebrew words urim and thummim, both plural, mean lights, and perfections.[30]

The first part of Elder McConkie's definition is fairly standard, something with which church members are familiar. Then Elder McConkie's description becomes eye-opening. The Hebrew word *urim* means "lights" and the Hebrew word *thummim* means "perfections." We know that with light comes understanding and knowledge. The word *perfections,* on the other hand, points to a couple of ideas. One is that these stones help the holder or benefactors to become perfect; a second thought might suggest that the stones are perfect and can only be used to obtain information that is perfect and true in every sense.

Further research on the Urim and Thummim revealed some surprising facts. I came across various interesting definitions regarding the purposes and uses of a Urim and Thummim from Jewish and Catholic sources that at first glance appear to be only slightly different than standard LDS thought:

> JEWISH ENCYCLOPEDIA:
>
> [The Urim and Thummim are] objects connected with the breastplate of the high priest, and used as a kind of divine oracle. Since the days of the Alexandrian translators of the Old Testament, it has been asserted that [the Hebrew words for Urim and Thummim] mean "revelation and truth," or "lights and perfections" . . . Exodus xxvii, 13–30 describes the high-priestly ephod and the breastplate with the Urim and Thummim. It is called a "breastplate of judgment" ("hoshen ha-mishpat").

The teachers of the Talmud, however, if their own statements may be believed . . . regarded [the Urim and Thummim] as the "great and holy name of God" written on the breastplate of the high priest, and they etymologize "Urim" as "those whose words give light," while "Thummim" is explained as "those whose words are fulfilled."[31]

CATHOLIC ENCYCLOPEDIA: Urim and Thummim
The sacred lot by means of which the ancient Hebrews were wont to seek manifestations of the Divine will. . . . Urim is derived from the Hebrew for "light" or "to give light," and Thummim from "completeness," "perfection," or "innocence." In view of these derivations it is surmised by some scholars that the sacred lot may have had a twofold purpose in trial ordeals, viz. Urim served to bring to light the guilt of the accused person, and Thummim to establish his innocence . . . in Numbers 27:21: "If anything is to be done, Eleazar the priest shall consult the Lord for him" (Heb. "and he [Eleazar] shall invoke upon him the judgment of Urim before the Lord") . . .

From this and various other passages which it would be too long to discuss here (e.g. Deuteronomy 33:8, Hebrews, 1 Samuel 14:36, 1 Samuel 23:6-12 etc.), we gather that the Urim and Thummim were a species of sacred oracle manipulated by the priest in consulting the Divine will, and that they were at times used as a kind of Divine ordeal to discover the guilt or innocence of suspected persons.[32]

In comparing LDS doctrine to that of Jewish and Catholic thought, all three definitions similarly use the terms *light* and *perfections* for urim and thummim. Even so, there are aspects of the definitions that seem to be somewhat different. The Jewish Encyclopedia call the apparatus upon which the stones are fastened a "breastplate of judgment"; the Catholic Encyclopedia similarly states that the stones were used "to discover the guilt or innocence of suspected persons." When I first read this I mulled it over and thought, "Well, here is difference of thought between The Church of Jesus Christ of Latter-day Saints and other major religions. The LDS Church sees the Urim and Thummim as a tool for inspired translation of ancient records, while both the Catholic and Jewish religions perceive that the stones were used as tools to judge the guilt or innocence of people." For several months I pondered these seemingly distinct notions. Then one day, while reading from the Book of Mormon, I came across a block of scripture I had read a hundred times yet had ignored or not understood. It was as if a light turned on in my head. There, in one of my favorite chapters (Alma 37), Alma is writing to his son, Helaman, and is describing something he found in the ancient Jaredite record, the Book of Ether:

> For behold, the Lord saw that his people began to work in darkness, yea, work secret murders and abominations; therefore the Lord said, if they did not repent they should be destroyed from off the face of the earth. And the Lord said: I will prepare unto my servant Gazelem, a stone, which shall shine forth in darkness unto light, that I may discover unto my people who serve me . . . the works of their brethren, yea, their secret works, their works of darkness, and their wickedness and abominations. And now, my son, these interpreters were prepared that the word of God might be fulfilled, which he spake, saying: I will bring forth out of darkness unto light all their secret works and their abominations; and except they repent I will destroy them from off the face of the earth; and I will bring to light all their secrets and abominations. (Alma 37:22–25)

Immediately it was made clear to me that Gazelem, who had been a Jaredite prophet, was given a set of interpreters (Urim and Thummim) so that he could judge the righteousness and wickedness (guilt or innocence) of his people. This was exactly the same use for the Urim and Thummim described by the Catholic and Jewish encyclopedias. As I contemplated those Book of Mormon verses, it was enlightening to one more time be persuaded of the truth and consistency found in that great book.

Now that we have a combined definition (Catholic, Jewish, and LDS) for the uses of the Urim and Thummim (translation, revelation, judgment), we can move on and see if there is any scientific rationale for these mysterious stones.

Pondering on how a Urim and Thummim might work, I came to realize that a scientific basis was right under my nose—and had been for many years. There is a good chance that the two stones that make up a Urim and Thummim are crystals. But, either way, in our time, both stones and crystals contain unique properties that are used in industry and in communications. For instance, vibrating crystals make up the main time-keeping component in wristwatches, clocks, computers, cell phones, oscilloscopes and even electric pianos (to produce different tones).

The use of crystals in radios, past and present, however, is even more intriguing and, in my mind, most pertinent to this writing. Crystals can be used as both radio transmitters (to modulate frequency) and as passive radio receivers. Most of us have heard of crystal radios, which were first invented in the late 1800s. At one time a crystal radio graced most homes, many of them built from spare parts found around the house or at the local hardware store. Today, crystal radios are rare and not universally understood. But if you have a grandfather or great-grandfather in his eighties who is still alive, he could tell you all about crystal radios, as he probably had one in his home when he was a boy.

It would not be a stretch to say that it is quite possible that a Urim and Thummim functions something like the amazing crystal radio. Let me explain how one works and you can be the judge.

Radio stations convert sound into radio waves and send out the waves in every direction. At some point within reach of those waves, a crystal radio receives the transmission and converts the waves back into sound. Most important, a crystal radio does not need any external power source. Yes, you read that right. No batteries and no electric wall-plug are necessary. The radio needs nothing more than the following components:

- An antenna
- A ground wire
- Some sort of tuner
- A crystal detector
- Ear phones

Again, as you can see, no battery or *any* other power source is on the list. Why? Because the radio waves actually *become* the power source. As the radio waves reach the antenna, the waves themselves become the source of electricity and flow between the antenna wire and the ground wire. The radio uses a simple tuner to receive a particular station from the electrical impulses. The tuner can be as simple as an adjustable one-slider that resonates with the antenna. Then, as the electricity leaves the tuner, it arrives at the crystal, which acts as a detector. When earphones are connected to the crystal, they convert the electricity to audible sound.

Thanks to Wikipedia, here is a pictorial representation of a crystal radio:

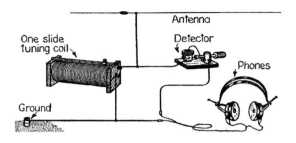

Pictorial diagram showing parts and connections for a crystal radio.

In addition to converting radio waves to electricity, one of the other reasons a crystal radio doesn't need an external power source is because of the amazing capabilities of the human ear. The ear is extremely sensitive to very faint sounds. As was mentioned before, the radio acts as a receiver and uses only the energy of the waves sent by radio transmitters, which send out enormous amounts of energy. However, because they are usually far away and because our radio antennas aren't large, the amount of energy received by the crystal radio is very small, measured in billionths of a watt. Even so, the human ear can detect sounds that are less than even a millionth of that.

Now that you can see how a crystal radio operates, let's compare that to how Urim and Thummim might work. The physical description given by the Book of Mormon prophet Moroni for a Urim and Thummim is that it is made up of two stones held in silver bows, connected to a breastplate (Joseph Smith—History 1:33–35). This sounds about the same as the description given in the Old Testament, which describes the one that Moses similarly possessed. I am not sure that we have any detailed record as to how these devices were used by the prophets who had access to them. We know that one could look into the stones and receive knowledge, but that knowledge came with a warning. In Mosiah 8:13 Ammon says, "No man can look in them except he be commanded, lest he should look for that he ought not and he should perish." From this we at least know that the eyes were involved and that this vital, revealed knowledge could be gained by sight.

With these facts in mind, let's stretch our imagination a bit. The bows that hold the two stones could be something like eyeglasses the user puts on so that he can look through or into the stones. For now, let's suppose that the Urim and Thummim functioned something like a crystal radio, with no external energy source except the particular light waves sent from God to power the device. So, is it possible that God gave the ancient prophets devices that could be used to tune into God's revelatory broadcasts?

Recently I visited my dentist. Just before he began work on a tooth that needed a crown, he offered me a set of space-age like eyeglasses to use while he worked. With these glasses, I was able to watch one of my favorite movies. If we can invent devices like that, surely God can, too.

Early Book of Mormon scripture offers yet another instance of stones being used as a source of power and light. Included in Ether's account of the Jaredites, the Lord commands Jared's people to leave the area where the Tower of Babel is being built. After a long journey over land and water, the Lord commands the people to cross a great sea/ocean. Through their prophet, the brother of Jared, they are told to build barges that are small, light on the water, completely enclosed, and tight like a "dish" (waterproof). Once the barges were completed, the Lord instructs them to cut holes in the top and bottom (that can be stopped up), so they can let air into their crafts. Then the brother of Jared goes before the Lord to discuss a problem:

> Behold, O Lord, wilt thou suffer that we shall cross this great water in darkness? And the Lord said unto the brother of Jared: What will ye that I should do that ye may have light in your vessels? For behold, ye cannot have windows, for they will be dashed in pieces; neither shall ye take fire with you . . . For behold, ye shall be as a whale in the midst of the sea; for the mountain waves shall dash upon you. (Ether 2:22–24)

After this conversation, the brother of Jared, having great faith, treks to a nearby mountain and smelts sixteen small, white, clear stones, and brings them before the Lord saying: "I know, O Lord, that thou hast all power, and can do whatsoever thou wilt for the benefit of man; therefore touch these stones, O Lord, with thy finger, and prepare them that they may shine forth in darkness" (Ether 3:4).

In answer to the prophet's plea, the Lord touches the stones, changing their molecular structure in some fashion so that they can serve as a source of light inside the barges while the Jaredites cross the great waters. Two stones are placed in each of the eight crafts. Then, loaded with provisions, with holes top and bottom for air, and with a light source, the Jaredites successfully venture across the ocean, ending up on one of the American continents.

I have often thought about this remarkable light source and wondered how the Jaredite stones worked. Armed with the simple knowledge of a crystal radio, we can understand that the Lord may have prepared the stones to receive waves of power from some source in the universe (similar to radio waves and light waves) that caused them to generate light. How amazing!

Now that we have some idea as to how stones or crystals can be used for power and communications, let's turn back to the initial reason for even bringing up the subject of the Urim and Thummim. After the earth has fulfilled is mortal purpose, it will be "resurrected" and become a great Urim and Thummim, the very habitation of those inheriting the celestial kingdom.

I think we can assume that the main purpose for the earth's becoming a Urim and Thummim is so it can serve as a great source of communications and power for its inhabitants. If we turn again to the Doctrine and Covenants and review the verses quoted earlier, we find yet another one to help us better understand God's purpose in all of this: "The place where God resides is a great Urim and Thummim. This earth, in its sanctified and immortal state, will be made like unto crystal and will be a Urim and Thummim to the inhabitants who dwell thereon" (D&C 130:8–9).

In a prior verse it states that these globes are like a "sea of glass and fire" where all things are manifest, past, present, and future, and are continually before the Lord.

These two massive globes, Urim and Thummim, where God resides and where we will reside if we are counted among the righteous, will provide their inhabitants with tremendous power, stored knowledge, and celestial communications capability. Those who inherit the earth in its glorified state will also know all things past, present, and future. They will inhabit a remarkable planet, a sanctified earth that provides access to great stores of knowledge, a powerful tool for communication with God and other celestial peoples throughout the universe.

Once again, we find in science something as simple as a crystal radio, a device that can help us better understand the way God works. There may be more scientific worth in the scriptures than most think. Do possibilities exist for scientists to take advantage of just these verses in Ether? If they did, we might find them working more with stones and crystals for power sources, lighting devices, and communications. Who knows what other marvelous discoveries might be made by just taking seriously the revelations God has given us.

III. Law of Opposition: What does physics have to do with this?

The previous subchapter was written about a physical universe designed and created by a loving Eternal Father who wants you, me and all His children to become like Him and return to live with Him. In that regard, science can bring into focus some of the remarkable detail behind what had to be done for God's plan to work. One of those details was the establishment of something we call the "law of opposition." You may ask: How can physics help us understand the law of opposition? Isn't that simply a spiritual law? Read on and see.

In the beginning, prior to the Big Bang, there was no matter. Everything in the universe was energy. This energy was compacted into a space a trillionth the size of an atom. The onset of the Big Bang sent temperatures in the early cosmos soaring. In less than a millionth of a trillionth of a trillionth of a trillionth of a second after the Big Bang, the temperature in the universe was 100,000,000,000,000,000,000,000,000,000,000,000 degrees Kelvin. If we had calculated the heat in Fahrenheit terms, the number would have been far larger. Either way, it was 100,000 times hotter than the sun's core. Then, an instant later, just ten thousandths of a second after the Big Bang, a portion of the energy formed into matter. During those early moments, matter was an ultra hot, super dense soup of particles called quarks and gluons. Because of the tremendous heat, they were incredibly active, zipping around everywhere and crashing into one another.

As the cosmos began its expansion, temperatures plummeted. Quarks and gluons slowed down enough to begin sticking together. After a few more microseconds had elapsed, these tiny particles became bound together by strong "nuclear" forces between them. Quarks and gluons became locked together permanently within protons, neutrons, and other particles that physicists collectively call "hadrons." The protons and neutrons that are part of every atom today are ancient droplets of that first great genesis that produced an ocean of tiny subatomic particles.[33]

As the universe expanded and cooled, the density of matter and the associated radiation gradually decreased. The particulate matter began to disperse outward and the universe took on an emptiness that gradually became what we see today. Because there was now so much empty space, the overall values for both matter fields and force fields began to approach zero. These fields included the electromagnetic fields (light is included in this group), the gravitational field, the strong nuclear force, and the weak nuclear force. Each of these fields/forces will be more completely described in future sections.

We all have an innate idea as to what light and gravity are. The strong and weak nuclear forces, on the other hand, though less familiar, are not difficult to understand. In a nutshell, the strong nuclear force is what holds atoms together, and the weak nuclear force is what prompts the gradual decay of matter and turns it back into energy. Many readers may be familiar with radioactive decay as it pertains to something like uranium. All the forces being discussed came into being at the time of the Big Bang.

In addition to light, gravity, and the nuclear forces just described, many physicists strongly believe that still another kind of field or force plays an elementary role in governing our universe. Created some time after the Big Bang, it is know as the *Higgs field*, named after the Scottish physicist Peter Higgs. This field wasn't formed until the temperature of the cosmos cooled sufficiently. An ocean of sorts formed filling the universe. We call this formation a *Higgs ocean*. As was mentioned a few paragraphs back, the universe spread out and the other fields (including electromagnetic and gravity) all dropped to a near zero value in empty space. However, the Higgs field did not. It never made it to zero. It uniformly permeates the universe, so that's why we call it a Higgs ocean. It fills all of space throughout the entire universe.

The question is: If empty space—nothingness—carries a value of zero, and if the Higgs field carries a nonzero value, and if we are all immersed in an ocean of Higgs field, why can't we see it, or feel it, or in some way be aware of it?

In fact, modern physics claims we do. For instance, pick up

something heavy like a brick or a dumbbell and swing it back and forth. Your muscles have to work hard to put the weight into motion, and then they must work hard to stop the motion and bring it back the other way. In this sense, the mass of an object represents the resistance it has to being moved. The greater the mass is, the greater the resistance.

The atoms that constitute your arm—and those that make up the brick or dumbbell you picked up—are all formed from protons, neutrons, and electrons. The protons and neutrons are broken down into even smaller particles known as quarks. So, when you swing the dumbbell back and forth, you are swinging all the electrons and quarks in both the object and your arm back and forth. The Higgs ocean that we have been talking about interacts with the electrons and the quarks. Thus, the more electrons and quarks there are (in other word, the more mass there is) the greater the resistance to moving those electrons and quarks.

One way to think about a Higgs field is to compare it to a gyroscope, a toy with which most have played. The spinning of a gyroscope creates energy, a kind of field. When you attempt to move it, it resists that movement. Another way to think about how a Higgs field affects mass is to, while you are in a swimming pool, hold a volleyball in your hand beneath the water of a swimming pool, then try to aggressively push and pull it back and forth. The water resists the movement of the ball. A Higgs field is something like that. The Higgs ocean that is all around us interacts with the electrons and quarks. It hinders movement and resists the particles accelerations and decelerations much as water resists the motion of a volleyball. So, we really do feel the Higgs ocean all around us, the field that creates resistance to every physical move we make.

The amount of resistance put up by the Higgs ocean when something is accelerated or decelerated, varies with each specific object because it depends on the particles that make up that object. It takes more effort to put a ball of steel in motion than a similarly sized ball aluminum. That is why airplanes are not made of steel.

It is essential to note that once you put an object in motion, if there is no resistance (like gravity, water, and so forth) to slow it down, it will continue moving forever. If you were to toss a ball while out in empty space, it would fly out of your hand with little effort and would continue to speed along forever because there is no resistance to slow it down.

A photon (particle of light) is one particle that can instantly move from a resting position to the speed of light in the Higgs ocean without resistance. A photon has no mass. So, its instantaneous movement to the speed of light is not affected by the Higgs ocean. Photons accelerate and pass unhindered through the Higgs ocean. If there were no Higgs ocean, all fundamental particles would be like the photon and would effectively demonstrate no mass whatsoever. That means we could put in motion a real airplane made of iron as easily as we could a model airplane made of balsa wood.

In such a condition there wouldn't be any resistance to anything. Automobiles, airplanes, and rockets could accelerate and decelerate instantly without energy and force to do it.

Athletes could instantly accelerate to top speed and just as easily stop on a dime. A baseball pitcher throwing a 100 mile fast ball would be commonplace. However, we wouldn't have muscles developed to even throw a ball because we couldn't practice doing it. There is an oxymoron there some place, but you get the idea. Without any resistance there would be no reason to practice.

The Higgs ocean is just one of a number of forces God may have put in place to regulate and bring order to the universe. We can also see that since the Higgs ocean provides resistance, it provides opposition to the movement of all things. "Opposition in all things"—that is something we have heard before. The physical laws of the universe, forces like the Higgs field and gravity, bring opposition into play, albeit a sort of temporal opposition, not a spiritual one like sin. But in some ways these physical forces are just as important.

Let's read about opposition in the Bible and also from a well known chapter in the Book of Mormon. When Eve and Adam were expelled from the Garden of Eden, they were *blessed with a curse.* I am sure that sounds contradictory. I am also sure that there are days when each of us feels that the effect of that blessing really is a curse.

In Genesis we find: "Cursed is the ground for thy sake. . . . In the sweat of thy face shalt thou eat bread, till thou return unto the ground" (Genesis 3:17, 19).

And we read in the Pearl of Great Price: "Cursed shall be the ground for thy sake; in sorrow shalt thou eat of it all the days of thy life. . . . By the sweat of thy face shalt thou eat bread, until thou shalt return unto the ground" (Moses 4:23, 25).

So that is the curse: we must work all the days of our life. At least a portion of that sweat is a result of the Higgs ocean and the gravititational force that God caused to surround us. If we didn't have to overcome these forces, there certainly would be no sweat of the brow.

In terms of work being a blessing ("cursed shall be the ground for thy sake"), here are a few statements from great men expressing how they feel about work:

Albert Einstein about 1947

- From author John Steinbeck, we get, "Work is the only good thing."
- Albert Einstein said, "Work is the only thing that gives substance to life."
- Egyptian peacemaker and former President Anwar al-Sadat said, "Without a vocation, man's existence would be meaningless."
- Finally, Theodore Roosevelt said, "Far and away the best prize that life offers is the chance to work hard at work worth doing."

All of these individuals were Nobel Prize winners and each believed that work is a blessing. That is why the scriptures were written as: "The Lord cursed the ground *for our sake.*"

The Book of Mormon prophet Lehi describes the law of opposition as given to us by God. At least part of that opposition has to do with physical or temporal things as well as that which is spiritual.

> For it must needs be, that there is an opposition in all things . . . Wherefore, all things must needs be a compound in one; wherefore, if it should be one body it must needs remain as dead, having no life neither death, nor corruption nor incorruption, happiness nor misery . . . Wherefore, it must needs have been created for a thing of naught; wherefore there would have been no purpose in the end of its creation. Wherefore, this thing must needs destroy the wisdom of God and his eternal purposes . . . And now, my sons, I speak unto you these things for your profit and learning; for there is a God, and he hath created all things, both the heavens and the earth, and all things that in them are, both things to act and things to be acted upon. (2 Nephi 2:11–14)

Lehi is talking about several kinds of opposition. Spiritual opposition was certainly part of it, but I believe he was also speaking of physical/temporal opposition. At the beginning of these verses, Lehi indicates how important opposition is to our bodies. He says that without opposition there would have been no reason for God to create for us a physical body (in other words, it would have needed to remain dead having no life). Anyone who has ever worked hard undergoes a combination of misery and joy. Joy and peace come from doing something worthwhile and doing a job well. Whether we have just finished planting a garden or painting a fence, we find joy in having done a good job and in having worked hard. Of course, there was also some misery along the way— heat, sweat, and long hours.

I remember that on a few occasions working as a missionary in Argentina, at the end of the day it felt like we had lived the perfect day. We had given everything possible to the Lord and His work; we couldn't have done more. It was on these occasions that I felt real joy and com- plete peace. We had worked hard spiritually, but we had also worked hard physically.

In Doctrine and Covenants section 93, we are told how important our bodies are to our overall happiness: "For man is spirit. The elements are eternal, and *spirit and element, inseparably connected, receive a full- ness of joy*; and when separated, man cannot receive a fullness of joy" (D&C 93:33–34). Of course, the element refers to the body that one's spirit inhabits. What good is a body that doesn't feel any opposition to its muscles? Our bodies are meant to bring us joy. Without opposition (Higgs ocean and gravity) our bodies would be sickly and anemic; there wouldn't be any reason to have one.

The creation of these forces and fields (Higgs, electromagnetic, gravity,and so on) provided a background and stage for life in the uni- verse. Without these basic, universal, all-encompassing forces, there would be nothing.

Of course, we have barely touched on what God has created. We have examined just a couple of forces that help make His plan work. How- ever, I hope this scientific perspective helps you to better understand this remarkable universe that was created for our joy and happiness. Maybe science will also help us to be more grateful for our marvelous exis- tence!

IV. Predestination: What does science have to say?

Before getting into the meat of this section, a few of definitions from the Merriam-Webster Dictionary are in order:

Predestine: To settle beforehand.

Predestination: The doctrine that God in consequence of his foreknowledge of all events infallibly guides those who are destined for salvation.

If one looks at predestination from the perspective of the average person, the term simply suggests that everything was planned out in advance and that we will all end up where we should be once this life is over. Predestination infers that one really doesn't have a say in regard to the outcome of this life and the reward hereafter. Indeed, if the universe and our part in it is predestined, as we lead our lives it won't much matter what we do because God knows all along the outcome of all things. Nothing can be changed for the better or, for that matter, for the worse.

Now let's examine a couple more dictionary definitions:

Agency: The capacity, condition or state of acting.

Free will: Voluntary

Obviously, the online Merriam-Webster Dictionary definition for *agency* is not complete when it comes to religious thought. So, we will turn to the meaning given by Bruce R. McConkie in *Mormon Doctrine*:

Agency is the ability and freedom to choose good or evil. . . . Agency is given to man as an essential part of the great plan of redemption. As with all things appertaining to this plan, it is based on the atoning sacrifice of Christ. As Lehi expressed it: "**Because that they are redeemed from the fall they have become free forever, knowing good from evil; to act for themselves** . . . " (2 Nephi 2:26–30)[34]

Strange as it may seem, quantum theory as it may pertain to our world of relativity (the world of the "big" that we live in) is important to understanding "predestination" from a scientific perspective. In a preceding section we considered the following: quantum theory is based on the concept that there is a probability that all possible events *might* occur, no matter how crazy or wacky they may be. Physicist Niels Bohr, who was instrumental in defining Quantum Mechanics, championed the thought that *before one measures an electron's position, there is no sense in even asking where it is.* It does not have a definite position. Even though the probability wave creates the *likelihood* that the electron, when properly examined, will be found here or there, it simply doesn't have a definite location until a measurement is done. The act of measuring the electron, though, somehow helps create the reality of the electron's location.

In 1927, Werner Heisenberg postulated the following regarding the uncertainty principle: A particle, according to quantum theory, cannot have a definite position and a definite velocity; a particle cannot have a definite spin (clockwise or counterclockwise) about more than one axis; a particle cannot simultaneously have definite attributes for things that lie on opposite sides of the uncertainty divide. Apparently, according to Heisenberg, particles hover in quantum limbo, in a fuzzy, amorphous, probabilistic mixture of all possibilities; and only when they are measured is one definite outcome selected from many.

In order to better understand this concept, let's consider again the fact that a proton, an electron, or any other subatomic object is both a particle and a wave. Since it is a wave, the particle can be anyplace in the wave; in reality it is anyplace and everyplace until it is measured or viewed. One way to consider this is if you imagine that you are outside, standing by a still pond and you toss a pebble into the water. A concentric ring of small waves instantly forms circles that expand out in all directions from the place where the pebble hit the water. That is sort of the way electrons or other subatomic particles move. Even though they are individually single objects, each independently functions as a wave.

When a particle is measured or viewed, we immediately see its location. Until then we don't know for sure where it is. We can determine the probability that it is in one location or another, but don't really know

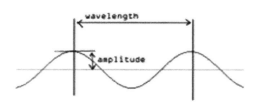

for sure. The reason we can forecast or guess at the probability is because waves have peaks and valleys.

A particle's location will most likely be near or at the

peak of the wave rather than on the downslope or in the valley. When scientists calculate the probability of the location of a particle they call this measuring its "wave function." Again, you can never know precisely where something like an electron is. The best you can do is calculate its wave function, which tells you the probability of it being in any particular location on the wave. If the wave function is large at a certain point, it means that there is a high probability that the electron is at that location.

Since an electron can seemingly be in two—and even many—places at the same time, how do we finally determine where it actually is? Scientists hypothesize that the wave functions we see in the quantum world may even apply in our world of relativity.[35] If we could see the wave function of a person, it would look very much like the person himself; however, over time the wave function would seep out and away from the person like ripples from the stone tossed in a pond, spreading so far away that the wave would reach places like New York or Tokyo. The probability that you or I might be found in a far away location compared to where we are right now is very small. But it may be possible. It is important to remember that the location of a particle in the quantum world is never definite; rather, it is based on probabilities that its location could be anywhere and everywhere until it is observed. Again, is it possible that the *relative* world we live in functions the same way?

Yet another example: one of my hobbies is mountain biking. Let's assume that one fine spring day I am riding up Mueller Park Canyon in Bountiful, Utah, and that I decide to ride all the way to the top and down into North Canyon. Let's also assume that I am the first rider of the year to make it over the top after the snow melts enough to let me through. A veritable forest of trees hugs the trail and every year a few of them, weighed down by snow, fall across and block the trail.

Now it is our task to analyze this situation. In reality, each of those trees may have a wave function that determines the probability as to whether it is standing or it has fallen. Obviously, a young, strong tree has a higher probability that, come spring, it is standing, while an old less stable tree has a higher probability that it has fallen. Just the same, both young and old trees have some chance that they are both standing and fallen. If I could calculate the probability of the wave function for each tree, it would tell me their likely state (standing or fallen) before I rode to them. But even then I would not have the ability to definitely know the condition of the trees. Common sense tells us that the objects are in definite states because when you look at the trees they are either standing or fallen, but not both. Is there anything to quantum physics in our world of general relativity? Is it possible that those trees were actually in *both* states—standing and fallen—until I observed them?

Sounds crazy, right? And to some contemplating such notions it may feel like a waste of time. But I assure you it is not, so try to stay with us on this.

Now, let's keep the aforementioned examples in mind as we try to resolve the discrepancy between waves of probability and our common-sense thoughts about our existence. One of the first to try to resolve this discrepancy was Niels Bohr, a contemporary of Einstein. Bohr concluded that after the measurement of an electron is made by an outside observer, the wave function magically "collapses," and the electron is found in a definite state. In other words, *the process of observation determines the final state of the electron.* Bohr essentially found that observation is vital to existence. The electron isn't in a definite state until we observe it. When we look at the electron, its wave function somehow collapses and we are able to see its definite state.

Scientists have speculated how remarkable it would be if one could control the wave functions, and then ensure that the electron's final state was exactly where they wanted them to be. Then, they would be able to control everything, small and large, as if by magic. You or I might be able to instantly appear in New York or Hong Kong, as our personal wave functions could be manipulated and collapsed at any point along the wave.

You may recall in the previous section on the creation, that this wave function concept was used as one of the postulates for how the universe was created. At the time of the Big Bang, it is possible that the universe just sprang into existence. Maybe God decided in what state He wanted the universe to be and controlled the collapse of the wave function so that His creation would be exactly as it is, as it needed to be. If it can be done, then God, if he so chooses, can do it!

Niels Bohr put forth a couple of the postulates that pertain to quantum mechanics. They can be loosely summarized as follows:

- Matter is made up of particles, and the probability of finding the particle is a factor of a wave.

- Before an observation is made to see where the particle is, the particle exists in all possible locations at the same time. To determine the particle's state, we have to observe it. This observation collapses the wave function and the particle shows up in its final state. The act of measuring/observing the particle destroys the wave function and the particle takes on a definite reality.

Philosophically and scientifically there is a possibility that our large world of general relativity functions like the small world of quantum physics; if that is true, it could in turn be possible that as I rode up the trail on my mountain bike, none of the trees would have been in a fallen or standing state until I or someone else observed them.

As you might guess, no matter how documented or experimentally proven quantum theory is, it is based on concepts that have created tremendous controversy in the worlds of theology and philosophy over the past century. Did God somehow create a universe for us that doesn't exist until we observe or affect it? And that question leads to a bigger question: Do we, in fact, have the free will or agency to determine our own reality? Or is everything predestined by God?

Both Isaac Newton and Einstein rejected the notion of free will and agency. They believed in what religionists refer to as *predestination* and they called *determinism*. In their minds, God, in the beginning, created a universe in the form of a giant wound-up clock. Ever since then the universe has been ticking in a precise and predictable way. "Determinism" insinuates that the future can be predicted as easily as the past has been determined.

Accordingly, Newton and Einstein felt that we live our lives out in a preplanned state. The idea of agency or free will—that we are the masters of our destiny—is an illusion. Maybe this is what was at the heart of Einstein's comment to Niels Bohr regarding quantum theory when he said, "God does not play dice with the world." Whereupon Bohr reportedly fire back, "Stop telling God what to do."[36]

Most members of The Church of Jesus Christ of Latter-day Saints take the side of quantum physics. We don't believe in absolute predestination/determinism. Rather, we believe each of us has the right to make choices and decisions; to a great degree, we control our own destinies.

Taking that a step further, the scriptures demonstrate that people with sufficient faith can move mountains and change the courses of rivers. Think about it for a moment. Is it possible that quantum theory works for rivers and mountains? Do wave functions for mountains and rivers exist? Could it be that even rivers and mountains are in many different places and states at the same time until someone observes them and causes their wave functions to collapse? If that is the case, then is it possible that Enoch, through his faith and priesthood, could have controlled wave functions and have caused mountains and rivers to be moved to different places (see Moses 7:13)? Based on a grand blend of science (Quantum Theory) and faith, who is to say that these events didn't occur?

Christ had the faith, authority, and knowledge to instantly heal the sick and blind, and even raise individuals from the dead. Think how those acts must have affected the lives and destinies of those who were healed as well as those who witnessed such miracles.

So, how does the "uncertainty principle" (wave function scientific theory) mix with faith to bring about healings? It is definitely possible that there exists a wave function for each of us. All of the potential scenarios we might experience may be bound up in such a wave or series of waves. We in the Church believe that there are certain blessings just waiting for us if we will worthily seek them. Is it possible that agency allows us to collapse our individual wave functions at an appropriate point to unlock that heavenly store? Is it possible that our lives don't begin to unfold and don't become reality until we collapse our personal wave functions?

In God's eyes we can be as great or as base as we desire. He cares about us, patiently coaxes us, and generously responds to our petitions. But our individual realities don't happen until we make our own decisions. Every day we make decisions that affect our own lives and the lives of those around us. Things like: "Will I go on a mission or will I stay home?" "Will I read the scriptures with my children or will I sleep in?" "Will I pay my tithing or will I spend it on something I want or feel I need?" We determine the outcome of an almost infinite variety of possible events through the exercise of our agency.

I know of at least one physics professor (Michio Kaku) who asks his PhD students to calculate the odds that they will suddenly disassemble and rematerialize on the other side of a brick wall. The reason he asks them to do that is because, according to quantum theory, there is the calculable probability that this can take place. According to Dr. Kaku and quantum theory, there is even probability, albeit very small, that one could rematerialize on a different planet. The probabilities of some of these events occurring are so small that in our everyday lives we dismiss them outright. Just the same, every probability includes a possibility!

Probability, the foundation of quantum theory's "uncertainty principle," is crucial to our very existence. If this uncertainty principle capability didn't exist at the quantum level, our world as we know it would collapse. If atoms obeyed Newton's laws, they would disintegrate whenever they bumped into another atom. What keeps the two atoms locked in a stable molecular state is that the electrons can simultaneously exist in so many places at the same time. When one atom gets to close to another, the electrons that surrounds the atoms, in a kind of cloud, seem to instantly and intelligently appear where they are needed so as to cause the atoms to deflect away from one another. These "electron clouds" act like *force fields* to protect the nucleuses of atoms and keep them from colliding. Thus, the reason why molecules are stable and why the universe doesn't disintegrate is because electrons can be in many places at the same time.

As a matter of fact, if we look at the universe—and even empty space—as a whole, everything seems to possess both intelligence and free will—the ability to act voluntarily. Even subatomic particles can act spontaneously and, it seems, voluntarily. In scientific vernacular, everything, even gravity, is subject to the quantum fluctuations inherent in the uncertainty principle.

Although scientific reasoning implies that empty space has a zero gravitational field, quantum mechanics shows that, in reality, it is only *on the average* zero, but that its actual value changes dramatically due to quantum fluctuations. So, even though portions of outer space appear to be completely devoid of gravity, there is actually a tremendous amount of ongoing activity. When viewed at a subatomic level is a frothing, frenzied world of gravity fluctuations, some positive and some negative. John Wheeler (one of the fathers of the atom bomb) came up with the term *quantum foam* to describe the frenzy that exists in the subatomic layers of space and time. When one recedes to more ordinary distances, the random, violent, small-scale undulations cancel each other out. Expressed another way, when viewed from a distance, space appears to be smooth and without activity. However, if you get close enough you find a tremendous amount of weirdness going on at a subatomic level.

A similar comprehension comes when one views the earth from afar, as when viewed from an orbiting satellite. Up close, the earth is filled with mountains, canyons, valleys, and gullies—and all kinds of physical anomalies. But from outer space, things appear to be fairly level. And the further away one gets the more smooth things appear.

Every object in our universe, it seems, no matter how large or small has some capacity for intelligence and decision-making. However, does that mean everything has agency? I think not. Agency is the gift given to Adam in the Garden of Eden, the special ability to know good from evil and to act freely in that knowledge.

God obviously considers the concepts of intelligence, free will, and agency as incredibly important. He created a universe that involves intelligences and their free will; and for man, it is a universe based on agency, the ability to know and choose between good and evil. In a sense, the overall outcome of the universe is somewhat predetermined. In the beginning—and I mean the *real* beginning, before God created the universe either spiritually or temporally—He must have made a tremendous effort to think things through, to plan and prepare. God wanted to create a place where mankind could be linked with Him and obtain eternal life. And, one of the most important tenets of God is that He will never force man, or any of His creations, to do His will. It all needs to be voluntary. He will provide guidance and even on occasion some coaxing, but *he will never, ever force* mankind, animals, plants, or any other entity, spirit or intelligence, to march to the beat of His divine drum.

So, when God planned this universe (our home), even though He offered free will to us, every creature, and every particle, and even offered agency to man, He knew overall how it would turn out. Like quantum foam, from a distance, everything would be fine in the end. However, up close, there would be lots of ups and downs. Mankind would make countless decisions that are wrong for us and disappointing to God. Along the way, we would learn from our mistakes, apply faith and repentance, accept and live His plan, and gradually become more like Him. Mortality brings its ups and downs, kind of like the quantum foam described in the subatomic world. It is interesting to note that God gave us all a way to even out the quantum foam of our lives. That is, He gave us the Atonement and repentance as a way to smooth things out.

You may recall an earlier reference to Enoch's dealings with God

(Moses 7), where God showed Enoch all His creations. Enoch also saw angels descending out of heaven, bearing testimony of the Father and the Son, followed by the Holy Ghost, who descended on many—but not all—God's children. Then as God looked on this residue of people that the Holy Ghost hadn't touched, those who hadn't been caught up to Zion, He wept. "And Enoch said to the Lord: How is it that thou canst weep . . . ?"

Indeed, the fact that God can weep over His children is significant. If all things were completely predetermined/predestined, God would have little concern for the way things turn out, as it would all have been decided long ago. But God *does* care about his children. At the personal level for each of us, everything is *not* predetermined. We individually have the right to choose our own paths, decide what our future will be. Do we actively choose to dwell in a world separate from God, in either the telestial or terrestrial kingdoms? Or do we so live our lives that we can dwell with our Eternal Father, becoming like Him, obtaining eternal life and exaltation in the celestial kingdom?

Recently while studying John the Revelator's magnificent and mystifying revelation, I came to the conclusion that God really does know everything from beginning to end. As you know, the book of Revelation includes a description of mankind's history from beginning to end. Seven general time periods for man's earthly history are represented by the opening of seven seals.

In addition to knowing the complete history of mankind on earth to the most minute detail, God's knowledge expands to the complete geologic and prehistoric history of the earth and all of its creatures. He knows the history of everything: all other planets, stars, and galaxies clear down to a level that includes every particle. He knows what each of us will do, how we will individually respond to any given situation in life.

When one begins to understand the remarkable light and knowledge He possesses, that realization often leads to a couple of questions: If God knows the end of every soul, why doesn't He just judge people now and place them in their appropriate kingdoms? Why do we need to go through all the hardship of mortality?

These questions make at least two false assumptions. The first assumption suggests a connection between what God knows and how a person behaves. It does not. No connection exists between what He knows about us as individuals and our behavior.

The second false assumption, as author Richard Draper eloquently puts it:

> . . . is that God as a magician who, by the wave of some divine wand, can make us into creatures of celestial, terrestrial, or telestial glory. But God is not a magician, and he cannot make us into anything. He can protect, guide, and empower us. But we are the ones who make us into something, and we do it through the millions of choices, both big and little (but mostly little), that we make during the course of an entire lifetime. Thus, we shape our eternal character, and in the resurrection what we have shaped is what we become.[37]

God does all in His power to see that we have every opportunity to return to Him and obtain Eternal Life. However, our futures are not predestined. *He will force no man to heaven!* We make our own decisions.

V. Prayer: Is it a scientific possibility?

Einstein postulated that nothing travels faster than the speed of light. Our galaxy is hundreds of light years across. Even if prayers could travel at the speed of light, how is it possible for God to hear and answer prayers?

The closest star to us is four light years away. If God lived there, it would take four years traveling at the speed of light for our prayers to get to him, and another four for him to deliver a response. If he resided *as close* as the center of our galaxy, it would take hundreds of years for prayers to be answered. Or God might live in yet another galaxy millions or billions of light years away. So how is it that we can communicate with Him?

Because the author and readers of this book are largely English speaking and of Christian ancestry, many have prayed and believe their prayers have been answered. Most would emphatically state that God *does* communicate with us through something we call prayer. In this modern age we could be a bit more descriptive and call prayer by another name, like "interstellar personal communications." Whatever we call it, it is the same. We know that we can communicate with God. But how does it work? Does physics have anything to say about the intricacies of prayer? It just might.

In order to understand how prayer works across infinite distances, let's first digress and look at how computers function. (The following is a bit technical, but you should be able to understand.)

For computers to be possible, scientists had to come up with some way of creating a language that computers could electronically utilize. Such a language needed to be extremely efficient, one that could be translated for human users. The invention of transistors made this possible. Using them, scientists realized they could create a very fast and simple language by just turning on and off electrical switches connected to the transistors. A series of *on* switches and *off* switches were used to create computer languages. One of those languages, ASCII, which is based on numbers, was developed a long time ago. You may be aware of the terms *bits* and *bytes*. A bit is a set of four transistor switches turned on or turned off. A byte is a combination of two of those bits. Thus, a byte is two sets of transistor switches (or 8 switches) that can be turned on or off.

Now remember, computers can only understand numbers. So in order to invent such a language, letters and symbols must be represented by numbers. Using the ASCII language for computers (a hexadecimal, base 8 numbering system), the alphabetic letter 'A' is represented as the number 41. The computer uses eight on and off switches, to produce the number 41. In computer language this number (41) is 0100/0001 and the letter 'B' is the number 42 or 0100/0010. These representations (0100/0001 and 0100/0010) simply show which of the eight switches is turned on and which is turned off. The zeros represent switches turned off and the ones represent switches turned on.

Even if you didn't follow all of this, the point is that man, through the use of transistors, was able to create an electronic, numerical language for computers using on and off switches.

Now, let's turn to physics and consider how God might create a language, similar to what we have done with computers, so that He can communicate with us and the rest of His creations across vast, infinite distances. In this regard, physicists have come across a rather remarkable phenomenon, one described by Bill Bryson in his *A Short History of Everything*: "Perhaps the most arresting of quantum improbabilities is the idea, arising from Wofgang Pauli's Exclusion Principle of 1925, that sub-atomic particles in certain pairs, even when separated by the most considerable distances, can each instantly 'know' what the other is doing. Particles have a quality known as spin and, according to quantum theory, the moment you determine the spin of one particle, its sister particle, no matter how distant away, will immediately begin spinning in the opposite direction and at the same rate."[38]

Experiments performed over the past twenty years show that something we do to a particle over here will likewise cause an effect on a particle over there, without any sort of obvious communication being sent between the particles. Einstein called this phenomenon "spooky."

Physicists have proven that there is something they call entanglement, which affects all atoms. This word is highly descriptive in that it references the fact that every atom here on earth and every atom located on other worlds light years away, are united or knitted together in some fashion. Physicist Michio Kaku's book *Parallel Worlds* describes this curiosity in a very straightforward fashion:

> Since all matter came from a single explosion, the Big Bang, in some sense the atoms of our body are linked with some atoms on the other side of the universe in some kind of cosmic quantum web. Entangled particles are somewhat like twins still joined by an umbilical cord (their wave function) which can be light years across. What happens to one member automatically affects the other, and hence knowledge concerning one particle can instantly reveal knowledge about its pair. Entangled pairs act as if they were a single object, although they may be separated by large distance.[39]

These results are derived from both theoretical and experimental efforts, and support the conclusion that the particles in our universe are interconnected, even if separated by vast distances. Quantum connections between particles can persist even if they are on opposite sides of the universe with trillions of miles of space between them. Instead of acting independently, it is as if they are right on top of each other. What affects one will affect the other.

> It is as if, in the words of the science writer Lawrence Joseph, you had two identical pool balls, one in Ohio and the other in Fiji, and the instant you sent one spinning the other would immediately spin in a contrary direction at precisely the same speed. Remarkably, the phenomenon was proved in 1997 when physicists at the University of

Geneva sent photons seven miles in opposite directions and demon-
strated that interfering with one provoked an instantaneous response
in the other.[40]

The idea that interfering with or acting upon one particle can instantaneously influence another particle light years away (trillions of miles)
is incredible. Even though the theory of relativity states nothing is faster
than the speed of light, somehow, at the quantum level, we know that
information can be instantaneously (far faster than the speed of light)
passed between two particles separated by large distances. No mortal
being on this earth can explain how the particles achieve this feat. Still,
we know it works.

Now, back to the way computers communicate. Remember, they
function through a series of on and off switches. It doesn't take a gigantic leap of reason to fathom that, at the subatomic realm, pairs of particles like photons could function as series of on and off switches. And
whatever affects one particle affects its sister particle. These *particle pairs*,
variously turned on and off, could then be used to create a language
that would instantly allow for communication between man and deity,
regardless of the distance.

If we can use physics to envision a way to instantly communicate
across large distances, it is more than likely that God has created a communication method—a language of prayer—capable of transferring
information between beings billions of light years apart. Those with faith
who have experienced the power of prayer may not need to know how
it is done; but, it is faith-promoting to know that even with our limited
knowledge of physics, we can see how it may be possible to communicate
instantly across vast distances. In the world of science, the concept of
communication with God, even though He may be on the other side of
the universe, 13 billion light years distant, is not all that farfetched.

As a matter of fact, the theory of entanglement suggests it is possible
that, in conjunction with the Big Bang, the particles that make up our
bodies are somehow connected with other particles on the opposite side
of the universe. With this in mind, we can infer that God, wherever He
is, could view the particles that are entangled with ours to see exactly
what is going on with us. It would be like watching a real-time video
of what we are doing and experiencing. From that we can reasonably
deduce that God could communicate with us through our entangled

particles by activating and observing kindred particles on His side of the universe. Then, we would instantly sense, feel, hear, or see what God imposes on our linked particles.

In one of Hugh Nibley's essays we find the following quote: "The sustaining Word of God . . . reaches all alike, since it possesses . . . the capacity for traveling for unlimited distances with inexpressible speed."[41]

VI. The Temple and the Universe: What is the similarity?

If someone were to ask you what the overall shape of the universe is, you would likely find it difficult to answer. Your answer might include something like this: we live on a small planet, orbiting a star on the fringe of an insignificant galaxy that is just one of hundreds of billions of galaxies thinly spread through the immensity of space. But, even knowing that, how in the world could you tell someone what the shape of the universe is? Is it pear shaped; is it in the form of a tube, an egg, or like the interior of a spiral seashell?

Symmetry again comes to the rescue. If you consider that scientists believe the universe is symmetrically the same in all locations and in all directions you might be on your way to answering your inquisitor's question. Since almost all shapes fail to meet the criterion of symmetry, the cosmos can be narrowed to a few common ones. Three dimensional shapes like eggs (ellipses), pears, tubes, and pyramids just don't fit the bill. They are either narrow in the middle or pointed at the top and square at the bottom. They are not symmetrical. However, there are some symmetrical shapes that can be considered. One that is obvious is the completely round *sphere* (a ball or balloon). But, this is not the only shape that offers symmetry. Another is the *cube*. Imagine for a moment a universe that is like a rubbery, infinite, expanding cube that has galaxies sprinkled evenly throughout it.

One nice thing about both the sphere and the infinite cube is that you can travel endlessly and never reach an edge or a boundary. However, with the sphere there is one major difference. If you travel forever across a universe that is spherical, there is a good chance that you will one day round the bend and find that, like the earth's fifteenth century's seafaring explorers, you have eventually returned to your point of origin. However, in a cosmos that has the shape of an infinitely sized cube, you will find that you can keep going and going and going, and you will never encounter an edge. You will also never return to the start of your journey.

So, if I were God and wanted to select a shape for my universe I would certainly consider the cube.

Since this book is about science and religion, we offer the question: Do the scriptures or the prophets have anything to say about cubes?

Leading up to an answer of this question, Hugh Nibley in his book *Temple and Cosmos* offers the following:

> The words ***temple*** and ***cosmos*** appear together in the title of this volume because the "temple is a scale model of the universe" . . . Participation in the instruction and ordinances of the temple enables "one to get one's bearings from the universe." The temple is the link between the seeming chaos and dissolution of this temporal world and the beautiful configuration (cosmos) and permanence of the eternal order. "The mystique of the temple lies in its extension to other worlds; **it is the reflection on earth of the heavenly order.**"[41]

> [The temple] . . . is **a scale model of the universe,** for teaching purposes and for the purpose of taking our bearings on the universe and in the eternities, both in time and in space.[42]

When we consider the temple we correctly include the City of New Jerusalem which will be on the earth during the Millennium and also after the earth dies and is renewed. From the Prophet Moroni (Ether 13:3–11) we are taught the following: "New Jerusalem, which should come down out of heaven . . . the holy sanctuary of the Lord . . . should be built upon this land [North America]. . . . And there shall be a new heaven and a new earth; and they shall be like unto the old save the old have passed away, and all things have become new."

Then, in his wonderful commentary on the Book of Revelation, Richard Draper provides the following regarding the City of Zion: "Many a Jewish apocalyptist . . . waxed rhapsodic over the splendor of the New Jerusalem, expressing the glory of God's kingdom in terms of a jeweled city with streets of gold and surrounded with splendor (see, e.g.,

Isa. 54:11–14; Ezek. 28:11–17). In Revelations 21, we get a feel for the resplendent power of God, which shines forth from the city to give life, light, and law to all things."[43]

This great city, New Jerusalem, resembles the temple of Ezekiel (see Ezekiel 48:31–35). However, one of the major differences between the two is that in Ezekiel only the temple is holy while in Revelation the whole city is a holy sanctuary.

One of the similarities in the descriptions of the two temples is that both John and Ezekiel indicate the measurements for their respective temples were taken by an angel (John 21:15–17 and Ezekiel 40:3–5).

> **The city is four square, the same shape as the holy of holies, an exact cube,** symbol of perfections and eternal stability. This suggests why the angel does the measuring [instead of John]. As great as John is, he is yet mortal. . . . The task of measuring the height, depth, and breadth of celestial perfection is beyond any mortal man's capability. This is emphasized by the city's size—12,000 furlongs (just short of 1,400 miles) in length, breadth, and (if it can be imagined) height. The term furlong (a distance of 220 yards) is used consistently in the KJV to translate the Greek stadion (a distance of 202.3 yards).[44]

Elder Bruce R. McConkie said the same thing:

> Here is a city, in size and dimensions, in splendor and glory, which is so far beyond human experience or comprehension that there is no way to convey to the finite mind what the eternal reality is. Hence, expressions relative to precious stones, to streets of gold, and to pearly gates. It is noteworthy that **the city is cubic in shape.** Calculated on the basis of 606 feet, 9 inches to the furlong, its outer limits will stretch nearly 1400 miles in length and breadth and height. This means there will be approaching 2,744,000,000 cubic miles of dwelling space within its sacred portals.[45]

Another author, Matthew B. Brown, in his contemporary book *The Gate of Heaven* indicates, while speaking of the Tabernacle of Moses and the temple built by King Solomon, that:

> The **Holy of Holies was shaped like a perfect cube.** In the temple built by King Solomon, this room was decorated with pure gold (see 1 Kings 6:20). When these two themes are considered together, the possibility arises that the Holy of Holies was an earthly representation of the heavenly city of Zion, for it was also perfectly cubical and

adorned with pure gold (see Revelation 21:10–18). The perfect square, when "amplified into a cube, was the symbol of truth, because from whatever point of view it may be contemplated it is always the same."[46]

Elder Franklin D. Richards taught that "the houses of our God, when acceptably dedicated, become to us the gates of heaven. They are esteemed most holy unto the Lord of all places upon the earth; therein the faithful approach nearest unto God."[47]

Bruce R. McConkie also commented, "The holy of holies in the Lord's earthly houses are symbols and types of the Eternal Holy of Holies which is the highest heaven of the celestial world."[48]

From all of the above we can conclude that temples are representations of the cosmos and the universe, that the most important part of the temple, the holy of holies, is always built in the shape of a cube, and that even the City of Zion the New Jerusalem, which will come down from heaven, will be in the form of a cube.

Once again we see that physics and religion offer some support for one another. The temple is symbolic of the universe; cubes play a major role in temples, and physics suggests the universe may well be in the shape of a cube.

VII. Interstellar Travel: How does God travel about His universe?

When it comes to traveling about His universe, two main facts about God are helpful to understand.

One: Joseph Smith's "first vision" verified that God does in fact have a body of flesh and bones. In section 130 of the Doctrine and Covenants he writes: "The Father has a body of flesh and bones as tangible as man's; the son also; but the Holy Ghost has not a body of flesh and bones, but is a personage of Spirit" (D&C 130:22).

And second: God has a lot of territory to cover. As we discussed earlier, Moses was told by God that "worlds without number have I created . . ." Speaking of those worlds, God went on to say that "[they are] innumerable unto man; but all things are numbered unto me, for they are mine and I know them" (Moses 1:33, 35).

In the previous section we were able to infer that science helps establish the possibility that God can communicate with man on distant worlds through something we call prayer. However, in addition to communication through prayer, we assume that God and His Son, Jesus Christ, travel to their various worlds and on occasion even appear to select individuals who live on these worlds. The scriptures indicate that on numerous occasions they have appeared to Adam, Moses, Abraham, Joseph Smith, and others.

The question is: How do they do that? Since they are flesh and bone, and since nothing can travel faster than the speed of light, how is it done?

The following topical discussions set forth some theories to explain how celestial beings might travel through the cosmos. These ideas have been extrapolated from current physics research. Should we take them with a grain of salt? Maybe . . . However, the important thing to remember is that physics demonstrates different ways that *God* could move about His universe in a timely fashion even in His tangible form.

Wormholes

If I asked you whether or not you had ever heard of the famous physicist Lewis Carroll, most of you would recognize that name but would likely answer no. The Lewis Carroll you know wrote a wonderful book called *Alice in Wonderland*. As you may recall, it is a story of a looking glass, a mirror, that connected the countryside of Oxford, England, to a place called Wonderland. A girl, Alice, was able to venture through the looking glass into a completely different and magically odd world.

Lewis Carroll was the pen name for Charles Dodgson, a professional mathematician and Oxford don. Dodgson was familiar with the concept of something called wormholes, or, as mathematicians call them, "multiply spaces." The name isn't important, but the concept is.

Wormholes create a shortcut between two points, between two different worlds. Of all things, the concept of wormholes has a foundation in Einstein's research. Einstein's theories of relativity are simple enough on the surface. With a few assumptions, one can understand a lot about the universe because of Einstein's marvelous work, including things that have been measured with amazing accuracy like the bending of starlight and the Big Bang itself. Even the ongoing expansion of the universe is understood because of general relativity.

Yet other things lurk within the theory that, as one writer put it, are the "demons" and "goblins" of science.[49] These demons and goblins include imaginative notions such as *wormholes, black holes, white holes, time travel*, and even *parallel universes*. Early in the twentieth century when Einstein came up with his relativity theories, these fanciful concepts seemed so bizarre that even Einstein himself thought that they would never be found in nature. However, today we have actual observation and experimental proof for many of these notions. Some are commonplace in our world. Who hasn't heard of black holes? Did you know that until 1990 the existence of these anomalies was still considered science fiction? Then out of the blue, with the help of the Hubble space telescope, astronomers were able to positively identify several hundred black holes. They really do exist, and there are a lot of them. We now even have a device invented by the military that can pinpoint the location of new created black holes. Today's astronomers can watch them form right before their eyes.

In the 1960s, at the height of the Cold War, the U.S. military, concerned about the Soviet Union's movement and testing of nuclear weapons, put a satellite in orbit—the Vela satellite—to watch for and identify nuclear flashes on earth and in space. The satellite worked. It picked up some unauthorized nuclear flashes off the coast of South Africa as well as signs of huge nuclear flashes in outer space. At first the military wondered if the Soviets were testing nuclear bombs in deep space. In order to better understand what was going on, scientists were brought in to analyze the data and see if the Soviet Union was gaining the upper hand in the arms race. The experts learned that something remarkable was going on in outer-space all right, but it didn't have anything to do with the Russians. However, because what they discovered was militarily classified, they couldn't tell the world about any of it.

Finally, in the 1990s after the breakup of the Soviet, Union there wasn't any need to keep the information secret, so the Pentagon passed a ton of this information on to astronomers. From the data provided by the Vela satellite, by other satellites, modern telescopes, computers and such, astronomers realized that the flashes being detected in deep space were monstrous explosions that released colossal amounts of energy, even as much energy as our sun will produce in its entire lifetime. By 2003, these explosions were identified as "hypernova," gigantic exploding stars that were in turn creating massive black holes.

To reiterate, using black holes as an obvious example, some of the strange things that were first theoretically conceived from general relativity are now proven reality.

But remember, the purpose of this section is to consider, through the use of physics, how God might travel about His universe. So what are some of the physics-related theoretical possibilities that could allow Him the freedom to instantly move across the vast cosmos?

Could black holes play a part? As mentioned, Einstein came to the initial conclusion that black holes were too strange to exist in nature. Oddly enough, he then went on to show that they were even more unusual than anyone thought. In 1935, he and his student, Nathan Rosen, introduced into the world of physics the concept of wormholes. Einstein's Theory of Relativity allowed for the possibility of wormholes lying at the center of black holes. These wormholes, he surmised, could serve as shortcuts between two points, celestial passageways that one day could provide man with the ultimate means of travel throughout the universe, and even into parallel universes and dimensions.

Today, scientists speculate that Einstein's wormholes (which they refer to as Einstein-Rosen Bridges) can act as gateways between universes. They speculate that something could go through a black hole and emerge on the other side through a *white hole* (so described because of the tremendous energy and light coming out of it). Einstein eventually came to have more confidence in his own theory. He believed that all aspects of his relativity equations were correct, including things like black holes, wormholes, white holes, parallel universes, the expanding universe, and much more. We have seen many of these ideas actually realized over the past 80 years; and more, if not all, will likely come to fruition in the future.

Most readers are familiar with the name Carl Sagan, the well-known astronomer and producer of the popular "Cosmos" TV program of the 1980s. A few years ago, prior to his death, Sagan appeared a number of times on public television in an effort to provide information and education about science and the universe. He shared with his audience how, back in 1985, when he was writing his novel, *Contact*, he sought to come up with a way that his heroine could travel to the star, Vega, then return to earth. Such a feat would not be possible using the Einstein-Rosen Bridge, because passing through a black hole (via a wormhole) would not allow her to go to Vega. Instead, it would spin his heroine right into another universe.

Shut down in his writing by this conceptual roadblock, Sagan turned to a physicist in southern California for advice. This man, Kip Thorne, after considering Sagan's predicament, shocked the world of physics by finding and announcing new solutions to Einstein's equations that allowed for interstellar travel and even time travel, all without needing to deal with the problems of black holes. In 1988, with the help of colleagues Michale Morris and Ulvi Yurtsever, Thorne showed that it is possible to build a machine for travel across the universe and even through time, if one could somehow obtain strange forms of matter and energy such as "negative matter" and "negative energy."

The great advantage of negative matter and negative energy is that they make it possible for movement through wormholes *in both directions*, a cosmic two-way trip. In fact, Thorne and his colleagues surmised that this kind of travel would be less stressful and far easier than flying on a commercial airplane. Plus such travel would be much better than passing through a black hole with all the problems of tremendous gravity and, with its one-way parallel universe trip capability. Now one could return to his or her original world.

Negative matter is amazing. If it existed on earth, it would most likely fall up instead of down. Why? It is repelled by mass instead of being attracted to it. Because of this trait, no person on earth is likely to have seen this exotic matter. What's more, it would be near impossible to find in nature, as it would have floated away into deep space, far away from any planets and stars. So, for man, it would be pretty difficult to acquire negative matter for interstellar or time travel, unless he could somehow create it.

On the other hand, "negative energy" is another thing entirely. Unlike negative matter, negative energy, while extremely rare has been experimentally detected. Yet like negative matter, negative energy could be used to power a machine that would allow for time travel and near instantaneous travel across the universe through wormholes. Remember, man has already experimentally detected negative energy. If we can detect it, God surely can produce it in great quantities.

If travel through wormholes rings a bell, it's because the concept has liberally appeared in fantasy and science fiction books, in the movie theatres, and on television the past few years. *Stargate Atlantis*, a fairly recent movie and television series, makes frequent use of wormholes for travel throughout the universe, utilizing a tunnel that stretches from one point in space to another along a new, previously nonexistent tube of space. Another way to express it is: "A wormhole is a new part of space that connects with ordinary space only at its ends." If you have ever watched *Stargate Atlantis*, you have seen the actors step through a portal from our world and instantly appear at a door in another world. This is similar to how Kip Thorne theorized space and even time travel could work.

Of course, experimentally, we don't really know for sure if wormholes exist. But many decades ago physicists established that they are a mathematical construct of general relativity. One day though, they will likely be applied on a practical level. It seems that everything touched on by Einstein's theory of general relativity eventually comes to fruition.

In the 1950s, John Wheeler, father of atomic energy, together with his coworkers became among the earliest researchers to investigate wormholes, and they unearthed many of their fundamental mathematical properties. More recently, as was previously described, Kip Thorne and his colleagues revealed the full richness of wormholes by hypothesizing that not only can they serve as shortcuts through space, they can be shortcuts through time.[50]

Today, there is some belief in the scientific community that human travel through wormholes will not be practical because it will require incredible quantities of exotic matter and energy (negative matter and negative energy) to sustain the wormholes. Still, as we shall discuss in a future section, God has at his fingertips all the energy in the universe and could make time travel through wormholes a reality. Possessing all power and all knowledge (even of wormholes), there is no doubt that God can instantly travel to any part of the universe and appear in whatever time He wishes.

The Doctrine and Covenants offers an astounding account of what may be a "God-supported" wormhole. In Section 137 we read of a vision given to Joseph Smith in the Kirtland Temple on January 21, 1836. The occasion was the administration of the ordinances of the endowment as far as they had been revealed.

> The heavens were opened upon us, and I beheld the celestial kingdom of God . . . I saw the transcendent beauty of **the gate through which the heirs of that kingdom will enter, which was like unto circling flames of fire;** Also the blazing throne of God, whereon was seated the Father and the Son. I saw the beautiful streets of that

kingdom, which had the appearance of being paved with gold. I saw Father Adam and Abraham; and my father and my mother; my brother Alvin, that has long since slept; And marveled how it was that he had obtained an inheritance in that kingdom, seeing that he had departed this life before the Lord had set his hand to gather Israel the second time, and had not been baptized for the remission of sins. Thus came the voice of the Lord unto me, saying: All who have died without a knowledge of this gospel, who would have received it if they had been permitted to tarry, shall be heirs of the celestial kingdom of God; Also all that shall die henceforth without a knowledge of it, who would have received it with all their hearts, shall be heirs of that kingdom; For I, the Lord, will judge all men according to their works, according to the desire of their hearts. And I also beheld that all children who die before they arrive at the years of accountability are saved in the celestial kingdom of heaven. (D&C 137:1–10, bold added)

Did you see at the beginning of this marvelous vision a reference to what might be a gate opening to a wormhole? Joseph Smith said he saw (while viewing the celestial kingdom) the "beauty of the gate through which the heirs of that kingdom will enter, which was like unto circling flames of fire." Perhaps once this life is over and the time is right, if we are worthy, we will be allowed to enter into a Celestial abode, by way of a wormhole that is supported by the power and energy of God.

String Theory and the Energy Needed for Wormholes

A later section of this book will focus more fully on something called "string theory." Yet, let's take a moment and briefly consider aspects of this theory as they pertain to God's possible methods of travel. One might surmise from its name that string theory is based on the idea that the universe is made of very small *strings*. As a matter of fact, such building-block strings would be billions of times smaller than the atom. The essence of these tiny strings is that they combine to form energy, atoms, and hence the elements. Even though the strings may differ slightly, their primary function is to vibrate like the strings of a violin or guitar. The strings' different vibration patterns correspond to different kinds of particles. Indeed, as these strings vibrate differently, they form a distinct variety of atoms, elements, energy particles or waves, and energy fields. Strings vibrating at one frequency might create the properties of an electron, while those vibrating at another frequency might form the components of protons or neutrons. So, a single class of string may lead to a great variety of particles being formed because the strings can vibrate in a multitude of different patterns. Hence, hydrogen may be different from gold because of the different vibrating strings that make up the disparate elements.

When one considers this theory in relation to God, it is as if He is a master orchestral leading the wonderful symphony of the universe. With all the power and knowledge He has, is it not possible that He can cause the strings that may make up cosmic matter to vibrate one way or another to create different types of particles? Is that also how Christ may have performed His miracles while he was on the earth? In His first recorded miracle, did He change water to wine by causing the strings that made up the water molecules to vibrate differently?

It is likely that God made travel through wormholes a reality at the time the universe was formed. Then when He needs to power the wormholes, He can easily create all the negative matter or negative energy needed for wormhole travel simply by causing the strings of the particles that make up the matter/energy to vibrate a certain way.

Teleportation

In addition to wormholes, another possible mode of travel from one location to another is by way of *teleportation*. Many of us grew up with the long-time television series *Star Trek*. In the early years of the show one particular phrase was used so often that it became household vernacular. Captain James T. Kirk was always calling upon his engineering officer to "Beam me up, Scotty!" Kirk was referring to a method of transporting or teleporting a person from one location to another without passing through the space between locations. Fans of the show and associated movies understood that the basic particles of the persons and objects being transported were disassembled at the point of origin and reassembled at the destination. The show was made even more intriguing in that the technology didn't seem to be perfect. Thus, on several occasions something went wrong with the teleporting process for crew members, whereupon, it became difficult to reassemble their particles.

It may surprise you to know that in 1997, about thirty years after the first *Star Trek* episodes were aired, two teams of physicists actually carried out successful teleportation experiments. One research group was led by A. Francesco De Martini of the University of Rome; the other was based at the University of Innsbruck, headed by Anton Zeigler. Neither group was able to teleport a person or any kind of living organism, but did manage to transport *photons* a short distance across their laboratory. The important thing is that they really were able to teleport matter from one place to another without physically moving it there.

In 2003, scientists at the University of Geneva in Switzerland were able to teleport photons a distance of 1.2 miles. Another significant experimental breakthrough came in 2004 when physicists at the National Institute of Standards and Technology teleported an entire atom, not just a photon of light.

Today, clearly we don't have the technical ability to transport complete organisms from one location to another. But as time passes, our ability to map atoms, elements, compounds, cells, and organisms will increase. Someday we may well be able to successfully teleport plants, animals, and even people. Because we mere mortals have had some actual success and believe in the future possibilities of teleporting objects, think how easy it must be for God to do it.

Again, instead of disproving God, science seems bent on providing a foundation for the reality of an all powerful Being who is the Creator and Master of the universe. Who knows, He may well utilize what we call "wormholes" and "teleportation".

Examples from the scriptures suggest teleportation could have been used by God to further His purposes. When Joseph Smith was just a boy, he was visited by the Angel Moroni (Joseph Smith—History 1:29–47). Joseph was in an upstairs bedroom when Moroni, a resurrected being of flesh and bone, just appeared. He didn't open any doors; he didn't come in through any windows or break down any walls. Similar visitations occurred in other scriptural settings. Christ and multiple ancient prophets appeared to Joseph Smith and Oliver Cowdery in the Kirtland Temple (see D&C 110). Then after His resurrection, the Savior appeared to his disciples in an upper room where He allowed them to feel the wounds in His hands and feet: "The same day at evening, being the first day of the week, when the doors were shut where the disciples were assembled for fear of the Jews, came Jesus and stood in the midst, and saith unto them, Peace be unto you" (John 20:19).

On yet another occasion: "And after eight days again his disciples were within, and Thomas with them: then came Jesus, the doors being shut, and stood in the midst, and said, Peace be unto you" (John 20:26).

In both appearances, the author (John the Apostle/John the Beloved/John the Revelator) calls attention to the fact that the doors of the room were shut. Somehow the resurrected Christ just appeared without entering through the door. Then, in both situations, so as to make sure His disciples understood the truth, He showed them the terrible wounds in his hands and side. He even had them touch the wounds. It was Christ! He had a body of flesh and bones. What better example could there be of some sort of teleportation?

The Uncertainty Principle

Thus far we have solely been using physics to describe how God and Christ might move about the universe. The Holy Ghost is another member of the Godhead who must have the ability to instantaneously travel through time and space. Inasmuch as He does not have a physical body, unlike the Father and the Son, it might actually be easier to describe how He moves about the Cosmos: "The Holy Ghost has not a body of flesh and bones, but is a personage of Spirit. Were it not so, the Holy Ghost could not dwell in us. A man may receive the Holy Ghost, and it may descend upon him" (D&C 130:22).

With a spirit body made up of matter that is more fine and refined (D&C 131:7) than a body of flesh and bones, the Holy Ghost likely travels about and interacts with us according to the laws that govern the quantum world. As already expressed in a prior section, in the realm of quantum theory, an object or particle can exist in more than one state at a time and in more than one place at a time. In this way an electron protects the nucleus of its atom. It forms an electron cloud around the nucleus binding the atom together, establishing a sort of force field to keep it from disintegrating when it comes in contact with other atoms. If the electron did not have this capability of being in many places at once, the world we live in would cease to exist.

As was mentioned—and as will be reiterated in other sections—experiments conducted on electrons demonstrate that an electron acts both as a wave and as a particle. What does this mean? Because of the wave function, you can never know where the electron particle is at any given point in time. You can calculate the probability as to where it might be, but in reality it is likely to be in multiple locations or everywhere at the same time.

Today, using nanotechnology, scientists can manipulate individual atoms and carry out actual laboratory experiments to show that atoms can be in more than one place at a time. Recently, further experiments were performed with something scientists call a "buckyball" to prove that objects can be in more than one place at a time.[51] And experimental physicists are even now contemplating what it would take to show that a virus (containing thousands of atoms) can be in two places at once.

So, if we think it might be possible for atoms and viruses to be in two or more places at the same time, why not an entity as remarkable as the Holy Ghost? One of the more intriguing questions of LDS thought is: How can the Holy Ghost be in more than one place at any given time? How can it simultaneously attend to me, you, and a host of other good people? Until now, we didn't have a really good answer. The question was always answered in some vague way like, "It can't; the Holy Ghost can only be in one place, but its influence can be everywhere at once."

Now, from a standpoint of physics, we can actually explain that, according to quantum theory and laboratory experiment, it's possible for the Holy Ghost to be in many places all at the same time.

Who knows, maybe this everywhere-at-once capability is even available to the Father and the Son. Do you recall in the Book of Mormon, prior to Christ's birth in Bethlehem, He appeared to Nephi and assured him that He would come into the world later that day. How could He have been in two places at once, both with Nephi and in Bethlehem about to be born? Commonly we rationalize and say that it must have been an angel who appeared to Nephi, speaking as if he were Christ. However, it doesn't say that at all—it says that it was the Savior who appeared.

Earlier in this book I warned that it is dangerous for us to always think of God from our limited, mortal perspective. Just because we can't be in more than one place at one time, it doesn't mean that the Holy Ghost and God can't accomplish this feat. Physics seems to promote this possible conclusion.

You may think this all sounds too crazy to be true. But the laws of mathematics and theories of physics God has given us attest to the truth of the accounts found in the scriptures.

Several times in this book a particularly key scripture is quoted. Found in Doctrine and Covenants section 88 verse 41, it supports the concept of an "uncertainty principle"—that God can be in many places and even all places at all times: "He comprehendeth all things, and all things are before him, and all things are round about him; and he is above all things, and in all things, and is through all things, and is round about all things; and all things are by him, and of him, even God, forever and ever."

So, how does God do it? How can He comprehend all things? How is it that He can have all things before Him? How can all things be round about Him? How can He be in all things and through all things and round about all things?

On three occasions while in Nauvoo, the Prophet declared from the pulpit: "If I revealed all that has been made known to me, scarcely a man on this stand would stay with me." To a priesthood group he once said: "Brethren, if I were to tell you all I know of the kingdom of God, I do know that you would rise up and kill me."[52]

Is it possible that Joseph Smith understood aspects of the uncertainty principle as it pertains to God? Because of the marvelous insight found in D&C 88:41 (God is through all things, round about all things, and so on), we see that God may utilize the uncertainty principle—or something like it—to be omnipotent and omnipresent. In some real way, God can be everywhere at once in all times. Yet, He also has the ability to be in just one place at a time.

It is no wonder that so much religious confusion occurred at the time of the "Great Apostasy." After the apostles were killed and darkness filled the earth, certain remnants of truth that had been taught during and after Christ's lifetime were lost. Over time, without inspiration and without someone to guide them, it became impossible to understand the truth about God. Without a knowledge of something like the uncertainty principle, how could anyone in any age ever understand that God, having a body of flesh and bones, could ever be in many or all places at all times?

Of course, we don't know for sure how He does it. But it is nice to see how the laws of physics validates that God, being all-powerful, can both control His universe and know, love, and draw near to us individually, across such vast distances.

VIII. Time: What is it scientifically—and what is it to God?

Joseph Smith said the following about God: "The great Jehovah contemplated the whole of events connected with the earth, pertaining to the plan of salvation, before it rolled into existence, or ever 'the morning stars sang together' for joy; the **past, the present, and the future were and are, with him, one eternal 'now.'** "[53]

This statement from a modern-day prophet indicates that, for God, time is "one eternal now." He sees the past, present, and future together. This concept seems to correlate with the view scientists have of our universe. That is, the laws of physics seem to be time-symmetrical, which means they are unaffected by the direction of time:

> The laws of physics that have been articulated from Newton through Maxwell and Einstein, and up until today, show **a complete symmetry between past and future.** Nowhere in any of these laws do we find a stipulation that they apply one way in time but not in the other. Nowhere is there any distinction between how the laws look or behave when applied in either direction in time. The laws treat what we call past and future on a completely equal footing. Even though experience reveals over and over again that there is an arrow of how events unfold in time, this arrow seems not to be found in the fundamental laws of physics.[54]

Additionally, Albert Einstein's general relativity theory allows for the possibility of wormholes and time travel. Because his theory links time and space inseparably together, wormholes that can connect distant points in space also have the ability to connect distant points in time.[55]

Does this mean that from the point of view of physics, it is possible that the past and the future exist simultaneously; and that travel between times, past and future, is possible? Yes, it does. Of course, this notion goes against our everyday reasoning and common sense. However, thus far, every shred of Einstein's relativity theories have proven to be true. So we expect that time travel is possible.

Another key axiom of classical physics is that, in theory, if we knew exactly how things are now and if we knew the positions and velocities of all particles making up the universe, we could use that information to predict how things would be at any given moment in the future as well as how they were at any given moment in the past.[56]

So, one way or another, whether through time travel or through the ability to predict future and past events, even physics suggests that God could, as Joseph Smith taught, have the ability to see and know the past, present, and future.

In regard to these thoughts, let's reread the scripture found in Doctrine & Covenants 88:41. Speaking of Christ, it states: "He comprehendeth all things, and **all things are before him,** and all things are round about him; and he is above all things, and in all things, and is through all things, and is round about all things; and all things are by him, and of him, even God, forever and ever" (bold added).

Somehow then, God is aware of everything throughout all time—past, present, and future. As Joseph Smith said: for God, this universe is "one eternal 'now.' "

The following conceptual queries will be developed in this section:

- What is time?
- What does modern-day physics tell us about time?
- What is time to God? Does He measure time?

First, *what is time?* The online Merriam Webster Dictionary provides two principal definitions:

> *Time*: **a**: the measured or measurable period during which an action, process, or condition exists or continues **b**: a nonspatial continuum that is measured in terms of events which succeed one another from past through present to future

In other words, time, according to the first definition, is simply a measured sequence of events. The second definition uses the term *nonspatial*, which means not occupying or taking up space. We live in a world of four dimensions: three (forward/back, side to side, up/down) take up space; the other, *time*, does not.

In order to define time in our lives, we count the number of instances the sun rises and sets and compare it to how long it takes us to traverse our orbit around the sun. We call this a calendar. When we figure time, we count our days, nights, and years and put them into some practical order.

A man-made device that both defines and measures time is a watch or clock. The clock counts orderly, sequential ticks that, added together, correspond to the days, nights, and years that make up the calendar we just considered. In a sense, a clock actually "creates" time, each tick counting an event that can be measured and ordered into seconds, minutes, and hours. From those ticks of a clock and the rotation of the earth around the sun, human beings proceed to order and live out their lives in sequential, systematic blocks of time, hour by hour, day by day.

It is generally accepted in the world of cosmology that time travel is possible. However, the idea of time travel bothered Einstein when he first formulated his thoughts on the subject. In his theory, time and space are treated kind of like a piece of rubber that can stretch, bend, and warp. Because of these properties and the overall physics of time, Einstein was concerned that time travel might indeed be possible. If one really could travel back and forward in time, he worried that events *could* be changed from their natural course irreparably damaging the universe along the way.

Before we begin considering travel through time, we first need to review the basics of general relativity in regard to time and how it works. This body of theory is really not as complicated as one might think.

Special relativity is largely based on the supposition that what appears as "space" and what appears as "time" depends on the position and motion of the observer. If an observer could stand back and compare the effects of time on two separate individuals (for example, for one that is stationary compared to the observer and for another that is moving very fast compared to the observer), time would appear to the observer to move much faster for the stationary person than for the person in motion. The faster a person travels in relation to the person who is stationary, the slower time appears to pass for the traveler.

An example: One of two twin brothers hops on a spaceship and blasts off, eventually achieving a high rate of speed, approaching the speed of light. Following a two-year journey, he returns to the earth. When he steps out of the spaceship, he finds that everything has changed. Though he had aged only two years, while he was gone, his brother and everyone else he knew had lived out their lives and died long ago.

One of the greatest achievements in scientific history was Einstein's theory of special relativity. Special relativity declares: "The combined speed of any object's motion through space and its motion through time is always precisely equal to the speed of light." Einstein discovered that the motion of time and the motion of an object through space are inherently related. When you watch a jet airliner take off and fly away from you, what you are really seeing is that some of the airliner's motion through time is being diverted to motion through space. Thus, the speed of the airline and its movement through time keep their combined total (speed of light) unchanged. Because some of the airplanes time is being diverted to its speed, the clocks in the airplane run slightly slower than the clocks on the ground. Since airplanes don't travel very fast compared to the speed of light, the time difference is not significant. Just the same, there is a definite difference.

If we further analyze relativity, we may come to better understand why time stops for an object when it travels at the speed of light. It is because all of the object's motion through time has been taken over by its motion through space. Remember, time and motion are inherently related. Hence, if an object travels extremely fast compared to you, but not at the speed of light, you will perceive that its time slows down but that it doesn't entirely stop. Again, as the major tenant of special relativity states: "The combined speed of any objects motion through space and its motion through time is always precisely equal to the speed of light"

Later on, when we discuss "light" as it pertains to God, we will learn that light doesn't age. Now, we can see why. *Nothing* ages that travels at the speed of light. Even though we haven't discovered the fountain of youth sought by Ponce de Leon long ago, we can at least see that light has. It doesn't age, dim, or diminish in speed. Not ever!

However, there is more to understanding time than just considering time travel relative to accelerated motion. Einstein taught that it is mathematically possible to travel forward through time.[57]

According to Einstein, time is variable and ever-changing. It even has shape. It is bound up . . . with the three dimensions of space in a curious fourth dimension known as *space-time*. One can better understand "space-time" by imagining a mattress or a sheet of stretched rubber on which has been placed something heavy like an iron ball. The weight of the ball causes the mattress (the fabric of space) to stretch and sag where the ball is resting. When one attempts to roll a small ball across the mattress near the large iron ball, the depression causes the smaller ball to curve and roll inward towards the large one.

This is similar to the effect that a massive object, like the sun, has on space-time. It causes the fabric of space to stretch and warp inward. Thus, gravity is one of the products of space-time, but it is not the only product of space-time. The fabric of time is also affected by mass. The more dense and heavier the object, the slower time moves on and around that object because the fabric of time is stretched and warped too. Hence, large quantities of dense mass create a lot of gravitational force, slowing time down.

Two different views as to how mass and gravity might affect spacetime.

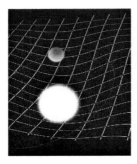 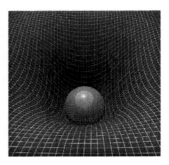

By way of summary: General relativity theory affirms that the relative passage of time is affected by both motion and mass. The faster one moves, the better one is able to push the envelope forward through time in comparison to a stationary universe. The greater the mass, the greater the gravitational pull, and the slower time moves. Therefore, a clock placed at the base of a very large mountain will run slightly slower than one placed on a satellite orbiting the earth.

There is still much to learn about time. Physicists are just beginning to come up with other clever theories about time. In a book called *The End of Time, The Next Revolution in Physics*, author Julian Barbour states that the unification of general relativity and quantum mechanics may well spell the end of time. By this he means that time will cease to have a role in the foundations of physics. "We shall come to see," he intones, "that time does not exist."[58] And you may recall from the information presented earlier that aspects of time such as "before" and "after" don't have meaning in the ultramicroscopic, quantum universe.

Even Brian Greene, a physicist who recently published two best sellers, *The Elegant Universe* and *The Fabric of the Cosmos*, says that "The laws of physics don't distinguish between forward and backward in time."[59] He also states that if you ply the combined equations of general relativity and quantum mechanics, they yield a single answer: *infinity*.[60] Infinity encompasses everything. Hence, time—an entity that we typically assign a beginning and an end, a before and an after—may cease to have boundaries and one day cease to have meaning.

Joseph Smith referred to this concept of infinity when he told us about how God relates to time and time to God. He said: "The past, the present, and the future were and are, with him, one eternal 'now.' "[61] All of time is instantly available to God, the present, the past, and the future.

I believe that many things we learn about the subject of time from today's scientific community mesh with truths that have been taught by God's prophets through the centuries. As a matter of fact, the plethora of scientific learning bursting forth in this day acts as a witness to the revealed, restored knowledge we find in both ancient and modern scripture as well as the words of living prophets. In Matthew 18:16 Christ says: "In the mouth of two or three witnesses every word *may* be established." Then in Second Corinthians a similar statement gets a little more definite: "In the mouth of two or three witnesses *shall* every word be established" (2 Corinthians 13:1). The truths found in science act as another witness of God and Christ. And, as written in Ether 5:4, scientific truth, as well as religious truth, "All . . . shall stand as a testimony against the world at the last day."

As Christians and more specifically as members of The Church of Jesus Christ of Latter-day Saints, we believe that all truth is revealed by the Holy Ghost. This being the case, we should compare the revealed word of God found in the scriptures to that of the truth (revealed/ inspired word) found in science. Speaking of time, the scriptures provide us the following:

> But beloved, be not ignorant of this one thing, that **one day is with the Lord as a thousand years**, and a thousand years as one day. (2 Peter 3:8; bold added)

> And the Lord said unto me, by the Urim and Thummim, that Kolob was after the manner of the Lord, **according to its times and seasons in the revolutions thereof; that one revolution was a day unto the Lord, after his manner of reckoning, it being one thousand years according to the time appointed unto that whereon**

thou standest. This is the reckoning of the Lord's time . . .

And thus there shall be **the reckoning of the time of one planet above another**, until thou come nigh unto Kolob, which Kolob is after the reckoning of the Lord's time; which Kolob is set nigh unto the throne of God, to govern all those planets which belong to the same order as that upon which thou standest. (Abraham 3:4, 9; bold added)

Correspondingly, from Einstein and his time honored theory of relativity, we learn that time is an individual phenomenon governed by the speed one is traveling relative to someone else, or by the amount of mass that the person is residing on or near (earth versus Kolob).

But of the tree of knowledge of good and evil, thou shalt not eat of it; for in the time that thou eatest thereof, thou shalt surely die. Now I, Abraham, saw that **it was after the Lord's time,** which was after the time of Kolob; for as yet the Gods had not appointed unto Adam his reckoning. (Abraham 5:13; bold added)

From the above scriptures, we learn that God lives in a location where time is reckoned differently than it is on the earth. A logical explanation for the difference in how time is measured on earth compared to the clock's ticking on Kolob may be that Kolob, a planet located near to where God lives, has tremendous mass compared to the earth. Therefore, Kolob's, space-time as described by Einstein, is warped to a far greater degree than it is on our world; so Kolob's time runs slower. According to the scriptures, God's time moves 300,000 times slower than ours. On pages 36 and 37 of the Pearl of Great Price there is a facsimile from the Book of Abraham that was translated by the Prophet Joseph Smith. As part of that translation Joseph states that Kolob is nearest to the residence of God. He also states that it is the *last* pertaining to the measurement of time, suggesting that time on Kolob is the manner in which celestial time is measured. "One day on Kolob is equal to a thousand years according to the measurement of this earth."

It is important we reiterate that Julian Barbour in his book *The End of Time, The Next Revolution in Physics* states that the unification of general relativity and quantum mechanics may well spell the end of time. By this he means that time will cease to have a role in the foundations of physics. Then he drops his bombshell: "We shall come to see that time does not exist."[62]

Many latter-day scriptures also testify to the possible truth of this statement:

> And Satan is bound and **time is no longer.** (D&C 84:100, referring to the Millennium; bold added)

> The seventh angel shall sound his trump; and he shall stand forth upon the land and upon the sea, and swear in the name of him who sitteth upon the throne, that **there shall be time no longer;** and Satan shall be bound, that old serpent, who is called the devil, and shall not be loosed for the space of a thousand years. (D&C 88:110, also referring to the Millennium; bold added)

> **There should be time no longer** . . . (Revelation 10:6, after the seventh seal is opened; bold added)

> Now whether there is more than one time appointed for men to rise it mattereth not; for all do not die at once, and this mattereth not; all is as one day with God, and **time only is measured unto men.** (Alma 40:8; bold added)

Clearly, God is not bound by time; and the scriptures also seem to indicate that during the Millennium man will not be bound by time either. What does this mean? For God, it means that He knows and can participate in everything, past, present, and future. We can only speculate, but during the millennium, if time is no longer a factor, we could cross time boundaries in such a way as to obtain all information for the ordinance work that needs to be done. For most people who have lived on earth there are simply no records that can be used for vicarious temple work. But if we could go back in time, we could easily obtain the necessary information about earth's past inhabitants and then vicariously perform the work for them. Thus the reason for the scripture in 1 Corinthians 15:29: "Else what shall they do which are baptized for the dead, if the dead rise not at all? Why are they then baptized for the dead?"

The fact that we perform ordinances like baptism vicariously for those who have passed away *bothers* some members of other churches. But Paul in 1 Corinthians openly addresses the fact that the Saints did such work in Christ's time. So, why not now?

Dr. Carl Sagan, the popular astronomer quoted earlier, likewise didn't shy away from proposing time travel. He believed that one day man would find a way to travel back in time. In an earlier section of this work, titled "Interstellar Travel," we brought up a discovery of physicist Kip Thorne that was influenced by Dr. Sagan. As you may recall, Sagan was writing a book in which his heroine needed to travel between earth and a planet in another solar system. He couldn't figure out how to make it work from a perspective of physics, so he sought out Thorne to glean his opinion. In an amazing set of events, Dr. Thorne and his colleagues, relying on the theory of relativity discovered new mathematical formulas which make room for both instantaneous interstellar travel and travel through time.[63]

The prophet Brigham Young had some things to say about time that support some of the theories being proposed by physicists today. In the *Journal of Discourses*, President Young, speaking of the Spirit World, is quoted as follows:

> The brightness and glory of the next apartment is inexpressible. It is not encumbered so that when we advance in years we have to be stubbing along and be careful lest we fall down. . . . But yonder, how different! They move with ease and like lightning. If we want to visit Jerusalem, or this, that, or the other place—and I presume we will be permitted if we desire—there we are, looking at its streets. **If we want to behold Jerusalem as it was in the days of the Savior; or if we want to see the Garden of Eden as it was when created, there we are, and we see it**.[64] (bold added)

How revealing that Brigham Young comprehended truths concerning time and time travel about which scientists are just now theorizing.

An event in time, for the most part, is either past or something we are looking forward to in the future. The "now" that we live in doesn't even last a second: The moment it occurs, it becomes and only exists in the past. So, we spend a lot of effort considering the past, seeing as that's where nearly all "time" for us exists. Almost all the news on television or printed in daily newspapers is past tense. We even measure our lives by the past years we have lived.

As members of the Church, we believe that through Christ, God created the universe and all that it contains. One aspect of that creation was time—space-time. However, prior to the Big Bang, we do not know how time may have been measured, or if it even existed. It seems likely that there have always been sequences of events, even prior to the Big

Bang. Still, we are certain that God was not then and is not now bound by time as we are.

The universe we live in is designed to have a beginning and an end. At least one purpose for which it was created is so that we could exist in mortality, in a state of high entropy—that is, an existence where we and even the universe eventually wear out. Time is incredibly important to us. Because of time, we can feel an urgency to live out our lives with purpose and joy that rest on a foundation of hope and faith in Christ. We exercise faith in God and hope in a life after death. Without the boundary of time in mortality, there would be little urgency to have hope and faith in God. The testing and character growth that we experience here on earth would likely not occur if we weren't bound by time and entropy (entropy essentially means that things wear out, that they move from a state of order to disorder). If we had all the time in the world and didn't wear out and grow old, we likely would not be motivated to live as we should and learn our life's lessons.

I once read a book about people from a parallel earth who could visit our world and, without impunity or permanent harm to them, slip into our earthly bodies. Once their, these alien visitors could do anything to us. They could even experience death before jumping back into their reality. Imagine that is how it would be for us if we weren't bound by time and entropy. This life wouldn't have the same meaning and purpose that it now has.

IX. God's Great Flood: Did it really happen?

Was there really a great, worldwide flood some 4,500 years ago? If a deluge of such epic proportions really did occur, where did all that excess water go? And where did such tremendous quantities of the water come from in the first place?

The primary written account we have of the great flood is found in Genesis and a lesser account appears in Moses in the Pearl of Great Price. The following excerpts quickly bring us up to speed:

> And it repented the Lord that he had made man on the earth, and
> it grieved him at his heart. And the Lord said, I will destroy man whom

I have created from the face of the earth . . . for it repenteth me that I have made them. But Noah found grace in the eyes of the Lord. . . . And God said unto Noah . . . Make thee an ark. . . . Thus did Noah; according to all that God commanded him. . . . And Noah was six hundred years old when the flood of waters was upon the earth . . . the fountains of the great deep broken up, and the windows of heaven were opened. . . . And the rain was upon the earth forty days and forty nights . . . And the waters prevailed exceedingly upon the earth; and all the high hills, that were under the whole heaven, were covered . . . and the mountains were covered . . . And the waters prevailed upon the earth an hundred and fifty days. And God remembered Noah . . . and the waters asswaged; . . . The fountains also of the deep and the windows of heaven were stopped, and the rain from heaven was restrained; and the waters returned from off the earth continually; and after the end of the hundred and fifty days the waters were abated. (Genesis 6, 7 and 8)

In the Genesis account we see that the water that caused the Great Flood came from three possible sources:

- Fountains from the great deep
- Windows of heaven
- Rain

Genesis specifically identifies all three sources when the flood begins and again when the flood abates. We understand the rain part, but what about the other two sources?

In Genesis 7:11 it states: "The same day were all the fountains of the great deep broken up, and the windows of heaven were opened." So, what was this "great deep" that was broken up to bring on such a cataclysm?

The following excerpts from two authors describe how water could have been wrung from the great deep: "The . . . subterranean aquifers, freed from their rocky chains by the mighty tremblings and tearings of the earth, burst forth from their hiding places in her bowels to join the swelling, surging, seas.[65]

The earth is endowed with great subterranean reservoirs that could adequately serve to flood the entire land surface of the earth . . .

. . . earth's scientists have been greatly surprised at the amount of water in the world aquifers (porous, underground rocks) that hold

97% of the world's supply of liquid fresh water. And, surprisingly, even the deepest accessible rocks beneath the earth's continents and ocean basins contain astonishing amounts of water locked up in their crystalline structure.[66]

Through both according to scripture and the possibilities given us from science, one can deduce that much of the water that covered the earth likely came from *beneath* the earth. Thus the scriptural term "great *deep*."

In addition to Genesis, a second scriptural reference supports the idea that there was a great amount of water above the earth in the expanse called heaven. Found in Abraham 4:6–8, it reads: "And the Gods also said: Let there be an expanse in the midst of the waters, and it shall divide the waters from the waters. And the Gods ordered the expanse, so that it divided the waters which were under the expanse from the waters which were above the expanse . . . And the Gods called the expanse, Heaven."

The water beneath the earth was in a liquid state. We don't know what form or state the water above the earth was in. Certainly the water that came down as rain was in a gaseous state before it formed as raindrops. However, we can't be absolutely certain what state the water from "the windows of heaven" was. Common sense tells us that it was a gaseous state and that it came down as rain. Another possibility is the atmosphere of the earth was different than it is today.

As Rodney Turner states in *This Eternal Earth*: "These waters were prepared in anticipation of the Flood which was programmed from the beginning."[67]

Was the water that fell from the "windows of heaven" already gathered in a predetermined canopy around the earth? The idea of a canopy of water has been widely promoted for years. Those who adhere to this model posit that during the creation, when God divided the waters, there became two divisions of water: one in the expanse beneath and the other in the expanse above (called heaven). Abraham 4:6–8 seems to suggest that was the case.

Scientifically, without more information, there could be a problem with the idea of a canopy of water surrounding the earth. In what form was this water? If it was hovering there in the gaseous state, would it have acted in some degree like the cloud cover that surrounds the planet

Venus? Would it have created a greenhouse effect and raised temperatures significantly on earth? Would life have been possible, given these
conditions? Without more information, this discussion really can't be
pursued further, except to note that the scriptures seem to make it clear
that in the beginning the waters were "divided" so as to separate that
water above the earth from that which was on the earth.

Returning to our Great Flood analysis, the prophet Moses indicates
in Genesis, the windows of heaven were opened so that water could be
poured upon the earth. Because of the combination of all these waters
(water from the windows of heaven, water stored inside our planet,
together with the rain), is it conceivable that the earth was entirely covered for a short time by water? Even the Book of Mormon testifies that
the extent of the flooding was tremendous: "After the waters had receded
from off the face of this land [America] it became a choice land above all
other lands" (Ether 13:2).

Perhaps no mortal man knows for sure how the Great Flood came
about. Still, through the scriptures and inspired scientific thought, we
have the testimonies of many declaring that it was not only possible but
that some sort of a Great Flood did unmistakably occur.

Evil in Noah's Day*

Before we leave this topic, it should be noted that preceding Noah's
day there were serious issues with humanity. The Great Flood wasn't just
an accident of nature and God didn't just do it on a whim. As Hugh
Nibley explains: "The wickedness of Enoch's day had a special stamp
and flavor; only the most determined and entrenched depravity merited
the extermination of the race. In apocryphal Enoch stories we are told
how humanity was led to extremes of misconduct under the tutelage of
uniquely competent masters."[68]

In the above quote by Hugh Nibley, he refers to "uniquely competent masters" who were especially adept at leading the people in their
depravity. These evil masters according to tradition, were variously des-
ignated as sons of God, as Watchers, and even as Fallen Angels. There
seems to be some question as to whether these individuals were angels
directly from heaven or special spirits sent to mortal bodies who became
enlightened sons of God. It is possible that they had become like Adam,
"sons of God."

In Moses 6:68 we find the following quote: "Behold, thou [Adam]

art one in me, a son of God; and thus may all men become my sons."
How is it that men may become sons of God in mortality? The answer is
that they need to *believe* in the gospel, *enter* into the new and everlasting
covenant, and *keep* the commandments of God. In short, sons of God
are those who accept and live God's laws.

Many of the wicked in Enoch's day were special individuals, enlightened men and possibly women blessed with great knowledge, who had
been strong in the faith and then purposely and knowingly partook of
all Satan had to offer.

> What made the world of Enoch so singularly depraved as to invite
> total obliteration was the deliberate and systematic perversion of heav-
> enly things to justify wickedness.
>
> The great danger to all existence was that the perverters knew too
> much: "Their ruin is accomplished because they have learnt all the
> secrets of the angels, and all the violence of the Satans, and all their
> powers—the most secret ones." The threat is from those "who have
> received the ordinances, but have removed themselves from the Way
> of Life." They have claimed the ordinances without keeping the law of
> God . . .
>
> As it was, their power for evil was almost unlimited, "for in secret
> places of the earth were they doing evil; the son had connection with
> the mother and the father with the daughter: and all of them with their
> neighbors' wives: and they made solemn covenants among themselves
> concerning these things . . .
>
> "While all nature obeys," Enoch tells them, "you do not obey; you
> are puffed up and vain . . . therefore your destruction is consummated
> and there is no mercy or peace for you." More aggressively they began
> to sin against the birds and the beasts . . . and against each other, eating
> flesh and drinking blood . . .
>
> Enoch never allows us to forget that the real tragedy is not what
> becomes of people but what they become. The people in the days of
> Enoch and Noah were quite satisfied with themselves as they were, and
> they hotly resented any offers of help or advice from God's messengers.
> "They denied the Lord and would not hear the voice of the Lord, but
> followed their own counsel." (Cf. Moses 6:43) . . . They know what
> they are doing when they say to God, "Turn away from us for the
> knowledge of thy ways gives us no pleasure!"
>
> Peculiar to the world of Enoch is not only the monstrously arro-
> gant quality of the sinning that went on, but the high degree of enlight-
> enment enjoyed by the sinners.[69]

There came a time when God simply chose to no longer send his spirit children into such a despotic and sinful world. In order to break the cycle of wickedness, He cleansed the earth with a Great Flood and started anew with Noah and his family.

We should count our blessings that we have been born since the Great Flood. Even so, though it may not now be as bad, there is plenty of opposition and depravity. We live in a great period of enlightenment (the fullness of times), yet a smorgasbord of wickedness is spread before us. We live in an age when most people intentionally bring sin and filth into their homes via the television, Internet, DVD movies, books, music, and magazines. Many either don't care or believe that their family members have the strength of character to control it. Who are we fooling? We are becoming a society of addicts. God's laws are openly scorned. If we aren't careful, the time will come a time when the Lord will once again wipe clean the earth—or chosen portions of it—from its wickedness.

As we know, the next major cleansing will come by fire:

> For the time soon cometh that the fullness of the wrath of God shall be poured out upon **all** the children of men; for he will not suffer that the wicked shall destroy the righteous. Wherefore, he will preserve the righteous by his power, even if it so be that the fullness of his wrath must come, and the righteous be preserved, even unto the destruction of their enemies by fire. Wherefore, the righteous need not fear; for thus saith the prophet, they shall be saved, even if it so be as by fire. (1 Nephi 22:16–17; bold added)

Is it possible that the earth again cries out as it did before the flood? "Wo, wo is me, the mother of men; I am pained, I am weary, because of the wickedness of my children. When shall I rest, and be cleansed from the filthiness which is gone out of me? When will my Creator sanctify me, that I may rest, and righteousness for a season abide upon my face?" (Moses 7:48).

We might address one other aspect of the Great Flood. In some circles it is believed that the flood did not cover the entire earth, that it was merely a regional phenomenon: "Mesopotamia, the region where Babel and Ur and presumably Noah's home as well are located, is bounded on three sides by the Tigris and Euphrates rivers. It is largely a plain. A massive flood approximately five thousand years ago produced a three-meter-thick sediment deposit in the vicinity of Ur. So a flood at the time of Noah is not without precedent."[70]

The expositor of this theory, author Gerald L. Schroeder, points out a variation in the Hebrew text that possibly translates as a local rather than a global flood:

> The first mention of the Eternal's plan to destroy animal life is: "And the Eternal said I will blot out man whom I have created from on the face of the earth (adamah), both man and beast and creeping thing and fowl of the heavens" (Gen. 6:7). For the entire Flood account, the destruction is related to destroying life from the face of the aretz, not the adamah. Though adamah and aretz may both be translated as earth, they can also mean local environs and not the entire earth. For example: "And the famine was on all the face of the aretz" (Gen. 41:56); and "There was no bread in all the aretz" (Gen. 47:13). Cane was banished "from the face of the adamah" (Gen. 4:14). He neither went to sea nor left earth for Mars! We see that these terms, aretz and adamah, often have implications of limited geological extent.
>
> The change in terminology from adamah to aretz may indicate a change in divine intent, a change from destroying all life to destroying life in the corrupt region of Mesopotamia. That change in intent is perhaps signaled by the verse following Genesis 6:7 . . . "But Noah found grace in the eyes of the Eternal" (Gen. 6:8).[71]

Does our reading of Schroeder's analysis of events, leave enough room to assume that Noah's a local event? Those in religious circles tend to believe it was global. Modern-day revelation suggests that the earth is a living intelligence, which has a spirit, and that it conforms to and abides by the law of the celestial kingdom (D&C 88:25). We believe that it had need of baptism by immersion just as we do. So, a great global flood, in addition to destroying the wicked, would have spiritually accomplished that baptismal, cleansing purpose.

Orson Pratt once said: "The first ordinance instituted for the cleansing of the earth, was that of immersion in water; it was buried in the liquid element, and all things sinful upon the face of it were washed away . . . As man cannot be born again of water, without an administrator, so the earth required an agency independent of itself, to administer this grand cleansing ordinance, and restore it to its infant purity. That administrator was the Redeemer himself."[72]

Calamities and God's Love

As we consider past calamities like the Great Flood, world wars, civil strife, famines, earthquakes and such, we are left to wonder how the Lord, being full of love, could stand to destroy his children. I think the answer lies not in the fact that He has less love, but because He has *more*. This life is a time for us to learn and progress. It is but a single step in a long staircase of steps that have been prepared by the Lord. Before mortality we lived with God and, as spirits, we progressed and learned. Then we came to this earth for an accelerated course. After this life, there comes a time in the "spirit world" where we will continue to grow. Then, after that comes the resurrection, and then even more opportunities to learn and progress. I am certain that God doesn't view this life exactly the way we do. Christ really did suffer for our sorrows as well as our sins so that He would know how to succor and save us; but, in all, He will do for us and the earth what is best. Some may have trouble with this idea, but the Lord has a very realistic understanding about death. All must die. The question is, when and how. Ultimate destiny is not determined by the moment or manner of death; rather it is by the manner in which we live. Those who are destroyed are not annihilated. They have further existence and further opportunity in the world to come.

X. The Ancients: Did they really live ten times as long as we do?

Having just reviewed Noah and the Great Flood, it is appropriate that we tackle a related question: How does one reconcile the differences between science and theology when it comes to the long life spans of Adam and Eve and the rest of their posterity up and until the time of the flood?

Turning once again to Genesis, Moses tells us that Adam lived 930 years, Seth lived 912 years, Jared, 962 years, Methuselah, 969 years, and so on (Genesis 5:5, 8, 20, 27).

Then, if that wasn't enough, verses in the same chapter indicate that men and women in their middle age—and by middle age we mean 500-plus years old—were conceiving children. Genesis 5:32 says that Noah was 500 years old when he "begat" Shem and Japheth. Genesis also tells us that Noah lived another 350 years after the flood, dying at age 950. So what do we make of this? Is it truth or fiction, fact or myth?

Today, many would write off these claims as make-believe. What do you say?

Can we turn to science for any sort of proof for or against the history written by Moses? We have fossil records, but can those records tell us anything about the life span of creatures? I think not. All they "prove" is that the creatures existed.

Some have surmised that prior to the flood, a layer of water hung in the atmosphere, blocking the sun's "killing" radiation, and that is why man lived longer in those days. However, that doesn't account for Noah and others living hundreds of years after the flood.

Yet another theory holds that until the flood, man didn't eat the flesh of other creatures, possibly accounting for a physically and spiritually healthier lifestyle. That may be true, but still seems like quite a stretch.

There is an additional plausible theory proposed in 1997 by Dr. Gerald L. Schroeder, author of *The Science of God*. Schroeder's contention is that aging is a product of genetics and that each species is programmed to die at a given age range. Elephants live to be a about hundred years old, dogs around fifteen years, fleas, five years, man about seventy-five, and so on. Each species' genetic package limits the age that the species can live. We accept that some trees can live 1000 years or more. Why can't man?

We read about terrible mutations that play havoc with the aging process. A genetic disorder called Progeria speeds up aging, so that children only eight or ten years old have already become shriveled old people. Most die as they enter their teenage years. If genetic mutations shorten life, can we not assume that changes in gene structure could lengthen life?

Dr. Schroeder's contention is within science's realm of possibility to reverse the aging process even ten-fold. "It would be surprising," he says "but not inconceivable that the manipulation of a flea's genome might allow it to live ten times longer than normal."[73]

Genesis describes a time when human metabolism was slower and life spans were lengthened. In times prior to the flood, the first child often wasn't born until a person was about 120 years old, and the average

age of the patriarchs was probably about 750 years. Today, puberty begins at around 12 years of age and civilized societies enjoy a lifespan of approximately 75 years—a number that is slowly creeping upward, year by year. As Dr. Schroeder points out, these numbers represent a possible metabolic shift of a factor of 10. That is 12 x 10 = 120 years to reach child-bearing age, and 75 x 10 = 750 years average life span. So, along with Dr. Schroeder, I suggest that it is possible that the ancients carried a DNA sequence that allowed them to live to ages ten times greater than today!

In the Pearl of Great Price, it states that when Enoch was about sixty-five years old, the Lord came to him in a voice from heaven saying, "Enoch, my son, prophesy unto this people, and say unto them—Repent, for thus saith the Lord: I am angry with this people." Enoch's response, as he bowed himself before the Lord, was, "Why is it that I have found favor in they sight, and am but a lad" (Moses 6:27,31).

How revealing! Enoch, at 65 years old, considered himself an inexperienced "lad."

Genesis bears witness that prior to the flood people lived ten times as old as they do today. Joseph Smith's inspired translation of Moses's writings offers up another account claiming ancient mankind lived to be that old. And from science we learn that genetics may hold a key to extending life. So, from the mouths of an ancient prophet, a modern prophet, and present-day geneticists alike, we can glean the truth.

We should, of course, always trust the venerable witnesses of the prophets over the claims of science. However, in regard to this issue, even scientists agree that our life-spans may have something to do with the state of our current genetic makeup.

XI. Evolution: Is it fact or fiction?

"The Lord made the world in some wonderful way that I can best only dimly comprehend. It seems to me sacrilegious to presume that I really understand him and know just how he did it. He can only tell me in figurative speech that I dimly understand, but that I expect to more completely comprehend in the eternities to come. He created the world, and my faith does not hinge on the detailed procedures he used."[74]

No topic in the sometimes conflicting worlds of science and religion has been argued more heatedly than evolution. Bitter debates have erupted, both in public and in private, over the past two centuries that continue—and will continue to rage on and on. Some believed that the science of evolution would spell the end of religion, while only a few would still cling to the notion that a Supreme Being made the earth and all that it is in just six days.

Long before Charles Darwin published his book The Origin of the Species, Galileo penned the following: "Long experience has taught me this about the status of mankind with regard to matters requiring thought: the less people know and understand about them, the more positively they attempt to argue concerning them, while on the other hand to know and understand a multitude of things renders men cautious in passing judgment upon anything new."[75]

I hope as you read the following arguments that you will keep an open mind. Please try to exercise patience and reason as our discussion attempts to bring a measure of common sense and enlightenment to the great, often ugly debate over evolution. Consider these last words from Galileo: "I do not feel obliged to believe that the same god who has endowed us with sense, reason, and intellect has intended us to forgo their use."

Keeping such wise thoughts in mind, we pose the following question: Are evolution and religion diametrically opposed? If one is wholly correct is the other wholly wrong?

As a place to begin, let's consider more words of the great chemist Dr. Henry Eyring:

> The scriptures record God's dealing with his children back to a "beginning" some six thousand years ago . . . The scriptures tell us of six creative periods followed by a period of rest. During these periods the earth was organized and took its present form. In the King James version of the Bible, the phrase creative periods is rendered as "days." The use of this term has led to at least three interpretations. In the first, the "days" are construed to mean the usual day of twenty-four hours. In the second, the days of creation are interpreted as thousand-year periods following such statements as occur in 2 Peter 3:8. "One day is with the Lord as a thousand years, and a thousand years as one day." The third interpretation accepts "creative periods" as times of

unspecified length and looks to a study of the earth itself to give added meaning to the exceedingly brief scriptural accounts.[76]

I suggest that the scriptural accounts we have of the creation of mankind may be "figurative." That is, it was written like a primer for school children. Dr. Eyring calls attention to three quite distinct scriptural accounts of the creation. These differing descriptions appear in Genesis, in the book of Moses, and in the book of Abraham. Both Genesis and Moses aver that man was created after everything else was created (Genesis 1 and Moses 2). At the same time, both books offer another story relating that man was created *before* all other flesh (Genesis 2 and Moses 3). Which is correct? Or are they both? Does one relate to the physical/temporal creation and the other to the spiritual? As far as I know, we aren't absolutely certain. All we can do is assume an educated guess. In this day and age it would be difficult to find anyone who believes that God actually created the earth and everything on it in just six earth days. As was described in a previous section, God is not bound by time, and even when He counts and measures time, it is probably not counted and measured the way we do it.

Then in Abraham we come across an account that doesn't use the word *day* to signify the period of time between phases of the creation. Instead, we see that no specific period of time is indicated, only that the durations were numbered. Again, the word *day* or *days* is simply not used. The scripture refers to each period of creation (the earth, the heaven, plants, animals, and man) as an indeterminate "time" (Abraham 4:8, 13, 19, 23, 31).

The intent of this writing is to combine the knowledge God gives us from scripture with the knowledge available from science to come up with a deduction of what actually took place. The obvious problem most have in accepting Genesis's literal version of the creation is that it took such a short time (six days). Alternatively, one difficulty most have in accepting the scientific version of earth's creation and its attendant theory of evolution, is that first it requires one to grasp the significance of extremely long periods of time required for the process (over four and a half billion years). And finally, it is hard to fathom as some scientists do, that it was all an accident.

In Psalms 19:1 we find: "The heavens declare the glory of God; and the firmament showeth his handywork." The universe (heavens) and the earth (firmament) are filled with such complexity and wonder that it is hard to believe in outright luck and pure happenstance

In this age of science and technology we thrill in our ability to glimpse back in time by gazing through instruments like the wonderful Hubble telescope. This remarkable device gathers light from galaxies that are so distant that it has taken 14 billion years for it to reach us. Other technology has finally made it possible for us to correctly date the age of the earth at 4.55 billion years. So, as we strive to find any truth that may exist in evolution, we can at least agree that it took a lot of time for things to change. Time, from that perspective is not a problem; it is a benefit.

Dr. Henry Eyring, whom I quoted earlier, had something to say about the amount of time it took to accomplish the creation: "In my judgment, anyone who denies the orderly deposition of sediments with their built-in radioactive clocks places himself in a scientifically untenable position."[77]

The venerable Eyring, then, apparently was able to accept many of the principles taught by evolution's advocates. He saw no major conflicts between an evolutionary explanation and a scriptural account of the creation.

But, clearly, that isn't and hasn't always been the case with scientists and religionists. Evolution has been a source of significant religious discomfort for the past 150 years. Again, when we are trying to learn the truth, we need to keep in mind that truth from any source comes from God. Because of the weight of scientific data supporting evolution, we would be well advised to look carefully at this theory of creation. As Eyring declares, few, if any, serious biologists today doubt the theory of evolution at some level.

Darwin proposed that all living species are descended from a small set of common ancestors—perhaps just one. He held that the variation within a species occurs randomly, and that the survival or extinction of each organism depends upon its ability to adapt to its environment. This is why he termed it "natural selection."

When one observes the complexity of life, it is extremely difficult to believe that everything evolved accidentally. What's more, God has told his prophets down through the ages that it *didn't* happen by chance. He tells us specifically, in Hebrews, that it was by His Son, Jesus Christ, that He created the worlds. Even though the accounts in Moses and Genesis differ slightly, God (Jehovah = Christ) says that He is the Creator (D&C 88). The question is: How did he accomplish it?

Spontaneous, Accidental Creation

In 1953 Stanley Miller, a graduate student at the University of Chicago, performed an experiment that produced amino acids by a series of totally random reactions. He filled a glass flask with the gases that might have been present in our atmosphere 3.8 million years ago: ammonia, methane, hydrogen, and water vapor. Since oxygen comes from life itself, it wasn't present at this time—and didn't appear until billions of years later.

Next, using electrodes and electricity, Miller sent sparks shooting into his soupy mixture, simulating a strike of lightning. The energy from these sparks produced random chemical reactions.

Finally after a few days, a red slime appeared on the inner walls of Miller's glass flask. This slime was found to contain amino acids. Amino acids are the building blocks of proteins, and proteins are the building blocks of life.

Miller's experiment energized the scientific community. The news media spread the results and significance of the study across the globe, but they went too far, trumpeting this experiment as fact that life itself had started by chance.

As a boy growing up in the fifties and sixties, I remember being taught about this experiment in grade school. Still, I wondered . . . Since then many published accounts have been revealed by the scientific community expressing doubt about life on earth being created accidentally.

In 1979, the magazine Scientific American printed an article that stated the following: "Can we really form a biological cell by waiting for chance combinations of organic compound? Harold Morowitz, in his book *Energy Flow and Biology*, computed that merely to create a bacterium would require more time than the universe might ever see if chance combinations of its molecules were the only driving force."[78]

Then, in February 1991, the same magazine printed a follow-up article written by John Horgan. "Some scientists have argued that, given enough time, even apparently miraculous events become possible—such as the spontaneous emergence of a single-cell organism from random couplings of chemicals." Then Horgan went on to state: "Sir Fred Hoyle, the British astronomer, has said such an occurrence is about as likely as the assemblage of a 747 by a tornado whirling through a junkyard. Most researchers agree with Hoyle on this point."[79]

Apparently modern-day chemists debunk Miller's original research. Somewhere along the line, his experiment contained some categorical flaws—as is quite often the case when small mistakes in procedures and measurements occur.

For that reason alone, it is good that we have God's revealed word in addition to science. In Genesis 1:19–20 we find the following: "And the evening and the morning were the fourth day. And God said, "Let the waters bring forth abundantly the moving creature that hath life." All life is water-based. Without water, there would be no life of any kind on earth. It is interesting to note that water first appeared on our planet approximately 3.8 billion years ago, and that is when fossils and carbon dating suggest life first appeared, too. About thirty years ago scientists first found micro-fossils of bacteria and algae in rocks that appeared about the same time water did. So, in the scriptures and in science there is no lag in time between when water appeared and when life occurred. There were no billions of years of time passing so that an evolutionary accident could cause life to appear on its own. As soon as there was water, there was life. Again, because of these recent discoveries, science and press have retracted their statements implying that life formed by chance over billions of years.

Scripture and science when combined can teach us a lot. As you can see, the scriptures reveal that life began when the waters were formed; and science offers corroborating evidence. To reiterate, both science and theology are in agreement that there was no lag in time between when water appeared and when life began. There simply weren't billion years of time available in order to give chance an opportunity to create something as complex as a single cell. However, it is important to also iterate that this doesn't mean there isn't some possible validity to other aspects of evolution. The earth has been here for a long time and God certainly could have taken advantage of ample time blended with the principles of evolution to modify and even develop His initial creation of life into different kinds of organisms. As Henry Eyring warned: "In my judgment, anyone who denies the orderly deposition of sediments with their built-in radioactive clocks places himself in a scientifically untenable position." He also went on to say, "The Lord made the world in some wonderful way that I can best only dimly comprehend."[80]

One of the early and foremost biblical scholars agreed in concept with Eyring. St. Augustine, who lived during the Great Apostasy, is generally known in the Christian world as one of the greatest of all religious intellects. As such, he was aware of the dangers of accepting all biblical texts, including the "Creation" story at face value. In regard to Genesis and the creation, Augustine wrote: "In matters that are so obscure and far beyond our vision, we find in Holy Scripture passages which can be interpreted in very different ways without prejudice to the faith we have received. In such cases, we should not rush in headlong and so firmly take our stand on one side that, if further progress in the search for truth justly undermines this position, we too fall with it."[81]

Even St. Augustine held that the scriptures don't tell us all there is to know. We need to be open-minded as further progress is made in the search for truth.

Fossil evidence found around the world challenges the classical notions of evolution. In North America, Africa, China, Europe, and almost everywhere, fossils have been found indicating that during the Cambrian period (530 million years ago) there was an explosion of life across the entire earth: "Jointed legs, food-gathering appendages, intestinal structures, notochords, gills, eyes with optically perfect lenses—all these 'evolved' simultaneously. Sponges, rotifers, annelids, arthropods, primitive fish, and all other body plans represented in the thirty-four animal phyla extant today appear as a single burst in the fossil record . . . Those are the data. No one disputes them."[82]

How can this sudden development of complex forms of life be explained? As I have read accounts from scientists and biologists, they unilaterally describe an interesting phenomenon. It seems that which we consider as primitive forms of life, like algae and protozoans, have cells that contain a huge genetic (DNA) library compared to those of man and modern mammals. Each cell of these primitive organisms contains as much as 100 times the DNA found in the cells of man or any other mammal.

Because nearly all forms of life appeared on earth almost simultaneously, many have wondered if the first cells that appeared on earth contained a code, a "plan," or blueprint for the development and creation of all future life. Then as the proper conditions occurred, life as we know it evolved from these complex cells. Scientists call this theory the "latent library" theory. According to this theory, all of the information for life is quietly present in the DNA code, waiting for a cue to be expressed.

We see many kinds of latent DNA expression in the world around us today. Chickens are known, on occasion, to grow hair. Sometimes human babies are born with gill slit openings. Horses are born with multiple digits on their feet instead of hooves. Some plants, when submerged in water form a leaf structure that is different than when they grow on dry land. And there are many more examples of latent DNA expression.

Let's consider such an expression that may have occurred millions of years ago. Is it possible that in the earliest beginnings of its existence a whale was a land mammal that gradually became an ocean dweller? If that happened, did some of its latent DNA kick in to make this evolution possible? It is such a huge creature. We can well imagine that millions of years ago, while living on land (with legs, feet, and so on), whales may have spent most of their time in water to help support their massive weight. Who is to say that they didn't gravitate back to the ocean as a full-time habitat? Fossil evidence in India and Pakistan show what appear to be primitive whales with small hind legs. If the fossil record is correct, both mammals and lizards are members of a phyla that were once primitive fish. Today we find fish-like genes in the DNA structure of land-based animals, the gill arches of mammal embryos being a prime example.

What does all this mean in terms of the creation of life? When God created the earth and first placed living organisms on it, did he also put into those early living organisms His plan for the creation or evolution of all living creatures? Did God make it possible for life to emerge from inauspicious beginnings and evolve from a self-generating DNA recipe into the complex life forms that exist in our world?

Take for instance, something as marvelous and elaborate as the human eye. Our eyesight brings us wonderful joy. All vertebrates (animals with a backbone) have the same basic "eye." It is certainly understandable that the eye of man would be similar to the eye of a horse, as vertebrates are quite similar in body structure. What is surprising is that other phyla such as mollusks have similar eye structures as well. Mollusks and vertebrates have been separated in their development for 530 million years, yet, their solutions for sight are almost identical. The octopus is a member of the phylum Mollusca—and a creature with eyes quite like man's. "Although the choice for proteins is different, both have eyes with cornea, functioning iris, lens, vitreous humor, three-layered retina with rods, pigments for moderating light intensity to the retina, a ganglion of nerves connecting the retinal photoreceptors to the brain, and most subtly of all, lateral inhibition, the mechanism by which adjacent optic neurons interact in order to enhance the perception of boundaries between two similar colors."[83]

How do we explain this similar evolution in extremely different animals? Do we really think it is random? If it was done as previously suggested, through the divine planting of DNA seeds that expressed themselves at the appropriate times, is this not as remarkable as a God who would visit the earth and plant each new form of life one at a time? In many ways, the use of millions of years, for evolutionary progress, along with a divine beginning is even more remarkable. Even as we "evolve" from less mature forms to higher states of being during our lifetimes—be it physically, emotionally, intellectually, or spiritually—perhaps God embraces evolution as a natural part of His divine plan.

In addition to the scriptures, is there any other case for divine creation? Absolutely! As was just shown, science of the twentieth century certainly has opened a door, and opened it wide—for that interpretation.

Famed LDS scientist Henry Eyring had the following to say: "In my mind the theory of evolution has to include a notion that the dice have been loaded from the beginning in favor of more complex life forms. That is, without intelligent design of the natural laws in such a way as to favor evolution from lower forms to high forms of life, I don't think the theory holds water."[84]

DNA and the Human Species

When considering the creation and the part evolution may have played in it, we need to look at the design of our human species. A number of years ago (1944), the experiments of Oswald Avery, Colin MacLeod, and Maclyn McCarty showed that DNA is the hereditary material that transfers the body's characteristics. Today we have a map of this DNA for our species. That map is the human genome, the text of which is three billion letters long and is written in a strange and cryptographic four-letter code.

The first draft of the human genome was announced in the year 2000. When this draft was announced, scientist Francis S. Collins, who had managed the gene mapping teams, said, "It's a happy day for the world. It is humbling for me, and awe-inspiring, to realize that we have caught the first glimpse of our own instruction book, previously known only to God."[85]

For each cell, the DNA molecule is like a software program, an instructional script sitting in the cell's nucleus. All the functions of the cell are directed by this script. This genetic code is universal in all known organisms. The human genome contains about 20,000 to 25,000 protein-coding genes. Gene counts for other, far simpler organisms such as worms, flies, and simple plants are similar in number, around 20,000.

In speaking of the human family, at the DNA level we are all 99.9 percent identical. That similarity applies regardless of where a person lives; whether one is a Kenyan, a Russian, a Native American, or a South Pacific Islander, we are all pretty much identical genetically. By DNA standards, we are truly all part of one close family. This low genetic diversity when remarkable compared to that of other species on the earth is remarkably symbiotic. In other species, the diversity is ten to fifty times greater than our own. As a human family, we are uniquely the same.

Despite so much sameness in human gene structure, we all have sixty new mutations that were not present in either of our parents. This helps account for the unique characteristics of each individual, differences both in body and personality. It is this human propensity for mutations that causes scientists to credibly consider the theory of evolution.

Just because we are, as human beings, remarkably similar to one another, it doesn't mean that we aren't also closely related to other organisms in terms of DNA design. When comparing the human to the mouse, we find that the overall size of the two genomes is roughly the same, and the inventory of the protein coding genes is remarkably similar. Even the order of the genes along the human and mouse chromosomes is maintained over substantial stretches of DNA. The evidence of a common design for humans and mice, then, is virtually inescapable. Because of this, it is easy for some to come to the conclusion (and many do) that humans and mice share a common ancestor.

Even if you find it hard to believe that we are related to mice, it is at least helpful to understand that the DNA of man and mouse is very similar. It also lends credence to an assumption that we have the same common **Creator**. Why wouldn't God use similar methods and molds for mammals, humans, and other animals?

When comparing man and the chimpanzee, we can see that there are small differences. (In fact, there are times when my wife might tell you there is *no* difference.) In reality, there really are only slight differences between the DNA of men and that of chimpanzees. One of the few differences is that the human has 23 pairs of chromosomes while the chimpanzee has 24.

In his book *The Language of God*, Francis Collins describes the comparisons between man and chimp as too remarkable to be an accident. He states: "For those like myself working in genetics, it is almost impossible to imagine correlating the vast amounts of data coming forth from the studies of genomes without the foundations of Darwin's theory." He goes on to say that "[Christian] believers would be well advised to look carefully at the overwhelming weight of scientific data supporting this view of relatedness of all living things, including ourselves."[86]

Throughout his book, Collins repeatedly affirms his Christian faith and his belief in the Bible, yet he also believes in evolution and teaches its precepts.

Like Dr. Collins, we could ask ourselves: "How did God create the earth and all organisms on our planet? Did he work from a basic DNA design for all creatures? Did the creation of animal and plant life take billions of years? And did evolution play a part?"

If considered seriously and with an open mind, it is likely that these questions will be answered in the affirmative because of the tremendous amount of scientific proof that exists today. Who are we to say that God couldn't accomplish His creation in any fashion He wanted. Why not create animals, man, and other organisms with a similar design?

Be advised that my intent is not to promote support for or a belief in evolution. The purpose of this book is to show the greatness of God and to demonstrate that there is much of His truth in science as well as religion. This truth can aid us in our understanding of the great Creator. We should always have inquisitive minds and be truth seekers at heart.

As was indicated previously, Dr. Henry Eyring seemed to favor some aspects of evolution: "I might say . . . that in my mind the theory of evolution has to include a notion that the dice have been loaded from the beginning in favor of more complex life forms. That is, without intelligent design of the natural laws in such a way as to favor evolution from lower forms to high forms of life, I don't think the theory holds water."[87]

Speaking of this evolutionary dice, you may recall Albert Einstein's disbelief pertaining to strange principles illuminated by quantum mechanics: "God does not play dice." Whereupon his good friend and colleague, Niels Bohr, replied "nor is it our business to prescribe to God how he should run the world."

So, when someone says that God could not have employed certain evolutionary precepts as a means to accomplish all or part of the creation, we might say in return, like Dr. Niels Bohr, that it is not our business to prescribe to God how He should run the world.

Speaking of just that as it pertains to the biblical account of God's creation, we are told that the first man, Adam, appeared on earth about 6,000 years ago. How can we reconcile this with the fact that museums are filled with human fossils that date back 50,000 years or more?

Most of us are familiar with C. S. Lewis; he's one of my favorite authors. In regards to the creation of man, Lewis made some interesting observations. He of course would have been the first to say that his thoughts were just that, thoughts—guesses, really, albeit enlightened ones:

> What exactly happened when Man fell, we do not know; but if it is legitimate to guess, I offer the following picture—a "myth" in the Socratic sense, a not unlikely tale.
>
> For long centuries God perfected the animal form which was to become the vehicle of humanity and the image of Himself. He gave it hands whose thumb could be applied to each of the fingers, and jaws and teeth and throat capable of articulation [speech], and a brain sufficiently complex to execute all the material motions whereby rational thought is incarnated. The creature may have existed for ages in this state before it became man; it may even have been clever enough to make things which a modern archaeologist would accept as proof of its humanity. But it was only an animal because all its physical and psychical processes were directed to purely material and natural ends. Then, in the fullness of time, God caused to descend upon this organism, both on its psychology and physiology, a new kind of consciousness which could say "I" and "me," which could look upon itself as an object, which knew God, which could make judgments of truth, beauty, and goodness, and which was so far above time that it could perceive time flowing past. This new consciousness ruled and illuminated the whole organism, flooding every part of it with light. . . . His organic processes obeyed the law of his own will, not the law of nature.

His organs set up appetites to the judgment seat of will not because they had to, but because he chose. Sleep meant to him not the stupor which we undergo, but willed and conscious repose—he remained awake to enjoy the pleasure and duty of sleep. Since the processes of decay and repair in his tissues were similarly conscious and obedient, it may not be fanciful to suppose that the length of his life was largely at his own discretion. Wholly commanding himself, he commanded all lower lives with which he came into contact. Even now we meet rare individuals who have a mysterious power of taming beasts. This power the Paradisal man enjoyed in eminence. The old picture of the brutes sporting before Adam and fawning upon him may not be wholly symbolical. Even now more animals than you might expect are ready to adore man if they are given a reasonable opportunity: for man was made to be the priest and even, in one sense, the Christ, of the animals—the mediator through whom they apprehend so much of the Divine splendour as their irrational nature allows. And God was to such a man no slippery, inclined plane. The new consciousness had been made to repose on its Creator, and repose it did . . .

We do not know how many of these creatures God made, nor how long they continued in the Paradisal state. But sooner or later they fell. Someone or something whispered that they could become as gods.[88]

What a provocative account of the creation of man and of his fall. When coupled with the anthropologic evidence we have of ancient man, with the theory of evolution, and with the comparison of our DNA to other creatures, Lewis's thoughts have merit and are certainly worth our consideration.

In an effort to paraphrase, he basically states his belief that mankind could have evolved under the direction of God. What's more, he surmised that man may have existed in a lesser form for countless years prior to being ready to be transformed by God so that man could become more like Him and become one with Him. Adam and Eve may in reality have been the first hominids with divinely created human souls.

With all the physical proof that surrounds us regarding the similarity of man to other creatures, there is something we haven't discussed that makes man unique. It is, among other things, the most important. It is his awareness of right and wrong, something that Lewis calls the "moral law." Only man has a conscience! The Book of Mormon prophet Moroni states: "For behold, the Spirit of Christ is given to every man, that he many know good from evil" (Moroni 7:16).

In effect, God gave man a conscience and, along with that conscience (free will), the freedom and ability to do as he pleases. Man can even knowingly do wrong. No other creature has the ability to distinguish right from wrong and to exercise *agency*, the ability to choose between good and evil.

More than two hundred years ago, one of the most influential philosophers of all time, Immanuel Kant, wrote: "Two things fill me with constantly increasing admiration and awe, the longer and more earnestly I reflect on them: the starry heavens without and the Moral Law within."[89]

As I reflect on God, I am ever in awe of His all-knowing intellect, His great goodness, His incredible creations. Like Moses I am forced to exclaim, "Now, for this cause I know that man is nothing, which I had never supposed" (Moses 1:10).

Compared to God we are *infinitely inferior*; yet, God states that his *work* and his *glory* is to bring to pass our immortality and eternal life. This mortal life is one of learning and probation. If we are successful, we will return to God, "who is our home"!

> Our birth is but a sleep and a forgetting;
> The soul that rises with us, our life's star,
> Hath had elsewhere its setting,
> And cometh from afar;
> Not in entire forgetfulness,
> And not in utter nakedness,
> But trailing clouds of glory do we come
> From God, who is our home.[90]

God is remarkable, whether He placed man on earth in one step or created Adam and Eve via some type of evolutionary process. We should always keep an open mind and not put ourselves in a position where we are stubbornly "kicking against the pricks." There is no point in fighting against it. Nothing in science proves there is no God. At the same time, much in science suggests there is.

XII. The Mystery of Light: The power of God!

"That which is of God is of light; and he that receiveth light, and continueth in God, receiveth more light; and that light groweth brighter and brighter until the perfect day" (D&C 50:24).

Light is a remarkable, marvelous, mysterious thing, an essence unlike any other! In fact, the intent of this section is to demonstrate that obtaining a correct understanding of light will aid you in discovering the true nature of God.

When God and Christ visited the boy Joseph, they appeared as beings filled with and surrounded by light. Likewise when Christ showed Himself to Oliver Cowdery and Joseph Smith in the Kirtland Temple: "The veil was taken from our minds, and the eyes of our understanding were opened. We saw the Lord standing upon the breastwork of the pulpit, before us; and under his feet was a paved work of pure gold, in color like amber. His eyes were as a flame of fire; the hair of his head was white like the pure snow; his **countenance shone above the brightness of the sun**" (D&C 110:1–3; bold added).

Because we hope to live with God some day, light may play a significant part in our lives. Hugh Nibley, gleaning teachings from ancient texts, stresses the importance of light as it pertains to our immortal and eternal existence: "One's station . . . hereafter depends entirely on the mysteries one has received on the earth. Without the performance of certain ordinances, no one, no matter how righteous, can enter into the Light. . . Hence the rites are all-important. . . . One becomes 'an heir of the Treasure of Light by becoming perfect in all the mysteries.' "[91]

What is this "Light" into which we must enter? What is the "Treasure of Light" to which we can become an heir?

In regard to Adam and man, Nibley quotes from another ancient text that describes the importance of light: "Three Great Men . . . are sent down to instruct and accompany Adam. . . . They are the Three . . . 'sent into the world to fetch the Elect . . . back to the House of Light.' "[92]

It doesn't take a stretch of the imagination to assume that the "House of Light" is the same house/home described by William Wordsworth in his poem when he says we come trailing clouds of glory, "From God, who is our home."

More or less a full hundred scriptures in the Book of Mormon, Doctrine and Covenants, and Pearl of Great Price refer to light. A few use the specific term "Light of Christ." Moroni 7:18–19 reads: And now, my brethren, seeing that ye know the light by which ye may judge, which light is the light of Christ, see that ye do not judge wrongfully . . . Wherefore, I beseech of you, brethren, that ye should search diligently in the light of Christ that ye may know good from evil; and if ye will lay hold on every good thing, and condemn it not, ye certainly will be a child of Christ."

It seems that one of the special functions of light is that it provides us with an ability to choose between right and wrong, good and evil. In other words, the Light of Christ provides us with a conscience. Regarding this conscience, in the last section we quoted Immanuel Kant: "Two things fill me with constantly increasing admiration and awe, the longer and more earnestly I reflect on them: the starry heavens without and the Moral Law within."[93]

Indeed, one of the intents of this section is to show that "the Moral Law within" and "the starry heavens without" are both functions of the Light of Christ.

What is light? Even in this age, light is still not well understood, but the following concepts sum up fairly well what we do know:

- No elemental particle can travel faster than the speed of light.
- Light simultaneously exhibits the characteristics of both a particle and a wave.
- Light never diminishes; it never wears out.
- It never slows down.
- Light is an individual phenomenon (relative to each of us).
- Light seems to have an intelligence of its own.
- Many forms of light come under the broad heading of electromagnetism.
- Light particles are extremely small; as such, they fall under the laws of Quantum Mechanics.

Albert Einstein gave us profound insight into the nature of light. Because of his research, we know that no object can travel faster than the speed of light. The speed of light (299,792,458 meters per second or

186,282 miles per second) is the universal speed limit.

As indicated in the second bullet point above, light exhibits the characteristics of both a particle and a wave. Individual particles of light are called photons. These particles, or photons, consist of packets of energy which move at the speed of light. You will see in the subsequent write-up that it may be possible that God includes both information and energy in these packets as they are sent to us. The diagram below shows light in its two forms, as particles and waves.

Light as Particles and Waves

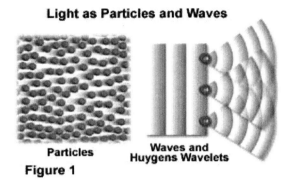

Particles

Waves and
Huygens Wavelets

Figure 1

Even young children learn and intuitively know that without light there is no life. Plants and animals depend on it. Hence, one of the reasons that light might need to be in the form of a wave as well as a particle is so that, as it emanates from the sun it can shine forth and touch everything in its path. If light was only made up of particles, as it traveled from the sun, it might be a hit or miss kind of thing. But since it has properties of a wave, it washes over everything, giving all in its reach an opportunity to receive light and life.

One of the reasons light may also need to be a particle is because, as it emanates from God, instead of touching everything in its path, on occasion it needs to reach one specific individual. From Doctrine and Covenats 88:11, we know that all understanding is derived from the light emanating from Christ. Therefore, light particles (photons) may contain packets of knowledge that can be individualized. God uses light as a medium to selectively bless each of our lives with truth and knowledge as we are receptive and prepared to receive it. The truth and knowledge with which we are blessed is tailored to our individual needs. Such custom-made light may be sent as a particle to specific individuals and not as a wave that washes over all in its path.

One concept mentioned in the list of characteristics of light is that it is eternal; it never diminishes. The light we can see (via the Hubble telescope) from distant parts of the universe is nearly 14 billion years old when it reaches us. Yet each particle is as strong and bright as it was the moment it left those ancient, remote galaxies.

Though presented earlier in the section on time, Einstein's observations also pertain to our discussion on light, and help us understand why light doesn't age, diminish or slow down. His theory of special relativity declares: "The combined speed of any object's motion through space and its motion through time is always precisely equal to the speed of light."

The simple equation for this can be expressed as $X + Y =$ Speed of Light, where X is the speed at which something is traveling and Y is its motion through time. If you increase the speed of an object, time will slow down for that object. If you decrease its speed, time will speed up.

It is important that this time-and-speed continuum is understood. Einstein theorized that the motion of time and the motion of an object through space are inherently related. For example, when you watch a jet airliner take off and fly away from you, you are really seeing that some of the airliner's motion through time is being diverted to motion through space. Thus, the airliner's speed and movement through time keeps its combined total speed-to-light ratio unchanged. Clocks on a jetliner actually run slower for two reasons. One is because of its motion relative to ours on the ground; the other is because the plane is farther from the mass of the earth than we are. However, this section will just focus on the theory of special relativity that pertains to speed and time, not on the theory of general relativity that also includes the law of gravity and its effects on time.

If we take the concept of speed and time to another level, we can better understand why time would stop for an object if it traveled at the speed of light. It is because all of the object's motion through time has been taken over by its motion through space. To reiterate: *The combined speed of any object's motion through space and its motion through time is always precisely equal to the speed of light.*

Nothing ages when it travels at the speed of light because, at that speed, all of the object's motion through time has been assumed by its motion through space. So, even though we haven't discovered the fountain of youth that Ponce de Leon was looking for, we can at least understand that light has. It doesn't age, grow dim, or diminish in speed. Not ever!

In his research, Hugh Nibley found ancient documents that, if they are true, indicate how very important this "never aging, never diminishing" light is to God. He never lets it go to waste. According to these documents, God has even assigned particular angels to go around and collect it. The idea of "waste not, want not" seems to be a heavenly dictum, not just an earthly one. "God's assistants . . . the faithful servants . . . rescue and preserve the light particles lest any be lost in space. . . . It is like a tiny bit of God himself."[94]

Another surprising truth is found hidden in this quote. That is, that "[light] is like a tiny bit of God himself," a concept we will explore in this book.

Remember, light which was sent out from galaxies some 14 billion years ago, is traveling at the same speed it was the moment it was generated by the stars in that remote part of the universe. What's more, each particle still has the same amplitude (brightness) and wave length (color) as when it was first generated.

At the beginning of this section, I stated that one of the more intriguing characteristics of light is that it is an "individual phenomenon." What do we mean by this? We mean that it always travels at the same speed towards or away from an individual, regardless of the direction or speed at which an individual moves. The speed of light, Einstein declared, is 186,282 miles per second *relative to anything and everything.* In essence, you can't catch up to or outrun light, no matter how fast you move. As a matter of fact, by chasing after light at a high speed, you can't even slow down the widening gap that it is traveling away from you.

> Well, this is certainly a simple statement. . . . The problem is that it also seems crazy. If you run after a departing beam of light, common sense dictates that from your perspective the speed of departing light has to be less than 670 million miles per hour [186,282 miles per second]. If you run toward an approaching beam of light, common sense dictates that from your perspective the speed of the approaching light will be greater than 670 million miles per hour. Throughout his life, Einstein challenged common sense. In this case, he forcefully argued that regardless of how fast you move toward or away from a beam of light, you will always measure its speed to be 670 million miles per hour—not a bit faster, not a bit slower, no matter what.[95]

If you could chase after light at an incredible speed, it would still move away from you at the same speed as if you were standing still, 670 million miles per hour. If you fly at an incredibly high speed directly toward a beam of light coming towards you, you will find that it is still coming at you at the same speed as it was before you decided to fly toward it. The rate of speed of the light coming at you is still 670 million miles per hour.

To better understand this, consider the following example. Suppose there are two spaceships that, when first viewed, are about the same distance from earth. However, one of the spaceships (A) is heading toward earth and the other (B) is heading in the opposite direction away from earth. In this supposition, we will go way out on a limb and say that each of their rates of speed is 93,141 miles per second or half the speed of light. Now suppose that some earthlings send up a super sized-flare so that both ships can see it. Those on the earth rightly observe that light from the flare will reach the space craft heading toward the earth in half the time that it would if the craft were standing still relative to the earth. They also correctly observe that it is going to take twice as long for light to reach the craft that is speeding away from the earth.

However, the people on the spaceships observe a totally different scenario. The light traveling toward both ships is observed by the respective travelers as moving toward them at exactly the speed of light, not faster or slower. The speed of the crafts moving away from or toward the light has no effect at all. To the observers on the spaceships, the light moving towards their individual crafts is exactly moving at 186,282 miles per second, the speed of light. They can't close the distance or move away from the light any faster than the speed of light. So, the observers on the earth and those in the spaceships correctly observe that light is an individual phenomena. It acts differently for each set of observers: those on the spaceships and those on the earth. It always travels away from us or towards us at the same speed, no matter how fast we might be moving toward or away from it.

Kind of confusing? Yes. Our minds don't wrap that easily around such far-reaching concepts. Still, the concepts are true.

Einstein realized that experimenters who are moving relative to earth-bound observers or those on the spaceships, will not find identical values for measurements of distances and durations. When space travelers are moving relative to one another, their perceptions of space and time are different.

"We conclude that **space and time is in the eye of the beholder.** Each of us carries our own clock, our own monitor of the passage of time. Each clock is equally precise, yet when we move relative to one another, these clocks do not agree. They fall out of synchronization; they measure different amounts of elapsed time between two chosen events."[96]

Somehow, space and time adjust themselves perfectly for each individual, regardless of how fast or slow he or she is traveling, so that their individual observations of light's speed yield the same result. Another way of saying this is that light is tailored to fit each individual so precisely that we can't do anything to change the way light interacts with us.

Why do you suppose God made this space, time, and light relationship an individual phenomenon? Why does it matter? There is a reason. We just have to figure it out. As we try to find reason in this, we might want to take into consideration the fact that God personally loves each of us with all his heart. He is our Father, and as such He cares about us and watches over each individual. So, one of the things He did for His children was to create a universe that ticks distinctly for each person.

As will be described later on, all light is from Christ. It is the power He uses to create and sustain all life as well as to provide us with understanding, knowledge, and truth. Through the use of light, God can sustain our lives and the lives of all creatures that live on our planet. He can also enlighten our minds and give us understanding. The law that governs light is remarkable. It is a law that makes it possible for God to interact personally with each of us.

Because space is expanding and galaxies are moving away from each other at incredible speeds, is it possible that God made light an individual phenomenon because He wanted its beneficial effects to not be diminished by speed, distance, and time for each of His children? If God is, as we believe, both a personal and a collective God, He knows and loves his children collectively and individually. So, He wants His light to touch all of us collectively (sun gives life to all things) and each of us individually or personally (knowledge, truth, understanding, conscience).

As you may recall, light is both a wave and a particle. With this understanding we can fathom how God uses light to provide life to all living organisms. Since light can function as a wave, it can wash over everything in its path, providing a sustaining warmth and energy to every living thing.

Even so, God has another use for light besides sustaining life with warmth and energy. By manipulating light's properties, conveys understanding (D&C 88:11). As described earlier, the light of Christ gives us our ability to discern between good and evil. In addition, light is used by God and Christ to enlighten our minds and provide us with understanding of Him, ourselves, and the world/universe around us. Nearly every person can point to instances in his life when he sensed flashes of understanding and inspiration. Such "light" is tailored to each individual.

From a physics perspective, all light, as it radiates from its source, functions as a wave. In that capacity it washes over everything in its path until it encounters a living organism. Then in a miraculous transformation, its wave function collapses to provide life-giving energy in the form of individual particles.

This is likely the same way God can use light to enlighten mankind, to give him understanding and inspiration. Light is sent from its source in the form of a wave. When these waves encounter the person they are meant to touch, their wave functions collapse and the packets (particles) that contain information for understanding and inspiration coalesce on that individual.

A common colloquialism used to describe someone who receives inspiration includes the phrase "in tune" with the Spirit. I expect there really may be something to that sort of thing.

Nibley sites ancient religious texts that imply almost the same thing:

"The worlds borrow light from each other and exchange all they know . . . The heavenly bodies receive commands [light] from a single center . . . the affairs of 'the incomprehensible expanse of the structure of heaven' are directed from a command-post center. . . . The rulers dispatch 'letters from world to world and reveal the truth to each other' "[97]

How amazing! Ancient writings describe the use of light to send truth-revealing letters from world to world. This helps us understand how critical it is that light has the characteristics of both a wave and a particle. Just as critical is the fact that someone is able to control light's wave function and collapse it when needed, allowing appropriate individuals to access the information included in the packets of light.

Interestingly Nibley's text uses the term "borrow light" rather than "share light" when referring to light being used as a means of communication. Borrowing connotes something valuable that should be returned.

As we have seen, light is a valuable, possibly recyclable commodity. "God's assistants . . . the faithful servants . . . rescue and preserve the light particles lest any be lost in space. . . . It is like a tiny bit of God himself."[98]

Earlier we referred briefly to man's conscience (the Light of Christ), which is given to all (Moroni 7). This light emanating from God to us is certainly a collective as well as an individual phenomenon. The Light of Christ is bestowed on all of us as a *wave*. As we tune into that wave, we can recognize right from wrong. As you know, some people choose to tune out their consciences, enabling them to ignore or not receive the understanding coming to them through the Light of Christ.

It seems that light in fact does wash over everything without discrimination. However, as was mentioned earlier, one must be in tune (kind of like a radio receiver) to absorb the intended knowledge and understanding. If all knowledge and understanding was to be instantly available to every person everywhere, if it were a collective thing, its possible that we would all be and act and think similarly, a result not unlike the plan proposed by Lucifer in our premortal life. God's plan is to provide us with individualized instruction and understanding customized according to our merit and need. He wants us to learn and grow and make our own decisions. In order to accomplish that, He sends light to his children in the form of private, personalized particles/packets addressed to individuals. In that setting, the light brings specific and different enlightenment to each of us.

Intelligence of Light

One of the most interesting aspects of light is that it seems to have intelligence of its own. In 1926 German physicist Max Born asserted that an electron wave (light wave) must be interpreted from the standpoint of *probability*. If one were to focus on the spot where an electron might be found, it actually could be in any number of locations or everywhere at the same time. At a microscopic level, the best we can ever do is say that an electron has a particular probability of being found at any given location. This is truly peculiar. What business does probability have in the formulation of fundamental physics? Again, it is as if elemental particles like photons and electrons have minds of their own.

In order to better understand this concept, let's again refer to the fact that light takes on at once the characteristics of both a wave and a particle.

One can reasonably ask: How can it be both? The quantum, microscopic world requires that we shed our intuition that something has to be one or the other, either a wave or a particle. The only choice is to embrace the possibility that it is both. It is extremely hard to understand at a deep, intuitive level, this dazzling feature of the quantum world.

Yet another, even more unfathomable characteristic of light is that it seems to have the ability to make decisions, as if intelligent. Did God, when He commanded "Let there be light!" somehow endow that light with a measure of free will or is it possible all particles innately have free will? As was stated earlier, light waves/particles are probabilistic. That is, we can't always be sure we will find them at the place where we think they should be. Its as if they decide for themselves. Many—even Einstein—find this troubling.

A famous experiment first performed two centuries ago by Thomas Young, shows us the probabilistic nature of light. Termed the "double slit experiment," a beam of light is fired at two slits positioned side by side (either vertically or horizontally).

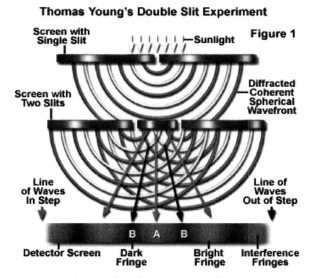

This experiment shows that light acts both as a wave and as individual particles. We even find that when a light beam is controlled to the point where only one photon is fired at a time that it exhibits both characteristics of a wave and of a particle simultaneously. In this experiment the light particles (photons/electrons) actually choose for themselves where they will go.

To substantiate this, we refer to the work of, renowned theoretical physicist Richard Feynman who, following World War II, picked up Thomas Young's research. Recreating the double slit experiment, he determined that an electron attempting to pass through the left slit actually "cares" what happens at the right slit. Until Feynman came along, physicists believed that when electrons were individually fired at a slit, they passed through one slit or the other, either left or right. Feynman proclaimed that each electron that makes it to the background screen behind the two slits *actually goes through both slits*. If you think that is crazy, hang on because it gets even crazier. In traveling from the source that is firing the electrons, each individual electron actually traverses every possible trajectory simultaneously. So, at the same time, the electron somehow proceeds in a nice orderly fashion through the slit on the left, and while accomplishing that, also travels in a nice orderly fashion through the slit on the right; but while doing this suddenly jumps back to the left slit. Then it meanders back and forth on a long journey, trying path after path. Incredibly it tries every possible route between its starting location and its destination (the left or right slit) before finally deciding to pass through both slits at once.

Mind boggling! How can one electron simultaneously take a seemingly infinite number of paths prior to going through both slits simultaneously? The quantum world, the microscopic world, really is a *wacky* world.

To add to that craziness, nothing at the subatomic level (electrons, photons, and all else) can be described as existing at a certain location and moving a particular speed. "In fact, if you were to capture a single electron in a big, solid box and then slowly crush the sides to pinpoint its position with ever greater precision, you would find the electron getting more and more frantic. Almost as if it were overcome with claustrophobia, the electron will go increasingly haywire—bouncing off the walls of the box with increasingly frenetic and unpredictable speed. Nature does not allow its constituents to be cornered."[99]

Because of the free will or intelligence, particles seem to posses, sub-microscopic reality is extremely turbulent. Even in the most calm, quiet setting imaginable, such as empty space (far away from the earth and even our galaxy), there is a tremendous amount of activity going on. And this activity gets increasingly turbulent on smaller and smaller scales. Quantum mechanics demonstrates that the universe is a wildly chaotic, frenzied place at super-microscopic levels; it is as if every particle has a mind of its own. Only when viewed from our perspective, our world of relativity (the world of the big), do things smooth out and appear to become orderly (law of averages). From our perspective, space seems uniform and empty. At the quantum level, however, it is teeming with activity.

Now, what does all of this have to do with God and man? First of all, it is interesting to note that *some aspect* of free will (the ability to choose and make decisions) may integrally affect everything that makes up the universe. This free will may not be as extensive as full-blown "agency" available to man, but it does suggest that some form of intelligence exists in all things.

Secondly, the study of quantum mechanics helps us see that God is not just interested in the whole, the law of averages, but He cares about the individual and each particle in His universe. When Christ told His newly-chosen Apostles that inasmuch as Heavenly Father notices every sparrow that falls to the earth, He surely would take care of His servants (Matthew 10:29–31), was He speaking in generalities? I think not. Somehow, God is so amazing that He is not only aware of each of us individually, but He is aware of each particle that makes up His universe.

What's more, it appears that He is not going to *force* any person—or even any particle—to do exactly what he wants. He leaves it up to us, and possibly every particle, to make free, independent decisions.

You may recall in an earlier section where we quoted from the Pearl of Great Price telling of a remarkable experience Moses had. He was able to behold the entire earth, all of it, every person, and *every particle* of it (Moses 1:28). Because Moses was given the ability to discern these things by the Spirit of God, we can safely assume that God maintains a watchful eye over all of it, even down to every particle. How amazing! How truly amazing that He knows the state of every particle of His great universe!

There are some wonderful things that man has scientifically been able to deduce about light. However, God has told us that there is much more to light than what science knows. For instance, Doctrine and Covenants 93:9 states that Christ is the *light* and *redeemer* of the world. It also says that He is the *spirit of truth* in the world. Then, in Section 88 verse 7 it adds, "Which truth shineth. This *is* the light of Christ." Section

88 goes on to say that Christ *is* the light and that through the light that emanates from Him, He is responsible for everything. The key word in each of these statements is the little, seemingly insignificant word *is*.

Section 88 verse 7 indicates that "Christ is in the sun" and that "He is the light of the sun" and the power by which the sun was made. Verses 8, 9 and 10 go on to state that "Christ is the power that lights the stars and is the power by which the stars, earth, and moon were created." Again, the key word is *is*.

Earlier we read a statement by Nibley quoting from an ancient text, asserting that God has commissioned angels to go out and collect light, because light is a "tiny bit of God itself." This may be literal. *Light* and *Christ* are synonymous; you can't have one without the other. *Christ is the fountain of all light, of all matter, of everything.*

Sometimes when we see or read something, we don't regard it literally or really understand it as it was meant to be understood. We understand things based on our current knowledge and experience. Most everyone reads about light in the scriptures and assumes that Christ controls light, that He manages it and sends it all over His universe. That, of course, is true, but may not be *all* the truth. Possibly what the scriptures are telling us is that the "light" is actually part of Christ. Every scripture cited in the past few paragraphs testify that "Christ *is* the light," and "He *is* the power."

Thus far, to illustrate the point that our Savior, God's remarkable Son, is literally the source of light and matter, we have exclusively referenced LDS scripture. In the book of Revelation, written by John the Beloved, the Revelator (translated from Greek to English by William Tyndale) we find the exact same language. In speaking of the heavenly city, New Jerusalem, John states: "And the city had no need of the sun, neither of the moon, to shine in it: for the glory of God did lighten it and **the lamb is the light** thereof. . . . And there shall be no night there; and they need no candle, neither light of the sun; for the Lord God **giveth** them light: and they shall reign for ever and ever" (Revelation 21:23; 22:5; bold added).

Isaiah while speaking of the millennium, when Christ will personally reign on earth, recorded similar thoughts: "The sun shall be no more thy light by day; neither for brightness shall the moon give light unto thee: but the **Lord shall be unto thee an everlasting light**, and they God they glory" (Isaiah 60:19; bold added).

Again, I find it fascinating and testimony building to see that Joseph Smith, John the Revelator, Isaiah and the translator, William Tyndale, use the same language when describing light and Christ.

As already mentioned, even children have an innate sense that without light there would be no life on earth. Plants and animals depend on it. Verse 13 in Section 88 provides more clarification: "[Christ is] the light which is in all things, which giveth life to all things . . ." So, all life exists because Christ *is* in all life; and without the sustaining influence of Christ, all life would cease to exist.

The Light of Christ is also that which gives us knowledge and understanding. Most everyone has experienced a time when it was as if a light had flicked on in their heads and they could understand something that they couldn't understand before. Section 88 verse 11 says: "[Christ is] . . . the light which . . . enlighteneth your eyes . . . that quickeneth your understandings."

Parley P. Pratt, a contemporary of Joseph Smith's, corroborates Doctrine and Covenants 88:11. It might be a fair assumption to say that this concept came from Joseph himself, as he was Elder Pratt's mentor: "The Light of Christ, in its less refined existence, is the physical light which reflects from the sun, moon, and stars. In its higher degrees, it serves as the means by which we reason, discern, judge, compare, comprehend and remember the subjects within our reach. Its inspiration constitutes instinct in animal life, reason in man, vision in Prophets, and is continually flowing from Godhead throughout all his creations."[100]

Finally, Doctrine and Covenants 88:13 states that the light emanating from Christ is also the power behind the law that governs all things (remember there are different worlds and kingdoms that have different laws). In this context, Elder Bruce R. McConkie said:

> The light of Christ . . . accounts for the omnipresence of God. It is the agency of God's power and the law by which all things are governed. It is also the agency used by the Holy Ghost to manifest truth and dispense spiritual gifts to many people at one and the same time. For instance, it is as though the Holy Ghost, who is a personage of spirit, was broadcasting all truth throughout the whole universe all the time, using the light of Christ as the agency by which the message is delivered.[101]

Remember, light is both a particle and a wave. The ability of the

Holy Ghost to use light to dispense truth to many people at one time is an example of light going forth as a wave. When the Holy Ghost dispenses a specific truth to a specific individual He is using light as a particle. Light may go out at first as a wave, but its wave function breaks down into a particle when it finds the intended person at the appropriate time. Can you see that it is kind of like a tuner on a radio? When one is tuned into God's broadcast, blessings of knowledge and understanding can be garnered from the light He sends.

Thus, we can see that without Christ and the light that literally comes from Him, there would be nothing. Everything owes its existence to Christ, as it may literally be a part of Christ. This reaffirms once more our understanding that "Christ comprehends all things, has all things before Him, all things round about him; that He is above all things, and in all things, and is through all things, and is round about all things; and all things are by him, and of him . . . forever and ever" (D&C 88:41).

This remarkable scripture, when we break it down, teaches us so much about Christ the Creator and Christ the Savior:

- He comprehends all things
  - o Christ has all knowledge, period!
- All things are before Him
  - o Christ has everything in front of Him. He knows what is happening everywhere and with every thing (every particle, every creature, everything!)
- All things are round about Him
  - o Christ is the center of everything
- He is above all things
  - o Christ has greater intelligence and more power than anyone or anything
- He is through all things
  - o Christ is intertwined into and through everything
- He is round about all things
  - o Before, we said that all things were *around* Christ. He is the center. Now the scripture tells us that *Christ* is around everything. He, in a sense, holds everything in the great hands of His power and influence.
- All things were made by Him and are of Him
  - o Christ made all things and all things are literally part of Christ.

Just think how excited scientists would be if they were privy to modern-day revelation (the Doctrine and Covenants, the Book of Moses, the Book of Abraham, the Book of Mormon, and so on) and understood the all-encompassing power of light and that it emanates from Christ. With that body of powerful knowledge, perhaps they could better focus their efforts and tune into more truth.

Light does not diminish or slow down. It does not age; it is infinite and eternal in nature. From the scriptures we may conclude that Christ is light, and that every photon of light, every particle of matter is an extension or a bit of Christ. Christ has always existed and He always will. Likewise, everything that comes from Christ has always existed and always will.

When we ponder profound truths such as this, we can see why during the apostasy there was a falling away, a loss of knowledge and understanding. It can be difficult to wrap our minds around a God from whom all light comes, who is light himself, yet who has a body of flesh and bones. Without the light from the Holy Ghost it becomes impossible.

To help us with that, let's consider the following: We all know that when matter is converted into energy, one possible outcome is light. We also know from Einstein's research and his famous formula, $E=mc^2$, that energy or light can be used to form matter. Because of these facts we can better understand how Christ was able to use his light and energy to create the earth, the worlds, the stars, and everything else in the universe around us. From a standpoint of physics, this also helps us understand how Christ can have a body of flesh and bone. Because energy and matter are interchangeable, He can use His energy to create both our bodies and His. Christ created the earth, and His body while on earth was made from its elements. When Christ was resurrected, the elements that became part of His resurrected body were an enhanced form of the same elements from his earthly body.

If you want to have a sacred experience, think about Christ and His great power while considering Doctrine and Covenants 88:6–13. We should stand in awe and reverence of a God and a Christ who are so powerful and who have such love for the children of their creation. How grateful we should be to think that God knows and loves and cares for each of us individually.

6 He that ascended up on high, as also he descended below all things, in that he comprehended all things, that he might be in all and through all things, the light of truth;

7 Which truth shineth. This is the light of Christ. As also he **is** in the sun, and the light of the sun, and the power thereof by which it was made.

8 As also he **is** in the moon, and **is** the light of the moon, and the power thereof by which it was made;

9 As also the light of the stars, and the power thereof by which they were made;

10 And the earth also, and the power thereof, even the earth upon which you stand.

11 And the light which shineth, which giveth you light, is through him who enlighteneth your eyes, which is the same light that quickeneth your understandings;

12 Which light proceedeth forth from the presence of God to fill the immensity of space—

13 The light which **is** in all things, which giveth life to all things, which **is** the law by which all things are governed, even the power of God who sitteth upon his throne, who **is** in the bosom of eternity, who **is** in the midst of all things. (bold added)

What can one say about this? Anything would be an understatement!

I was pondering a thought presented earlier in this section, the idea that time doesn't exist for light. After all, it doesn't diminish, grow old, or slow down. And I wondered about matter. Previously in this book I described the atom as being very durable and said that no one actually knows how many years an atom can survive. But it would be in the neighborhood of 100 million, billion, billion, billion years. That is, the atom, like light, is essentially eternal in nature.

We can logically see why light doesn't age or grow dim. It travels so fast, it does not experience time. But you may wonder how it is that matter (the atom) doesn't age, either. It may be because matter and energy (light) are interchangeable ($E=mc^2$). *Every basic particle of matter is made from light, the energy which comes from God.* That energy is eternal—it never ages. The eternal, everlasting light that Christ provides lends existence to everything.

Now, that doesn't mean that some forms of matter don't change as time marches on. We can definitely see and feel the aging of our bodies.

However, even though we wear out and cease to function, the atoms which make up our bodies don't age or diminish at all. And all of that has reference to time. Time doesn't really exist for light or for atomic and subatomic particles. Hence, in a sense, for God, as the source of all energy and matter, time doesn't have any affect. That is why Joseph Smith stated: "the past, the present, and the future were and are, with him [God], one eternal 'now.' "[102]

One day we will be resurrected and get our bodies back in an eternal form that won't wear out. Our bodies are remarkable, even more remarkable than we think! They provide a link to God. Without them it would prove to be disastrous for us. As has been explained, there is evidence that supports the concept that all light, all matter, everything, doesn't just come from Christ, but is *part* of Christ. The only thing that doesn't come from Christ is our eternal nature, our intelligence. Just as Abraham was told that we have an eternal intelligence or spirits, so the Lord has told us in modern times that "Man was . . . in the beginning with God. Intelligence . . . was not created or made neither indeed can be" (D&C 93:29).

As we make an effort to reason this out, I don't think we will be disappointed. God is eternal, and we also are separate and eternal—a portion of our being, our intelligence, has been around forever. The thing that links us permanently to God is the *element*, our bodies. Without our bodies we cannot have a fullness of joy because we can't be linked permanently to God. Our bodies are God's—part of God actually. This universe we live in was created not just by God but *from* God. It is part of Him. All light flows from Him. All matter is made from light, the light that *is* Christ. Light and matter like God and Christ are eternal.

Without our bodies, we are separated from God. As intelligences, we were distinctly separate from yet co-eternal with God. The distinction is: As corporal beings we are actually part of God. Hence, we are linked to God through our bodies. It is as if He lends part of Himself to us so we can eternally be one with Him. Without our bodies we are ultimately on our own, and without that link to God we will never experience a fullness of joy.

That is likely the reason it is so important for Satan to convince the world's people, through erroneous false religious teachings, that God doesn't have a body and that after death we won't either. Satan will never be linked to God; he will never have a body. He will be eternally unhappy and will *never* know what it is to have a fullness of joy.

Joseph Smith said: "We came to this earth that we might have a body and present it pure before God in the celestial kingdom. The great principle of happiness consists in having a body. The devil has no body, and herein is his punishment. He is pleased when he can obtain the tabernacle of man, and when cast out by the Savior he asked to go into the herd of swine, showing that he would prefer a swine's body to having none. All beings who have bodies have power over those who have not."[103]

Satan, through his enticing, exercises much power in this our probationary existence. Without our bodies, which are our link to God, Satan would be able to force his will upon us eternally. That is the fate of the third of the hosts of heaven who fell with him. That is the fate of those who are consigned to spirit prison after this life.

Revelation found in the Doctrine and Covenants helps clarify this point:

> Behold, here is the agency of man, and here is the condemnation of man; because that which was from the beginning is plainly manifest unto them, and they receive not the light. And every man whose spirit receiveth not the light is under condemnation. For man is spirit. The elements are eternal, and spirit and element inseparably connected, receive a fullness of joy; And when separated, man cannot receive a fullness of joy. **The elements are the tabernacle of God; yea, man is the tabernacle of God**, even temples; and whatsoever temple is defiled, God shall destroy that temple. (D&C 93:31–35; bold added)

How about that? There actually is a scripture, a revelation, which indicates that our bodies are part of God: "The elements are the tabernacle of God; yea, man is the tabernacle of God." It goes on to state that if we defile our bodies, we will in essence *lose* them, for God will destroy them.

We find a description of the various grades or types of eternal bodies in 1 Corinthians 15: 39–42, which teaches that there are bodies celestial and bodies terrestrial and so on. So, depending on how we live our lives, we will receive the body that we deserve.

How is it that we *defile* ourselves? We do it by not keeping the commandments of God, by consciously rejecting Him and His counsel. The prophet Abinadi paraphrased the basic commandments as they were given to Moses:

> Thou shalt have no other God before me. . . . Thou shalt not make unto thee any graven image, or any likeness of things which are in heaven above, or which are in the earth beneath, or which are in the water beneath. . . . Thou shalt not bow down thyself unto them, nor serve them. . . .
>
> Thou shalt not take the name of the Lord thy God in vain. . . .
>
> Remember the sabbath day, to keep it holy. . . .
>
> Honor thy father and thy mother. . . .
>
> Thou shalt not kill.
>
> Thou shalt not commit adultery.
>
> Thou shalt not steal.
>
> Thou shalt not bear false witness. . . .
>
> Thou shalt not covet thy neighbor's house, thou shalt not covet thy neighbor's wife . . . nor anything that is thy neighbor's. (Mosiah 12:35–13:24)

After delivering the bulk of his message, Abinadi went on to say: "Fear, and tremble before God, for ye ought to tremble; for the Lord redeemeth none such that rebel against him" (Mosiah 15:26). So, if we want to have a fullness of joy, we must submit ourselves to God. We must learn to control our appetites and passions. Everything else follows. If we do that, God will give us everything. He will enlighten us with whatever knowledge we desire and the universe will be at our fingertips. Not only will we be allowed to keep the bodies He has provided us during this mortal existence—indeed, which are part of Him—but our bodies will also become celestialized, exalted, and perfect following the resurrection.

As spirit combatants in the war in heaven, we fought on the side of God. We chose to remain with Him. Everyone who has ever been born on this earth chose His plan and chose to remain with Him. In turn, God chose to have us all linked to Him. He loves His children, every one. As a reward for our fealty in premortality, everyone who lives or ever did live on earth will have a body that is actually part of God. These resurrected bodies will, however, be of different quality depending on the glory or degree or kingdom the individual earned during his or her earth life.

All, except the sons of perdition, will *eventually* learn and choose to use their bodies as they should. Eternity, after all, is a *long* time. As mentioned, resurrected bodies will be different (see 1 Corinthians 15:39–42) and necessarily limited, because no individual will be able to abide, or "wear" a body that is not suited to him. That is, we each will be resurrected with the body that suits us best according to our obedience to the measure of God's light and law received while living on earth.

Joseph Smith revealed some interesting things about our bodies that may help us better comprehend the importance of having a body that is linked to and part of God Himself. In a meeting in Nauvoo, Illinois, on January 19, 1841, it was recorded: "Before the foundation of the earth in the Grand Council . . . the spirits of all men were subject to oppression and the express purpose of God in giving it a tabernacle was to arm it against the power of darkness."[104]

On another occasion, Joseph declared (punctuation inserted): "[The] spirits of the eternal world are [as] diverse from each other as here in dispositions. [They are] aspiring [and] ambitious. As man is liable to enemies there as well as here, it is necessary for him to be placed beyond their power in order to be saved. This is done by our taking bodies (keeping our first estate) and having the power of the resurrection pass upon us, whereby we are enabled to gain ascendancy over disembodied spirits."[105]

A key scripture from the Book of Mormon attests to the importance of our bodies, our link to Christ, which make it possible for us to defend ourselves against and overcome Satan:

> O the wisdom of God, his mercy and grace! For behold, if the flesh should rise no more our spirits must become subject to that angel who fell from before the presence of the Eternal God, and became the devil, to rise no more. And our spirits must have become like unto him, and we become devils, angels to a devil, to be shut out from the presence of our God, and to remain with the father of lies, in misery, like unto himself . . . O how great the goodness of our God, who prepareth a way for our escape from the grasp of this awful monster. (2 Nephi 9:8-10).

The fact that a body linked to Christ can exercise power over evil is also attested to by James, the half-brother of the Savior, the son of Mary and Joseph: "Submit yourselves therefore to God. Resist the devil, and he will flee from you" (James 4:7).

At the time Moses was confronted by Satan, he found that, because of his body and his link to Christ, he had power over that dark and evil being:

> And it came to pass that Moses looked upon Satan and said: Who art thou? For behold, I am a son of God, in the similitude of his Only Begotten; and where is thy glory, that I should worship thee? . . . where is thy glory, for it is darkness unto me? . . . Get thee hence, Satan; deceive me not . . . And now, when Moses had said these words, Satan cried with a loud voice, and ranted upon the earth, and commanded, saying: I am the Only Begotten, worship me. And it came to pass that Moses . . . commanded, saying: Depart from me, Satan, for this one God only will I worship, which is the God of glory. And now Satan began to tremble, and the earth shook; and Moses received strength, and called upon God, saying: In the name of the Only Begotten, depart hence, Satan. And it came to pass that Satan cried with a loud voice, with weeping, wailing, and gnashing of teeth; and he departed hence, even from the presence of Moses. (Moses 1:13–22)

Joseph Smith also taught: "We came to this earth that we might have a body and present it pure before God in the Celestial Kingdom. The great principle of happiness consists in having a body. The Devil has no body, and herein is his punishment . . . All beings who have bodies have power over those who have not. The devil has no power over us only as we permit him."[106]

We should be ever grateful that God loves us so much that He wants us to be with Him and have bodies that link us to Him. He will do just about anything to help us progress and become like Him— anything but force us. He provides mortality and the challenges of mortality so we can learn about ourselves and learn to choose Him over Satan.

It breaks God's heart when we don't achieve our potential and fall short of becoming like Him. He wants each of us to be eternally happy and forever with Him. He wants to protect us from the powers of darkness.

XIII. Spirit World: Is there any scientific proof for such a place?

Very little is as compelling and fascinating as the spirit world. We all have—or assuredly will have—loved ones who have died. In my own life I have lost many loved ones. When I was twelve, my five-year-old brother passed away. My father died at an early age in 1988. Then, recently my wife's aged parents passed away, dying of natural causes within a day of one another. I love all these people very much. It would be wonderful to know how they are doing and what their lives are like in the spirit world.

In this regard, I am intrigued by something found in the Doctrine and Covenants, section 93, verses 27 and 28, which basically states that if one keeps God's commandments, he will receive a fullness of what God knows. His promise is that through obedience to His laws we can receive truth and light *until we know all things*. I have hope in this promise, and believe that some portion of it can be fulfilled in this lifetime.

Nearly everyone would like to know more about death and what it entails without having to experience it. We have been taught that death is the separation of body and spirit. In a revelation given to Joseph Smith, the Lord states: "For man is spirit. The elements are eternal, and spirit and element, inseparably connected, receive a fullness of joy" (D&C 93:33). We believe that our mortal bodies are a temporary thing, "until death do we part." Then, as this scripture intimates, after the resurrection we can be re-connected with our bodies and receive a fullness of joy.

But that doesn't have to be the end of our knowledge of death and of our spirit existence following death; even now, there is much that can be learned. As science is brought into the picture, alongside scripture and the testimony of the prophets, we can know a whole bunch more about what takes place after we and our loved ones die. At the very least, our testimonies of the Gospel can be strengthened, as once again, science witnesses that the gospel is true.

The observable universe created for us here in mortality has just three spatial dimensions. Basic physics reminds us that a one dimensional object is simply a line. Previously we spoke of something called string theory. The strings included in that theory are one dimensional. Moving up the dimensional ladder, something like a photograph or the page of a comic book is two dimensional; and the third dimension is the one we live in, with all manner of curved and faceted shapes (cubes, cylinders, cones, and balls). This third dimension has height and width and depth. Then when we add the dimension of time, we come up with the four dimensions in which we live.

But in actuality, there are more dimensions that make up our universe, more than what we see and experience in our four-dimensional state. In the Doctrine and Covenants, section 138, the Lord informs us through the prophet Joseph F. Smith of another dimension, one we call the spirit world:

> On the third of October, in the year nineteen hundred and eighteen, I sat in my room pondering over the scriptures; While I was thus engaged . . . I opened the Bible and read the third and fourth chapters of the first epistle of Peter, and as I read I was greatly impressed, more than I had ever been before, with the following passages: "For Christ also hath once suffered for sins, the just for the unjust, that he might bring us to God, being put to death in the flesh, but quickened by the Spirit: By which also he went and preached unto the spirits in prison; Which sometime were disobedient, when once the long-suffering of God waited in the days of Noah, while the ark was a preparing, wherein few, that is, eight souls were saved by water." (1 Peter 3:18–20.) "For for this cause was the gospel preached also to them that are dead, that they might be judged according to men in the flesh, but live according to God in the spirit." (1 Peter 4:6.) As I pondered over these things which are written, the eyes of my understanding were opened, and the Spirit of the Lord rested upon me, and I saw the hosts of the dead, both small and great. And there were gathered together in one place an innumerable company of the spirits of the just, who had been faithful in the testimony of Jesus while they lived in mortality. . . . They were assembled awaiting the advent of the Son of God into the spirit world, to declare their redemption from the bands of death. . . . For the dead had looked upon the long absence of their spirits from their bodies as a bondage. These the Lord taught, and gave them power to come forth, after his resurrection from the dead, to enter into his Father's kingdom . . . (D&C 138:1, 5–12, 16, 50–51)

President Smith's attention was often drawn to the world beyond mortality because of his frequent confrontation with death. Both of his parents died when he was a young man, and among his greatest trials was the passing away of many of his children. At the time he received this revelation he was quite old, ill, and knew that his life was coming to an end. So it is likely that when he received his vision of the spirit world, President Smith held great interest in the world of spirits because that is where he was soon headed. Of this, Robert Millet wrote: "The stage was set: preparation of a lifetime and preparation of the moment were recompensed with a heavenly endowment."[107]

Where is this spirit world that is referenced in the New Testament and that was revealed to Joseph F. Smith? Brigham Young taught that the spirit world is "right here;" it is not "beyond the sun, but is on this earth that was organized for the people that have lived and that do and will live upon it."[108]

We also have the following quote from President Young: "Can you see the spirits in this room? No. Suppose the Lord should touch your eyes that you might see, could you then see the spirits? Yes, as plainly as you now see bodies."[109]

And this from President Harold B. Lee: "The spirit world is right here round about us. If our spiritual eyes could be opened, we could see others visiting with us, directing us."[110]

Elder Parley P. Pratt also explained that the spirit world "is here on the very planet we were born [on]. . . . A veil is drawn between the one sphere and the other whereby all the objects in the spiritual are rendered invisible to those in the temporal."[111]

Pratt's source for his statement was most likely the Prophet Joseph Smith. On one occasion Joseph Smith taught: "The spirits of the righteous are not far from us, and know and understand our thoughts, feelings, and emotions, and are often pained therewith."[112]

What do the spirits of the departed look like? Doctrine and Covenants 77:2 teaches us that the "spirit of man is in the likeness of his person." Taking this a step further, Joseph F. Smith taught:

> The spirits of our children . . . after bodily death, are like they were before they came. They are as they would have appeared if they had lived in the flesh, to grow to maturity, or to develop their physical bodies to the full stature of their spirits. If you see one of your children that has passed away it may appear to you in the form in which you would recognize it, the form of childhood; but if it came to you as a

messenger bearing some important truth, it would come . . . in the stature of full-grown manhood.[113]

You may be surprised to know that the Book of Mormon even tells us what spirits look like. In the Book of Ether, when the Brother of Jared sees the finger of God, he is instructed on the matter: "Behold, I am Jesus Christ . . . Seest thou that ye are created after mine own image? Yea, even all men were created in the beginning after mine own image. Behold this body . . . is the body of my spirit; and man have I created after the body of my spirit; and **even as I appear unto thee to be in the spirit will I appear unto my people in the flesh**" (Ether 3:14–16).

So, before Christ came to earth He possessed a "spirit" body which looked like the body He would take on while in mortality. Then, after dying on the cross, His spirit temporarily separated from His body. At this time, prior to His resurrection, Christ was able to enter into the spirit world.

Before the time of Christ's mission to the world of spirits, a gulf separated those in paradise from those in spirit prison. The Lord described this condition in a parable. He told of a rich man who went to "hell" and a beggar who was received into "Abraham's bosom." The rich man in torment asked for the beggar to come help him, but Abraham responded: "Between us and you there is a great gulf fixed: so that they which would pass from hence to you cannot; neither can they pass to us, that would come from thence" (Luke 16:26).

In our day, Elder Bruce R. McConkie explained that two separate divisions make up the spirit world: "[At the time of death] . . . the spirit undergoes a partial judgment and is assigned an inheritance in paradise or in hell [spirit prison] to await the day of the first or second resurrection."[114]

From both Luke's account of the rich man and beggar man and Elder McConkie's words, it appears that two distinct places are set aside to receive the spirits of the dead. It seems clear that individuals in paradise (prior to Christ's visit there) could not communicate with those in spirit prison, and vice versa. I believe that at the time of Christ's visit and ministry in the spirit world, the gulf that kept the righteous in paradise from visiting those in spirit prison was eliminated or at least a way was opened for those in Paradise to cross into that prison. We know from Joseph F. Smith's vision that Christ didn't actually go to those in spirit prison. Rather, he went to paradise and organized a missionary force, and opened the way for them to share the gospel with those "once disobedient" spirits. (D&C 138).

As a side note: I believe the gulf separating spirit paradise from prison is a *physical* one. If it hadn't been a physical gulf, it just seems natural that great men like Abraham, Isaac, Jacob, Noah, Adam, and others would already have been sharing the gospel with those in hell (spirit prison). But it wasn't until Christ came to paradise and physically opened the door, organized the spirits, and sent them armed with His gospel that it could be taken to all who had ever lived on the earth.

Another thought is that baptism for the dead and other vicarious work wasn't begun until after Christ's death and resurrection. It is likely, then, that only after these keys were given and exercised could the work for the dead allow spirits to escape hell and enter into paradise. Maybe the ordinances themselves protect those in paradise from Satan.

The ultimate blessing, of course, is that, through Christ's Atonement, death, and Resurrection, all mankind will be saved from the chains of death. That is one of the main reasons why Christ was born into mortality. As we have been taught since childhood, because of Adam's actions, death came into the world, and through Christ came the resurrection from the dead (1 Corinthians 15).

Beyond doubt, those deceased person who are in spirit prison are only able to cross the gulf into paradise based on conditions of acceptance of the gospel, repentance, and baptism. But how can they be baptized when they are no longer living, mortal beings? We have some reference to this in the Bible. The Apostle Paul, in 1 Corinthians 15: 22–29, tells us that because of Christ, we shall all be made alive and overcome death. Verses 23, 24, and 26 indicate that following Christ's millennial reign on the earth and His overcoming all His enemies, including death, He will deliver up this kingdom to God the Father. Verse 28 goes on to state that after subduing all enemies and offering His kingdom to God that Christ will subject Himself to God so that God may be over all and in all. Finally, as proof for the gospel being taught and ordinance work being done in the spirit world, verse 29 says, "Else what shall they do which are baptized for the dead, if the dead rise not at all? Why are they then baptized for the dead?"

In addition, Paul's testimony of the work that is being carried on in the spirit world to save souls and overcome spiritual death, modern day prophet, Lorenzo Snow pointed out the following: "I believe . . . that when the gospel is preached to the spirits in prison, the success attending that preaching will be far greater than that attending the preaching of our elders in this life. I believe there will be very few indeed of those spirits who will not gladly receive the gospel when it is carried to them. The circumstances there will be a thousand times for favorable."[115]

From an analysis of the scriptures we can see, so far, that there are three distinct locations for the living and the dead: the three-dimensional world we live in (four if you count time) and two other locations in the spirit world (paradise and spirit prison).

According to Brigham Young, Parley P. Pratt and Joseph Smith, the Spirit World is located on earth. If that is the case, why can't we see it and experience it? We are aware that, on occasion, individuals, are contacted by others from the spirit world; also on occasion, individuals have visited the spirit world in dreams, visions, and through out-of-body experiences.

On two occasions the Prophet Brigham Young reported that Joseph Smith had visited him from the spirit world: when Brigham himself was dying (he uttered the words "Joseph, Joseph, Joseph"); and, many years before, in February 1847, when the Prophet Joseph appeared to Brigham Young in a dream or vision, Brigham pleaded to be reunited with the Prophet. At that time he asked Joseph if he had a message for the Brethren. Whereupon Joseph replied: "Tell the people to be humble and faithful, and to be sure to keep the spirit of the Lord and it will lead them right. Be careful and not turn away the still small voice; it will teach them what to do and where to go; it will yield the fruits of the kingdom. Tell the Brethren to keep their hearts open to conviction, so that when the Holy Ghost comes to them, their hearts will be ready to receive it." Then he added: "They can tell the Spirit of the Lord from all other spirits; it will whisper peace and joy to their souls; it will take malice, hatred, strife and all evil from their hearts; and their whole desire will be to do good, bring forth righteousness and build up the kingdom of God."[116]

Jedediah M. Grant, an apostle and counselor to Brigham Young, said the following about his visit to the spirit world: "I have seen good gardens on this earth, but never saw any to compare with those that were there. I saw flowers of numerous kinds, and some with from fifty to a hundred different colored flowers growing upon one stalk. He also spoke of buildings . . . and said that the temple erected by Solomon was much inferior to the most ordinary buildings he saw in the spirit world."[117]

Heber C. Kimball taught: "If men and women do not qualify themselves and become sanctified and purified in this life, they will go into a world of spirits where they will have a greater contest with the devils than ever you had with them here."[118]

Again, we ask the question: Why can't we see and experience the spirit world? First, let's consider what the scriptures have to say about the makeup of the spirit world. In the Doctrine and Covenants, section 131 verses 7 and 8, the Lord says: "There is no such thing as immaterial matter. All spirit is matter, but it is more fine or pure, and can only be discerned by purer eyes; We cannot see it; but when our bodies are purified we shall see that it is all matter."

Therein is the answer to the question: Why can't we see the spirit world? It's because matter in the spirit world is too subtle, too refined for natural, unpurified eyes.

Science and the Spirit World

Now, what does science have to say about this spirit world? Well, using the exact term *spirit world,* not a lot. However, science does say an awful lot about other "dimensions" of existence that are hidden from our eyes. In addition to the three spatial dimensions we live in and the one dimension for time, which we experience, physicists believe there may be seven additional dimensions around us. Perhaps one or two of these seven dimensions could house the spirit world, paradise and spirit prison inclusive.

String Theory

Besides what has previously been discussed in this book, some readers may have heard or read about "string theory." String theory is important because it may lay the foundation for the discovery of the spirit world from a scientific perspective. It is not difficult to understand, so let us proceed.

String theory hypothesizes that the fundamental building blocks of the universe are ultra-small vibrating strings (vibrating filaments of energy), each some hundred billion billion times smaller than a single atom nucleus. That number is represented as 1 over 100,000,000,000,000,000,000. So, you can see that a string is infinitely smaller than an atom. Today, many if not most physicists believe that these strings are the universe's most elementary particles.

According to string theory, the different vibration patterns of these strands correspond to different particles (electrons, photons, neutrons, protons, atoms, elements and so on). For instance, strings vibrating one way might create the properties of an electron, and strings vibrating another way might form protons or neutrons. Thus, a single class of string can produce a great variety of particles because the string(s) can vibrate in any number of different patterns. Hydrogen is not gold because of the different vibrating strings that make up these dissimilar elements. This naturally leads one to ask: Is God managing or conducting the universe as if it were one grand, string symphony that is vibrating organized matter into existence?

At this point you may be asking, "Why all this talk about string theory?" The reasons for honing in on it are because most scientists hold to this theory and because string theory accounts for the visible and hidden/unseen dimensions—the ten spatial dimensions and one time dimension. I propose that at least one or two of these dimensions, if not more, account for that portion of our universe where the spirit world can be found. It may be that there are two locations for the spirit world as a whole, one for paradise and one for spirit prison.

There is still much about sting theory that physicists and mathematicians around the world are working to comprehend. But, as just stated, the theory has revealed that the universe is likely to contain many more dimensions than we perceive from the window of our four-dimensional universe. There are likely another seven dimensions (or more) that may be the key to resolving some of the universe's deepest mysteries, the spirit world included.

Earlier we quoted Brigham Young as saying, "Can you see the spirits in this room? No. Suppose the Lord should touch your eyes that you might see, could you then see the spirits? Yes, as plainly as you now see bodies."[119] Brigham Young was clearly aware that there is a world around us we cannot see, but could under the right conditions. Clearly one of the great questions to have answered is: What are those conditions? What do we need to do to peer into the other worlds around us?

Of all things, physics can provide a thought provoking answer to that question. And again the answer comes from string theory. A man by the name of Edward Witten, the world's most renowned string theorist, uncovered concepts that really brought credibility to string theory.

Witten came up with a single, unifying master theory that links together all of the string formulations. This master theory provides a framework for unifying quantum mechanics (the world of the really small) and general relativity (the world we live in), and may be considered the "holy grail" of physics.

Now, what does this unification of string theory have to do with the spirit world? Well, Witten's work led to the realization that the universe is made up of other basic ingredients besides strings. His analyses showed that, included in the cosmic recipe are things like membranes. As you know, a membrane can act as a barrier, wrapping itself around another object, such as a membrane around a single cell. Except now, we are talking about membranes that can wrap themselves around and through objects as big as the universe. Physicists have coined a term for these basic membranes: they simply call them *branes*. These branes can be two-, three-, four-, five- and six-dimensional. Actually, they can be any whole number of dimensions less than ten.

The work of Andrew Strominger, Brian Greene, and David Morrison shows that a brane may wrap itself around small as well as infinitely large objects, such as a dimension or many dimensions. They also found that these branes are like "cosmic Velcro"—they are very sticky.

One of the aforementioned researchers, Brian Greene, wrote: "The grand expanse of the cosmos—the entirety of the spacetime of which we are aware—may itself be nothing but an enormous brane. Ours may be a braneworld. . . . Might everything we know [our complete universe] exist within a three dimensional . . . brane . . . ? Could it be that what Newton, Leibniz, Mach, and Einstein called three-dimensional space is actually a particular three-dimensional entity in string . . . theory? . . . In short, might the universe as we know it be a brane?"[120]

As a paraphrase of what we just read, our three-dimensional world according to Greene, may very well be surrounded and permeated by a particularly sticky sort of membrane. I know that sounds a little wacky, but bear with me. Let's first consult the dictionary. As defined by Merriam-Webster, there are all kinds of membranes (cell, embryonic, mucous, periodontal, and so on). These are usually thin, soft, pliable sheets, or layers that surround something, especially of animal or plant origin. So, if one can envision it, our three-dimensional universe may well be enclosed by a membrane.

We haven't discussed it yet, but a key characteristic of string theory includes the fact that the vibrating strings can be either closed loops (like a rubber band) or open-ended like a section of cut string. That point is important to understand if we are to grasp the next point—and if we are to understand why we can't peer into the spirit world. *String theory says that only the open-ended strings (strings with endpoints which don't connect) can vibrate so as to create photons (light)*. This, as you will soon see, is a major reason why we can't peer into the spirit world and other dimensions.

Now remember, vibrating strings that make up particles can be of two sorts, open ended and looped, close ended. A physicist by the name of Joe Polchinski mathematically found that in some situations, the endpoints of open strings (the two loose ends) would be trapped or stuck within a region of space. He wondered: If the endpoints of these vibrating strings are stuck to something, what is it that they are stuck to? Finally, when Edward Witten discovered that branes (sticky membranes) are basic components of the universe, Polchinski was able to quickly deduce that these open strings might be restricted in space because of a *sticky* brane, a membrane wrapped around and through our three-dimensional universe. His calculations showed that these branes exhibit exactly the right properties to be so sticky as to maintain an unbreakable grip on open string endpoints. So, for this reason, open ended strings—such as strings that vibrate to create photons of light—can only move or vibrate within the brane space in which they exist. And so, they only exist in our three dimensional universe.

If science is correct, and the three-dimensional universe we live in is enveloped by a brane, we now have an explanation as to why we are not aware of other dimensions, the spirit world in particular. The open ended strings which vibrate to create photons (light) are stuck within the brane (membrane) of our three-dimensional universe. Because open string endpoints are not able to leave the brane by which we are surrounded, they are unable to move into the spirit world. Hence, the other dimensions. This implies that light as we know it is trapped in our world. It may be as Brian Greene puts it, "Our brane world could be floating in a grand expanse of additional dimensions that remain invisible to us, because the light we see cannot leave our brane [three dimensional universe]."[121]

How do we detect things? We generally use our eyes or some other medium that accesses a form of electromagnetic energy, like light.

Powerful instruments like microscopes and telescopes require light. The electromagnetic force is critical. But if, as we hypothesized, this light/electromagnetic force is constrained, confined, and stuck to our three-dimensional brane, it makes it impossible for us to look into the spirit world and the other dimensions, regardless of their size. The vibrating, *open-ended* strings that make up photons, cannot escape our three dimensions, nor can they enter other dimensions (the spirit world) and travel back to our eyes or our equipment (microscopes and telescopes) because they are stuck in the sticky brane that surrounds and permeates our dimensions. We simply can't see the *outside* dimensions because of the way our eyes work. Our eyes only respond to a single force (light) to probe anything and everything. So we too are stuck and can only detect our three spatial dimensions even though the others may be right next to us, on top of us, or all around us.

Nature exhibits four primary forces. The electromagnetic force (light) is just one of those. Two others are called the *strong* and *weak* nuclear forces. The strong nuclear force insures that the components making up protons and neutrons stay glued together; they keep protons and neutrons tightly crammed together inside atomic nuclei. The weak force is best known as that responsible for radioactive decay of substances, including uranium and cobalt.

The messenger particles for the strong and weak nuclear forces are gluons and W and Z particles. Early on, physicists wondered: Can we conceivably come up with a way to measure and use these forces and their messenger particles to somehow peer into other dimensions? The answer is no. Mathematical calculations show that these particles also consist of open ended vibrating strings. They are just as trapped by the membrane (brane) around us as are photons (light).

The same goes for particles of matter. Electrons, quarks, and all other particle species come into being through the vibration of *open-ended* strings. Hence, because our visible world is surrounded by a brane, we are permanently imprisoned in it with everything else we have ever seen— except for one thing. There is one more force in addition to the three already mentioned (electromagnetic, strong and weak nuclear forces). That force is gravity. Calculations show that the strings which make gravitons are closed, with no endpoints, much like a rubber band. So gravitons are able to leave the space our three-dimensional world. Because they are not open-ended, they do not stick to the brane that we live in.

If we knew how to manipulate and utilize the force gravity, we could influence the other dimensions, and be influenced by them. We might even be able to see into these alternate-dimensional worlds.

Again, because the strings which make up the force of gravity are closed loops, they don't stick to the brane that permeates/surrounds our three-dimensional world. Who knows, maybe we could invent eye glasses that instead of light utilize a force like gravity to allow us to see what is going on in the spirit world and other dimensions.

Research is currently being conducted to see if gravity could be used as a medium for detecting these other dimensions. The Laser Interferometer Gravitational Wave Observatory (LITGO) as run by the California Institute of Technology is a leading center for this research.

Over millennia humans have employed a number of ways to discover the universe around us. In earlier days we were limited to using our senses of sight, sound, smell, taste, and touch. Then the inventions of infrared radio and x-ray and gamma ray telescopes let us view the universe in wonderful ways we never had before thought possible.

Everything is subject to gravity; everything carries or produces an observable gravitational signature. Current scientific thought and actual research have put us on the brink of measuring and seeing the cosmos through the use of the gravitational force. Aside from going to the trouble of actually dying, such technology might be the way for us to escape the sticky, three-dimensional brane world in which we live and thereby peer into another dimension or dimensions.

As mentioned earlier, we know of individuals who have been granted the privilege of looking into the spirit world—Jedediah Grant being one. Maybe God has a way of opening our eyes, our senses, and our minds so that we can see gravitational waves and thus peer into the spirit world.

In addition to the gravitational studies being done, other types of research are focusing on detecting these dimensions. For instance, high-energy experiments are being conducted at both the newly upgraded facility at Fermilab and the Large Hadron Collider. Though mathematically and theoretically, physicists have long predicted other dimensions, it is hard to imagine a discovery that would be more exciting than finding actual empirical evidence for dimensions beyond the three with which we are all familiar.

When Christ ushers in the Millennium, we will be doing tremendous amounts of vicarious ordinance work for the dead—those who live in these other dimensions. The temples will be open and running night and day in order to accomplish all the work that needs doing before the end comes. Until all our ancestors' work is complete, *we* won't be able to move on. Yet, if things stay the way they are, we will find ourselves in a quandary. Records for most people who have lived on the earth just don't exist. How will we obtain the information needed to do the ordinance work which binds us together?

One obvious way to resolve this stalemate is to somehow access and form a connection with those who have passed on and are in the spirit world. To provide a way to accomplish this work, will God open communications between the dimensions of the spirit world and the one in which we live? Brigham Young said: "The names of those who have received of the Gospel in the spirit world will be revealed by the angels of God."[122]

We also have the following from Joseph Fielding Smith: "During the Millennium those on the other side will work hand in hand with those in mortality and will furnish the names of the dead which we are unable to obtain through our research. . . I fully believe that many among the dead, those who are worthy, are even now engaged in compiling records and arranging information, if it has not already been done for this very purpose."[123]

As a side note: Gravity may be the reason why the spirit world and the other dimensions are here on the earth. Because of gravity, the spirit world is as trapped as we are, even if the elements which for that dimension are more fine and refined than those of our corporeal world.

Miracles and String Theory

It is because of string theory that physicists and mathematicians have been able to determine that many other dimensions exist, some of which could include the spirit world. Still other facets of string theory are compatible with the gospel.

Let's consider one of Christ's miracles. His first recorded miracle is that of changing water to wine at the request of His mother. String theory helps us see how that miracle might have been accomplished. Christ may have simply caused the vibration patterns of the strings making up the water to change and vibrate in a different manner, thus creating wine.

Several sections back, while discussing light, we turned to both scripture and ancient texts to provide evidence that Christ *is* the light powering the universe. Light is a form of energy. In string theory, energy and mass are the same; the mass of a particle is nothing but the energy of its vibrating string. The reason one particle is heavier than another is because its strings are vibrating faster, with more energy (light), than those that make up the lighter particle. With that information, we can see how Christ might utilize his energy (light) to power the universe. It is as if He is conducting a cosmic symphony of vibrating strings.

An important footnote to this discussion: This helps us see how matter is eternal in nature, just as is light. It never ages or diminishes because it is made from the energy of Christ.

Space/Time, String Theory—and Repentance

When one considers string theory's role in space and time, some interesting things happen. The theory challenges the conventional idea that space and time are smooth, continuous entities. Instead, if string theory is right, when you get down to the Planck length (the length of a string) and Planck time (the time it would take light to travel the length of a string), you find that space and time can't be divided further. So, we see that space and time are not smooth and continuous. Instead, both are divided into sections or pieces.

With this in mind, it is conceivable that motion through space and time requires a series of sequential moves from one "string/strand" to another. Again, time may consist of a lattice-like structure, with individual moments packed closely together but not melding into a seamless stream of events. This way of thinking exposes the concept of ever smaller intervals of space and time down to the Planck scale. In this scenario, space and time are broken into sections the size of a string.

From a scriptural, gospel perspective, does it matter that space and time are not continuously smooth, but instead they are independent sections or pieces of a whole? Actually, this feature of space and time could be helpful in explaining certain principles God uses to carry out His purposes. It might mean that if God chose to, He could pull out a section of time and effect a change in history. Is it possible that He manipulates strands of space and time so as to make repentance work? Because of Christ's suffering for our sins, does God have the capability to change the events of our lives when we truly repent, so that He and we remember our sins no more? Could God accomplish this by extracting and "cleansing" sections of our lifetime? This is going out on a limb, but if time and space are just a sum of many independent Planck-length events, why couldn't select events be pulled out and the history and experience of our personal lives be altered? Aren't we promised in the New Testament that Christ will take away our sins (1 John 3:5) and remember them no more (Hebrews 8:12) when we truly repent? Wouldn't it be wonderful if this was a literal, physical event?

Years ago, while attending BYU, I agreed to head up a lecture series to be held in the Wilkinson Center on the Provo campus. Over a nine-month period we invited and scheduled a number of wonderful speakers. One of them was the noted chemist Dr. Henry Eyring. I recall that during his talk he indicated that, after this life, we might be able to review our lives here in mortality as if we were watching a movie. He also said as we watched the film, we would find some portions of it blanked out, blank spots perhaps representing times when we had exercised repentance.

Now, I don't know if that's the way it will work or not. But we do know that, when we repent, God takes away our sins and remembers them no more.

Now, let's return to our discussion on the spirit world. One of the express purposes for the existence of the spirit world is so that every person might have an opportunity to accept or reject the gospel prior to the resurrection. The vast majority of God's children do not have the opportunity to hear the gospel on earth, so their effective probation does not take place until they hear the principles of salvation in the spirit world. The fact that repentance will be possible for those spirits should not lead one to believe it is all right for us to sin a little in this life thinking that it will be possible to repent in the next. The Book of Mormon gives strong warning to those who have the opportunity of hearing and living the gospel while still on earth:

> For behold, this life is the time for men to prepare to meet God; . . . I beseech of you that ye do not procrastinate the day of your repentance until the end; for after this day of life, which is given us to prepare for eternity, behold, if we do not improve our time while in this life, then cometh the night of darkness wherein there can be no labor performed.
>
> Ye cannot say, when ye are brought to that awful crisis, that I will repent, that I will return to my God. Nay, ye cannot say this; for that same spirit which doth possess your bodies at the time that ye go out of

this life, that same spirit will have power to possess your body in that eternal world. (Alma 34:32–35)

Joseph Smith also taught: "A man can do as much in this life in one year as he can do in ten years in the spirit world without a body."[124]

Finally, a last thought on this topic: The spirit world may exhibit quantum characteristics. Brigham Young taught that *the righteous* in the spirit world will have marvelous powers of travel:

> [They] move with ease and like lightning. If we want to visit Jerusalem, or this, that, or the other place—and I presume we will be permitted if we desire—there we are, looking at its streets. If we want to behold Jerusalem as it was in the days of the Savior; or if we want to see the Garden of Eden as it was when created, there we are, and we see it as it existed spiritually, for it was created first spiritually and then temporally, and spiritually it still remains. And when there we may behold the earth as at the dawn of creation, or we may visit any city we please that exists upon its surface. If we wish to understand how they are living here on these western islands, or in China, we are there. . .[125]

In the quantum world an electron can move from one location to another without visiting the space between. Based on the quote by Brigham Young, when we are in the spirit world, laws of the quantum world may be in force as we will be able to move from location to location and from time to time instantly, without visiting the space and time between the locations.

So, a prophet, seer, and revelator tells us that in the spirit world we will enjoy marvelous powers of travel. We will be able to instantly go where we want to, whether it is Jerusalem during the times of Christ or the Garden of Eden during the time of Adam. In order to accomplish this, it seems that we will have to be able to experience and control the quantum world. We will then be able to travel to a different place and time without visiting the space and time in between. Again, this sounds a lot like the way things happen at the quantum level. As Einstein put it, it is "spooky."

XIV. Parallel Universes: Telestial, terrestrial, celestial, and more?

Both 1 Corinthians chapter 15 and section 76 of the Doctrine and Covenants reference the various glories or states to which we can be resurrected: celestial, terrestrial, and telestial. We are informed that bodies resurrected to these various glories will differ greatly, each attuned to its specified world.

In Corinthians the Apostle Paul tells us that the glory of bodies resurrected to the celestial kingdom are like the brightness of the sun, while the glory of terrestrial bodies can be compared to the moon's brightness and telestial are like the glory of the stars in the night sky. Then John 14 and a host of other scriptures (Enos 1, Ether 12, and in D&C 59) teach that many mansions have been prepared for us after this life.

When we are resurrected, we will leave the spirit world and be assigned to one of these other worlds. In D&C 76:71, Joseph Smith and Sidney Rigdon submit the following: "And again, we saw the terrestrial world, and behold and lo, these are they who are of the terrestrial, whose glory differs from that of the church of the Firstborn who have received the fullness of the Father, even as that of the moon differs from the sun in the firmament."

The oft inspired C. S. Lewis offers yet another perspective of heavenly mansions in his book *The Great Divorce*. Describing his impressions regarding the difference between heaven and hell, he says, "All Hell is smaller than one pebble of your earthly world: but it is smaller than one atom of *this* world [Heaven], the Real World."[126]

Needless to say, a number of credible sources describe other existences and other worlds where mankind may dwell following mortality. Where are these other worlds? Are they in a different part of our galaxy, in a different dimension, or in an entirely different universe? Science provides an inkling of insight into these other worlds.

Both the scriptures and science suggest that there are countless earths like ours. These most certainly would be considered other worlds. Additionally, there are trillions of stars in the universe. We have also shown scripturally and scientifically that the spirit world may exist in a separate dimension. Now we are going to delve into something that cosmologists call "parallel universes" or "parallel worlds."

As you may recall, in a prior section we described general relativity and Einstein's feelings regarding aspects of the theory. He initially had no problem with some of the theory's more obvious tenants, in particular those of gravity, motion, and time. But there were some things that were mathematically and conceptually part of the theory that really bothered Einstein. One of those was the inflationary cosmos. He just couldn't accept it and later indicated that it was one of the biggest blunders of his life to not have believed it.

Other things likewise lurked within relativity's shadows, defying our notions of common sense. Some of these concepts were so bizarre that Einstein initially thought they would never be found in nature, concepts like black holes, white holes, wormholes, and even time machines. For years, he fought against many of these ideas. Of course, over time Einstein warmed up to these ideas and many have since been observed and experimentally proven. Today, we know all of these concepts to be an integral part of general relativity.

Perhaps the oddest of all general relativity anomalies is the possibility of parallel universes and that there are gateways connecting them. One writer used the Shakespearean metaphor "all the worlds a stage" to help us understand parallel universes. Einstein's "relativity" not only suggests our world is a stage, but that there are many stages (worlds/universes) with trap doors (gateways) connecting them. These universes are parallel to one another and are somewhat like one another. As actors on one of these stages, we live out our lives oblivious to the fact that other stages exist all around us. If we could access the trapdoors (gateways) between these stages, we would likely encounter universes similar to—or the same as—the one we live in; and we would likely find some with entirely different laws, different rules, and different scripts than ours.

Appearing in the May 2003 issue of Scientific American is an article titled "Parallel Universes." The article's subtitle reads: "Not just a staple of science fiction, other universes are a direct implication of cosmological observations."

In describing these alternate universes we are told that each is merely a part of a larger "multiverse." This idea of a multiverse is grounded in the well-tested theories of quantum mechanics and relativity. Scientists hypothesize that there are as many as four distinct types of these parallel universes. Let's briefly review each in turn:

Level 1 Multiverse: Beyond Our Cosmic Horizon

The title alone of this type of parallel world offers a clue that it is far, far, far away outside the bounds of our universe. Since it's easy to believe in worlds, stars, and galaxies we can't see that are distant from us, for most of us a level 1 multiverse is the most acceptable kind of parallel world. It simply represents a region of space that is too far away for us to see it. Astronomical observations show that our universe is 14 billion light years across, and that it grows more distant every year as our universe continues to rapidly expand. A veritable infinity awaits us out there. None of us will live long enough to see the parallel worlds that exist beyond our universe, as the light from those worlds will take too long to reach us. It is worth noting that the galaxies we see shining on the edge of the universe some 14 billion light years distant now actually shine about 40 billion light years distant, due to cosmic expansion. In the past 14 billion years that it has taken for light to reach us from these distant worlds, the universe has expanded tremendously.

Scientists believe that the laws of physics in multiple distant universes are very similar as those in our universe, especially in terms of the way matter is spread around. This class of parallel universe will essentially appear like ours, except for the initial arrangement of matter that may have occurred as a result of their own creative beginnings (individual Big Bangs).

Level 2 Multiverse: Post-inflation Bubbles

Again, the name of this class of multiverse speaks for itself, suggesting that distant bubble universes will form as portions of our universe stop inflating. As one envisions this multiverse, it is important to remember that space didn't get pushed out from the initial creation; rather, it was stretched out. Even though space as a whole will continue to stretch and expand forever, this theory requires us to imagine that some part of space *stops* stretching.

When regions of space stop stretching, distinct bubbles may be formed, like gas pockets in a loaf of rising bread. Each bubble is an embryo of the Level 1 Multiverse just described. These bubbles themselves will likely become infinite in size and will be filled with matter produced by the Big Bang.

If you traveled forever at the speed of light, you could never reach one of these universes because the combinations of space between our bubble universe and its neighboring bubble universes are expanding faster than the speed of light.

These post-inflation bubble universes could be very different from our universe. Based on a scientific theory called "symmetry breaking," which suggests that the cosmic, quantum fluctuations that created our universe and that drive inflation likely produce different effects in other bubble universes. Also, it is possible that the dimensions of space were organized differently in these other universes. Instead of a four-dimensional world, like ours, maybe there are five, six, or even ten spatial dimensions represented in other bubble universes. Cosmologists have even postulated that *new* universes are constantly being sprouted through black holes, as matter from our universe is sucked into them.

In regard to the inflationary universe and its array of bubble universes, a fresh idea has been put forth by Russian physicist Andrei Linde of Stanford University. Because no one knows for sure how inflation started, there is always the possibility that the same thing can take place again and again. That is, some as yet unexplained mechanism in our universe may cause other distant bubble universes to explode or inflate into existence. According to this theory, a tiny patch of our universe might suddenly expand and "sprout" another infant universe. This sprouting process could continue on forever. In this sense, Big Bangs may have been taking place in a never-ending, infinite succession. Maybe that is how Abraham, Isaac, and Jacob came to be gods: "Abraham . . . as Isaac also and Jacob did none other things than that which they were commanded; and because they did none other things than that which they were commanded, they have entered into their exaltation, according to the promises, and sit upon thrones, and are not angels but are gods" (D&C 132:37).

We may live in a sea of universes, like bubbles floating on an ocean. Bubble universes from our universe may have other gods ruling over them (like Abraham, Isaac, and Jacob). Who knows, maybe our universe with our God is a bubble that came from yet another universe. Is it possible, as Andrei Linde hypothesizes that there exists a continuous, never-ending inflationary process? Theoretical evidence is mounting to support the existence of the multiverse, in which entire universes continually sprout from older universes.

Paul Davies, an internationally acclaimed physicist of our day, has said: "What we have all along been calling 'the universe' is, in this theory, just an infinitesimal part of a single 'bubble,' or pocket universe, set amid an infinite assemblage of universes—a multiverse—itself embedded in inflating space that exists without end."[127]

Do you recall the quote from Joseph Smith about God? "God Himself was once as we are now, and is an exalted man, and sits enthroned in yonder heavens! That is the great secret."[128]

Even the Apostle Paul testified to the truth of this concept when he proclaimed, "The spirit itself beareth witness with our spirit, that we are the children of God: And if children, then heirs; heirs of God, and joint-heirs with Christ" (Romans 8:16–17).

It seems that the early apostles were in agreement on this subject. The great Apostle Peter described the possibility of our partaking of God's divine nature and taking upon us His glory: "Grace and peace be multiplied unto you through the knowledge of God, and of Jesus our Lord, according as his divine power hath given unto us all things that pertain unto life and **godliness**, through the knowledge of him that hath called us to glory and virtue: **Whereby are given unto us exceeding great and precious promises: that by these ye might be partakers of the divine nature**" (2 Peter 1:2–4, bold added).

Over the years, members of The Church of Jesus Christ of Latter-day Saints have taken a lot of flak because of their tenet: "As man is, God once was. As God is, man may become." However, one can go back to early years of Christianity and find the same concept being taught. Many of today's Christian churches are beginning to consider these doctrines as well.

When one considers theories of multiple universes and considers the purposes and personality of God as revealed through prophets ancient and modern, some of this "bubble universe" stuff doesn't sound so strange.

Level 3 Multiverse: Quantum Many Worlds

The Level 1 and Level 2 multiverses just described suggest worlds and universes situated very far away from us, so that we well never physically detect them unless we do so via gateways (trap doors), like wormholes.

The use of *quantum* in describing the Level 3 multiverse indicates that parallel universes may be hovering right around us. The theory was spawned as a result of the highly controversial many-worlds interpretation of quantum physics, the idea that random quantum processes cause the universe to branch into multiple copies, one for each outcome possible in particle/wave theory.

As you may recall in an earlier section, we discussed features of wave theory as they pertain to quantum mechanics (the world of the very small). At the quantum level, a particle exhibits traits of both a wave and a particle. Because of its wave characteristic, the particle may exist in multiple locations at the same time. It's still kind of mind-bending to think about, isn't it?

Many scientists suggest that the wave function governing quantum particles also governs our world of large objects. That means you and I and the world around us may exist in multiple if not a huge number of places. Each of these parallel worlds would be slightly different. In one of these worlds you would not have read this book; in another I wouldn't have written it. In one world you are alive and well; in another you are no longer alive—and so on. A tremendous number of universes would exist for each possible outcome of the initial creation, and for each potential outcome of life itself. It is hard to visualize, but these universes are located "elsewhere," not in ordinary space, but in the realm of all possible states. Every conceivable way a world could be organized corresponds to a different universe.

This many-worlds explanation was first proposed by Hugh Everett III, a student at Princeton University in 1957. Since then, it has garnered a sizeable following in the world of science and physics. For decades, Everett's many-worlds explanation has sparked the imaginations of minds inside and outside of physics.

The passionate debates over this version of a multiverse are gradually subsiding, as we discover less controversial multiverses (like Level I and Level II), which are equally large in number.

I must say that this kind of multiverse is hard to grasp and accept, as we believe that our existence is so important to God. God loves each of us and wants us to return and live eternally with Him. If each person were actually to exist in multiple versions in multiple universes . . . how would one describe God's relationship to each of these copies? As you can see, it is difficult to conceive of an infinite number of creations and universes, all under God's watchful eye and all similar and somewhat indistinguishable.

Besides compromising our one-on-one relationship with Heavenly Father, this particular concept of a multiverse seems to also do away with agency and free will as every possible alternative to decisions and actions would exist at the same time in different universes. In fact, in that sort of multiverse it might not matter how you live, because every decision made would be reflected by a thousand different outcomes.

One appealing component of wave function theory seems to resolve many of these issues. Proposed in the 1920s, it states that every possible universe of outcomes goes away because the wave function of scenarios simply collapses when observed. That means there is just one "now." So, the wave function of many probable outcomes exists only until an observation is made. We can stretch this idea a little further and suggest that the wave function of many outcomes collapses when we make a decision and act on that decision.

This is really an interesting idea. Some of the decisions we make may not be as important as others—like which shirt to wear or which pair of shoes to buy. But other decisions, such as whether to view pornography or whether to steal from one's employer, are choices that can significantly affect us. The idea of a wave function that opens up almost infinite possibilities in our lives feels like part of God's plan. The fact that we can collapse that wave function(s) at any given point by making a decision (agency/free will) is a remarkable gift—and one which also feels like part of God's plan.

This sort of thinking suggests that, once we collapse a wave function by making a decision, a new wave function of possibilities open before us. However, because of previous decisions, this new array of possibilities may now exclude some possibilities that were open to us before. For instance, every healthy natural-born citizen could possibly become president of the United States. But each decision a person makes in life, even early on, either increases or lowers this possibility in one's personal wave function of opportunities. If you did well in high school, both academically and socially, your chances of being elected are slightly enhanced. On the contrary, if you've committed a felony, your electability becomes seriously impaired. And so on and so on. Every time we make a decision, we either open the door to numberless opportunities or little by little inch it shut. "I the Lord, am bound when you do what I say; but when ye do not what I say, ye have no promise" (D&C 82:10). If we do well, our list of possibilities is truly endless.

Level 4 Multiverse: Other Mathematical Structures

This version of a multiverse is a tad more complex than the others we've discussed. In a nutshell, a Level 4 multiverse suggests that different parallel universes may exist for many possible mathematical models.

With the advent and through the use of string theory (M Theory in particular), thousands upon thousands of solutions for universes have been mathematically found. There are cosmologists who believe that each of these solutions may represent an actual universe. Still, as yet, a string theory mathematical model that perfectly fits our universe has yet to be discovered. Michio Kaku, one of the world's leading string theory researchers, emphasizes how open-ended the possibilities are:

> [There have been] millions of solutions so far found for string theory, each one representing a fully self-consistent universe. In the past, it was thought that, of this forest of solutions, only one represented the true solution of string theory. Today, our thinking is shifting. So far, there is no way to select out one universe out of the millions that have been discovered so far. There is a growing body of opinion that states if we cannot find the unique solution to string theory, it's probably because there is none. All solutions are equal. There is a multiverse of universes, each one consistent with all the laws of physics.[129]

In a famous lecture given by Eugene P. Wigner in 1959, he stipulated that "the enormous usefulness of mathematics in natural sciences is something bordering on the mysterious." Wigner further inferred that the universe was in fact created from a bunch of mathematical equations, and that mathematics currently plays a huge role in understanding the universe.

Despite common belief, mathematical structures have a very real feel to them; they exist outside of space and time as a spiritual creation, of sorts. Mathematical structures can be thought of as a major part of our actual existence. For one, they are independently and totally rational;

they are the same, no matter who studies them. A theorem is the same whether it is proved by a computer or a human. Any intelligence that would be capable of discovering a mathematical theorem would find that it is the same no matter which intelligence found it. Mathematicians don't create mathematical theorems, they just discover them. In a sense, that means the mathematical structures or theorems have an existence of their own.

Modern theoretical physicists suspect that mathematics can perfectly describe our universe so well because the universe is itself mathematical in nature. Centuries ago a remarkable idea similarly came into the mind of Galileo Galilei, which he stated as: "Mathematics is the language with which God has written the universe." Taking that startling declaration at face value, one could deduce that *everything* in *all* sciences may simply be a mathematical problem that needs to be solved.

In this regard, modern day physicists have raised the following question: "If the universe is inherently mathematical, then why was only one mathematical structure singled out to describe it?"

Stating this another way, cosmologists wonder why there are so many possible mathematical alternatives, and why only one used as a model for our universe?

Cosmologists who study parallel universes believe in something called mathematical symmetry: that is, that *all* mathematical structures actually exist physically. They assert that every mathematical structure or theorem corresponds to a parallel universe. The elements of these parallel universes do not reside in the space with which we are familiar, but somehow exist outside of space and time.

This is more than just an interesting idea. Maybe God creates universes mathematically, and with those numerical blueprints is able to draw up and form other universes with different laws, characteristics, rules, and so on. These universes would function outside of space and outside of time. Likewise, perhaps it is through mathematical models that He creates varied kingdoms for celestial bodies, terrestrial bodies and telestial bodies. Is it possible that the physics for our universe is based on a telestial mathematical model? Is our cosmos a mathematically created place where our special kind of space and time exists, a place where millions or even billions of solar systems exist, providing homes where God's children can experience mortality?

That idea, of course, suggests the existence of mathematical models of universes for terrestrial beings as well as celestial beings. Something whispers that there may be some truth to this, as the laws governing such beings and such worlds would be so very different from those governing our planet.

It may be that the mathematical models used by God to create universes may be akin to the spiritual creation that precedes the actual physical creation. Einstein once offered this tantalizing tidbit: "I am convinced that we can discover by means of purely mathematical construction the concepts and the laws . . . which furnish the key to the understanding of natural phenomena. . . . I hold it true that pure thought can grasp reality."[130]

Earlier, in discussing the spirit world, we implied that parallel universes might simply be different dimensions within our universe. String theory, as mentioned, posits there are seven dimensions hovering around us that we cannot see. Indeed, the Spirit world may reside within one or two of these dimensions.

Should you believe in parallel worlds, these theoretical alternate universes? By all means! As members of The Church of Jesus Christ of Latter-day Saints, we already know a lot about them. For that matter, children and adults, alike, discuss parallel universes each Sunday in their various meetings—though without use that term. Rather, we learn of a premortal world, spirit worlds (paradise and spirit Prison), our mortal probationary world, resurrection's worlds (telestial, terrestrial, and celestial), and even worlds of perdition. Under God's divine leadership, there certainly is a multiverse of alternate worlds.

XV. Entropy: A testament to God!

Time and time again, the truths of science provide support for the existence of God. Yet some of the gatekeepers of science—physicists, cosmologists, and geneticists—go out of their way to deny it or ignore it whenever they can. Just the same, many scientists believe in God, men and women like Francis Collins, Director of the National Human Genome Research Institute, and Vera Kistiakowsky, physicist at M.I.T., who apply theology—or at least consider it—in their studies.

The purpose of this section is to consider something in science known as *entropy*. Entropy is a most compelling witness to the idea that there is a God who rules the universe.

First, let's consider a prior section in this book that dealt with the creation of the universe and specifically, the piece on inflationary cosmology, one of the most current scientific theories pertaining to the initial Big Bang and the universes ongoing expansion. This "Creation" section includes this statement: "During [its] earliest moments, the size of the universe grew by a factor larger than a million trillion trillion in less than a millionth of a trillionth of a trillionth of a second." Yes, somehow the universe apparently just burst into existence. In far less than a second, it was born and grew massive in size.

As you may recall, gravity was thought to have caused this instantaneous growth. Another theory held that the "uncertainty principle" found in quantum mechanics, had a major hand in the instantaneous birth and expansion of the cosmos.

No matter how it was accomplished, one thing the creation produced for certain: a universe that is highly ordered. *The order which exists throughout the universe and in nature is remarkable.* This order is directly opposed to another powerful mathematical concept: entropy.

Entropy is defined by Merriam-Webster as "The degree of disorder or uncertainty in a system. Also, the degradation of matter and energy in the universe to an ultimate state of inert uniformity. Also, a process of degradation or running down or a trend to disorder."

Synonyms for *entropy* include: chaos, disorganization, disorder, and randomness.

The notion of entropy was first developed during the early stages of the industrial revolution by scientists working in the field of thermodynamics. The three Laws of Thermodynamics affirm some of the most fundamental, universal tenets that form our knowledge and expectations as we go about our lives.

The first law of thermodynamics states that the total amount of matter and energy is conserved. That is, matter and energy cannot be destroyed; they continue to exist infinitely.

The second law is the one we will most focus on at this time. In general it states: "The universe's total amount of entropy (chaos and disorder) always increases. In other words, chaos and disorder always increase in nature and in the universe; things always move toward disorder."

The third law of thermodynamics asserts that it is not possible for the universe—or anything in it—to ever reach the temperature of absolute zero. Something can come within a fraction of a degree of absolute zero, but it will never reach a state of zero motion, where the particles that make up the atoms cease to vibrate.

To begin with, a couple of key thoughts need to be explored:

- First, given that one of the most powerful laws in our universe states that everything moves to chaos, disorder, disarray, and death: Why did the early universe manifest a low-entropy, highly ordered, uniform distribution of matter instead of a high-entropy, disordered, "clumpy" distribution? And after that initial creation, why have the universe and the earth progressed, morphed, and evolved in an orderly manner, a manner that would support life?
- Second, why in mankind is there some innate impulse that makes him strive to understand nature and to know the laws behind the complexities of the universe? Why do we seek to bring order out of disorder?

Let's consider the first issue: Why did the early universe manifest a low-entropy, highly ordered, uniform distribution of matter instead of a high-entropy, disordered, "clumpy" distribution? Why have the universe and the earth progressed, morphed, and evolved in an orderly manner, a manner that would support life? The universe on its own should not have blossomed into a uniform distribution of galaxies, stars, and planets. Plants, animals, humans, and other complex forms of life should not exist as accidents of nature. As a testament to this, when we observe our world, we find the second law of entropy running rampant—everything eventually ages or runs down. Buildings crumble, machines rust, empires fall, and the human body deteriorates, wilts, and dies.

When we consider the progression of time, on the face of it, it seems pretty simple, like a one-way street: eggs don't unscramble, laugh lines don't vanish, and your mom and dad will never be younger than you. Everything seems to flow in one direction—on a crash course toward disorder, destruction, and death. Still, scientists cannot explain why order lies in the past and disorder in the future. How did things begin with order when thermodynamics firmly states that it should have begun with disorder and continued down the road to greater and greater chaos and disorder?

For more than a century, scientists have proposed any number of explanations for this apparent contradiction. When considering the heavens, the cosmic microwave background radiation—a remnant of the Big Bang—provides a clue. Some 380,000 years after its birth, the universe, still in its infancy, was filled with hot gases, all evenly distributed and highly ordered. Eventually, as the early universe inflated and cooled, this harmonious, homogeneous soup began to coalesce into the universe of stars and atoms we know today. What remains puzzling is why the early universe was so orderly—a condition that physicists consider highly improbable.

In addition to the early ordered cosmos, the marvelous variety of living organisms inhabiting the earth are amazingly complex and full of order. Even the simplest are beyond our ability to duplicate. We cannot create a single cell, much less a complex, multi-celled entity. The order we see in nature is astonishing. How can it be? The second law of thermodynamics tells us that the total amount of entropy (chaos and disorder) in the universe always increases. If that is the case, why do we live in such an orderly universe? Some in the scientific community try to explain it away as merely an off-chance spasm in the law of averages. They submit that our universe (our planet, man, every organism) was completely an accident of nature, even though the second law of thermodynamics (entropy), which they so feverishly espouse, indicates that everything is supposed to have been spawned in disorder.

No matter how many billions of years may have passed, or how many billions of failed universes may have been formed, is it possible that there were so many trillions of remarkably ordered accidents in a single universe? To some degree, this question has to be answered independently by each of us. You and I have to take into account our knowledge of: (a) science, (b) scripture, (c) personal inspiration, and (d) our inherent God-given senses. When one of the most important laws of nature states that everything gravitates toward disorder, not order, how is this universe possible? How can one consider earth's creation—much less its evolution—without considering God?

In the February 1991 issue of Scientific American, John Horgan stated: "Some scientists have argued that, given enough time, even apparently miraculous events become possible—such as the spontaneous emergence of a single-cell organism from random couplings of chemicals. Sir Fred Hoyle, the British astronomer, has said such an occurrence is about as likely as the assemblage of a 747 by a tornado whirling through a junk yard. Most researchers agree with Hoyle on this point."[131]

Today, scientists say that the earth exists in a "Goldilocks zone." Coined from the well-known children's tale by physicist James Lovelock, the term provides an apt analogy The story traces an adventure of a little girl named Goldilocks who goes into and disturbs the home of a family of bears. Along the way she finds a bowl of porridge, a chair, and a bed that are just right for her. Our earth and universe are very similar in nature. We find ourselves with just the right components to support life. Our planet is just far enough from the sun so that water can exist in a liquid form (not too hot and not too cold). Because water is the universal solvent, it played a key roll in creating the chemicals of life as we know them.

If the earth were any closer to the sun, it would be Venus-like—an inferno of heat and carbon dioxide. Temperatures would soar to 900 degrees. The February 2008 issue of *Scientific American* describes just one of the ways as to how different Venus is: "Venus's atmosphere, unprotected by a magnetic field [such as earth's], encounters fierce solar winds that rip apart molecules and send them out into space. Investigators discovered that twice as much hydrogen is leaving Venus as oxygen, suggesting that water is being driven off. Based on the data, perhaps an ocean's worth of water has departed Venus since the planet formed."[132]

On the other hand, if the earth were situated farther from the sun, like Mars, it would become a freezing desert, devoid of life, a frozen chunk of dirt.

The Goldilocks analogy extends to numerous other "just rights," including:

- The moon is just the right size. If it were any smaller, earth's orbit would not be stable, but would wobble disastrously bringing on terrible climate fluctuations. Life as we know it would not be able to survive.
- The giant planet Jupiter is important for life on the earth. Most of the asteroids and space debris that has filled our space in the universe over the past 4.5 billion years has been cleaned up by Jupiter. Because of its massive gravity, it has acted like a big vacuum cleaner sucking most of the garbage in the solar system to it. If Jupiter's gravity were any less, our solar system would

still be full of asteroids, which would frequently plunge into our oceans, destroying life on earth.

- If earth were any smaller, its gravity would be so weak that it wouldn't be able to hang on to its oxygen. If it were fractionally any larger, it would still be covered with the poisonous gases that formed in the early days of its existence.

- Our Sun and its solar system are just the right distance from the center of our galaxy. If we were any closer to the Milky Way's center, we would be dangerously close to a black hole. The radiation field from that black hole would be so intense as to make all life impossible.

- Conversely, if we were located too far away from the galactic center of the Milky Way, there would not have been a sufficiently high level of heavy elements to favor the formation of planets.

- Even the soil on earth seems designed to support mankind. Its properties and reactions and the processes that occur within it, make it an ideal medium for plant growth. Without it, plant and animal life as we know it would not exist.

- Something as simple as the fact that a proton weighs just slightly less than a neutron is extremely important. If protons were just one percent heavier, they would decay into neutrons, causing atoms to fly apart. In this case, everything would cease to exist.

We could go on and on. Scientists have assembled hundreds and thousands of "happy cosmic accidents." A change in any one of these so-called accidents would mean that the stable earthly existence we know would be horribly altered, life would be impossible. We live in an improbably ordered world with a band of very narrow possibilities combining to allow a planet to teem with life. So, the natural question is: Why do the earth and the cosmos seem so bio-friendly? From the tone and nature of this book, you already know my answer. Earth and the universe were created intelligently, *on purpose*! Many physicists the world over, past and present, believe the same thing. Sir Isaac Newton saw no clash with his personal religious beliefs. In fact, he reasoned that the very elegance of the laws of the universe point to the existence of a God.

On the other side of the ledger, David, the boy shepherd who became king of Israel, testified: "The fool hath said in his heart, there is no God . . . The heavens declare the glory of God; and the firmament showeth his handywork" (Psalms 14:1, 19:1).

Many scientists, because of their experience with religion—or limited experience—argue that religion "puts the brakes" on creativity, research, and reason. Because most theologies promote the thought that: "We are here because we are here and we don't need to know anything else," scientists are naturally wary. If they would just take time to listen to the LDS missionaries, they would find something even more exciting than their scientific understanding. They would discover a world of modern-day revealed knowledge that correlates with and strongly promotes their scientific efforts.

Previously in this section we asked a pertinent question: Why in mankind is there some innate impulse that makes him strive to understand nature and to know the laws behind the complexities of the universe? Why do we seek to convert order out of disorder? The answer is quite simple and stems from what was stated at the preface of this writing. It is because, and I paraphrase, "We come, trailing clouds of glory, from God, who is our home." We are in the image of God, and we are Gods in embryo. We came from Him and hope to return "home" to be with Him for eternity. As we learn to be Gods, similar in character, love, mercy, and grace to our benevolent Father and Mother, one of our first instincts is to find and create order and beauty in the world around us.

David may have said it best: "When I consider thy heavens, the work of thy fingers, the moon and the stars, which thou hast ordained: What is man that thou art mindful of him? . . . For thou hast made him a little lower than the angels and hast crowned him with glory and honour. Thou madest him to have dominion over the works of thy hands; thou hast put all things under his feet" (Psalms 8:3–6).

God placed us on earth so that we could learn to be more like Him, so we could see for ourselves how we would do if we were in charge of a portion of His creation. We are here to learn and progress! If we do it well, we will be given the opportunity to return and live with God, be like Him, and go on to create our own orderly worlds.

XVI. Earth Rolled Up Like a Scroll: Is there any scientific rational?

Prior to beginning this section it may be good to have a little understanding about a principle of physics called *symmetry. Symmetry underlies the laws of the universe.* The word itself connotes *sameness.*

In the early moments of the creation, the universe was a primordial soupy mixture of super-heated matter. It was the *same* everywhere. Then, as the cosmos expanded and began to cool, its symmetry broke and the matter and gases in it began to coalesce into clumpy regions that eventually formed stars, planets, and galaxies. Hence, a cooler cosmos lost some of its early symmetry.

There is much in nature that suggests symmetry. When you hold a ball in your hand and rotate it every which way—it looks exactly the same. Snowflakes when laid flat and examined and rotated under a microscope look just the same from all vantage points. Even people when viewed face-on and divided down the middle demonstrate a form of symmetry. Generally, each side of a person's body is almost identical to the other. We have two eyes, two ears, two arms, two legs, and so on. A pear demonstrates the same kind of symmetry. When it is cut from top to bottom, one half is similar to the second half.

However, as we all know, some things are more symmetrical than others. A ball is more symmetrical than a pear because a ball looks the same no matter how you look at it, while a pear bulges and narrows as it is viewed from different angles. Hence, the more kinds of manipulations an object can sustain with no discernable effect, the more symmetry it possesses.

The laws of the universe and the forces that act under or within these laws are also symmetrical. That is they demonstrate the same properties anywhere in the universe. For instance, even though you might change locations, the laws of electromagnetism and of gravity still work. This symmetry is called translational symmetry or translational invariance. That is, these laws invariably work when translated or moved to different locations.

When thinking about this, you will note one important thing. Even though these laws still function, the details of your observations of these laws and forces may vary from place to place. For instance, if you were to test the effects of gravity on the earth and then on the moon, you would find that with the same effort, you could jump higher on the moon than you can on the earth. The difference between your earth and moon experiences doesn't mean that the law of gravity has changed from place to place. Instead, it simply reflects an environmental difference that the law of gravity has to accommodate. Where there is more mass, there is more gravitational force. So, a change in location doesn't require that we have to go back to the drawing board and come up with new laws. Physicists have confidence that nature's laws and forces demonstrate symmetry.

However, some laws in the universe look different when exercised in different locations. As was mentioned, gravity looks and feels different on the moon than it does on the earth. We call this *rotational* symmetry.

It is interesting to note that heat or the lack thereof affects symmetry in most objects. Take H_2O, common water, for instance. When extremely hot, it is in a gaseous, very symmetrical state. As it cools it becomes liquid water and is less symmetrical; then, when cooled to 32 degrees Fahrenheit it becomes even less symmetrical as it turns to ice.

At the beginning of this section I indicated that the early universe was hotter and hence, more symmetrical than it is today. Scientists believe that when the universe passed through particular critical temperatures it radically changed and drastically reduced in symmetry. Most physicists believe we are living in a condensed or frozen phase of the universe. It is very different than it was in earlier times.

We continue to see localized phase transitions in the symmetry of the universe. For instance, when gases and dust coalesce to form new planets we understand that symmetry decreases. However, when new stars are formed, we see that the heat in some fashion increases the symmetry of the molecules and atoms in those stars.

The laws of the universe still function when something is hot or cold or when there is more mass or less mass, however, the way they function may vary.

When we look at the universe close up it doesn't appear very symmetrical. An example of that is when we look at the sky versus looking down at the earth under our feet. Things don't look at all the same. If we then move to another location, say far into outer space away from our galaxy, the blackness of the universe looks pretty symmetrical. Again, we call this rotational symmetry.

Now, what does this have to do with the earth and with the scriptures?

In Mormon 9:2 we find: "Behold, will ye believe in the day of your visitation—behold, when the Lord shall come, yea, even that great day when the **earth shall be rolled together as a scroll**, and **the elements shall melt with fervent heat**, yea, in that great day when ye shall be brought to stand before the Lamb of God—then will ye say that there is no God?"

In other scriptures we find similar thoughts:

> And he did expound all things, even from the beginning until the time that he should come in his glory—yea, even all things which should come upon the face of the earth, even until **the elements should melt with fervent heat,** and the **earth should be wrapt together as a scroll,** and the heavens and the earth should pass away. (3 Nephi 26:3; bold added)

> And there shall be silence in heaven for the space of half an hour; and immediately after shall **the curtain of heaven be unfolded, as a scroll is unfolded after it is rolled up,** and the face of the Lord shall be unveiled;
> And the saints that are upon the earth, who are alive, shall be quickened and be caught up to meet him.
> And they who have slept in their graves shall come forth, for their graves shall be opened; and they also shall be caught up to meet him in the midst of the pillar of heaven— (D&C 88:95–97; bold added)

And all the host of **heaven shall be dissolved**, and the **heavens shall be rolled together as a scroll** . . . For *it is* the day of the Lord's vengeance . . . (Isaiah 34:4,8)

> Say to them that are of a fearful heart, Be strong, fear not: behold, your God will come with vengeance, even God with a recompense; he will come and save you. . . .
> And the ransomed of the Lord shall return, and come to Zion with songs and everlasting joy upon their heads: they shall obtain joy and gladness, and sorrow and sighing shall flee away. (Isaiah 35:4, 10)

The first four scriptures cited refer to the earth and/or the heavens essentially being "rolled [or wrapt] together as a scroll."

Both Book of Mormon scriptures tell us that earth's elements will "melt with fervent heat" when the earth is rolled up as a scroll, while Isaiah 34:4 states "the hosts of heaven shall be dissolved." I submit that the fervent heat will vaporize those on the earth not "dissolve" the hosts of heaven. It may be that William Tyndale, when he translated the Bible into English, didn't have a word for "vaporize" in his day, so he used *dissolve.*

From a scientific perspective, improved symmetry will be obtained as the earth is heated, melts (dies), and all of the planet's complexity returns to its primordial, symmetrically-ordered state. Of course, the heat that it takes to make this happen will vaporize men and everything else, possibly the earth itself.

In terms of the heavens and earth being literally and scientifically rolled up like a scroll, physicists who study string theory suggest that matter in some dimensions, even the dimensions themselves, can be compacted (compactified), or "rolled up." If the earth were to be compacted and rolled up, it is likely that it would first have to be in a symmetric state. Hence, that is part of the reason for its being heated and melted at the end of the millennium.

Compactification is string theory's version of "symmetry-breaking." For example, a simple symmetrical shape such as a big, six-dimensional sphere, might shrivel spontaneously into a complicated, multidimensional labyrinth of twisted bridges and bifurcating tunnels.[133]

The Prophet Joseph Smith taught: "This earth will be rolled back into the immediate presence of God, and crowned with celestial glory."[134] Brigham Young also stated that, "When it is celestialized it will go back into the presence of God, where it was first framed."[135]

Since the earth will one day be moved back into God's presence, one way to get it there may be to heat it to its symmetrical state, then cause it to roll up, to shrivel, and become compacted. Is it possible that in this state quantum physics might apply (including the uncertainty principle); and going one step further, is it possible that the laws associated with other dimensions might also apply? If so, once the earth is in this rolled up, compacted state, it might then just pop into a location that is in the presence of God, be de-compacted and eventually be reorganized into its heavenly state, there to function as an abode for celestial beings.

Is this crazy or what? Is it possible that science can actually theorize certain means that God might use to wrap up the final act of His creation? Could earth be rolled up as a scroll and be more easily moved to a region near His celestial abode? Whether it happens this way or not, it seems certain that the heating and melting of the earth to bring it into a state of symmetry is a requirement before it can be moved back into the presence of the Lord.

In regard to the earth's being rolled up like a scroll and moving back into the presence of the Lord, the Doctrine and Covenants offers the following: "The end shall come, and the heaven and the earth shall be consumed and pass away, and there shall be a **new heaven** and a new earth. For all old things shall pass away, and all things shall become new, even the heaven and the earth, and all the fullness thereof, both men and beasts, the fowls of the air, and the fishes of the sea; and not one hair, neither mote, shall be lost, for it is the workmanship of mine hand" (D&C 29:23–25, bold added).

A "new heaven" is mentioned in this scripture. It is unlikely that the galaxy or the universe will pass away when the earth is renewed. More likely this description in the Doctrine and Covenants was given because the earth, when it is consumed and rolled up like a scroll, will be moved to a new place in the universe where, from its new vantage point, the heavens will appear new and different.

As a side note, this scripture is interesting as it shows that not only will men be resurrected to live on the new earth, but so will *beasts, birds,* and *fishes.* So if you have ever wondered about the resurrection of animals, here is a great scripture you can reference, as it states that *all* things shall become new including men and animals.

Now, as we return to our previous discussion, please consider this related question: Is this melting of the earth and rolling it up like a scroll going to take place at the Lord's Second Coming or at the end of the Millennium? In section 29 we find our answer: "And again, verily, verily, I say unto you that when the thousand years are ended, and men again begin to deny their God, then will I spare the earth but for a little season; And the end shall come" (D&C 29:22–23)

Prior to leaving this section, there is one last thought that I would like to share regarding *heat, symmetry* and our *relationship* to God.

In this section we have considered heat and symmetry as it pertains to the universe and even as it pertains to the earth at the end of its life.

I think that these concepts relate to man as well as the earth. When the earth was created it was born; then it fell (along with Adam and Eve) when it was moved from its primordial state. It was baptized during Noah's time; and finally, fire will melt its elements at the end of its life. This fire and melting will bring the earth into a more symmetric state so it can be brought back into the presence of the Lord.

Is the life of a man not similar to that of the earth? We fall when we are born and leave the presence of the Lord. As we reach the age of accountability we can be baptized; then, when we receive the Holy Ghost, we are refined with fire. This fire brings us into a more symmetric state with God. We achieve a sameness with him, which one day allows us, like the earth, to come back into His presence.

NOTES

1. "Theology toward a Hidden God," *Time*, April 8, 1966, http://www.time.com/magazine/article/0,9171,835309,00.html.
2. Dan Cray, "God vs. Science," *Time*, November 5, 2006, http://www.time.com/magazine/article/0,9171,1555132,00.html.
3. Ibid.
4. Joseph Smith, *History of The Church of Jesus Christ of Latter-day Saints*, 6:308.
5. Hyrum L. and Helen Mae Andrus, *They Knew the Prophet*, 95.
6. *Teachings of the Presidents of the Church—Joseph Smith* (Salt Lake City: The Church of Jesus Christ of Latter-day Saints, 2008), 42.
7. Matthew B. Brown, *The Gate of Heaven*, 26.
8. Brian Green, *The Fabric of the Cosmos*, 337–38.
9. Ibid., 14–15.
10. Ibid., 277.
11. *Astronomy*, Kalmbach Publishing, Jan. 2009, 12.
12. Bruce R. McConkie, *Mormon Doctrine*, 237.
13. Stephen G. Morgan, *Hidden Treasures of Knowledge*, 156–59.
14. Ibid., 156–59.
15. Ibid.
16. C. S. Lewis, *Mere Christianity*, 205–206.
17. *History of the Church*, 6:303–305, 308.
18. Lewis, *The Problem of Pain*, 34.
19. Ibid., 47.
20. Ibid., 34–47.

21. *Teachings of the Presidents of the Church—Joseph Smith*, 209.
22. Lewis, *The Problem of Pain*, 88.
23. Ibid., 89.
24. Ibid., 94.
25. Ibid., 95–97.
26. Ibid., 95–97.
27. Ibid., 101.
28. *Journal of Discourses*, 15:137.
29. Robert R. Caldwell, "Dark Energy," May 30, 2004, http://www.PhysicsWorld.com.
30. McConkie, *Mormon Doctrine*, 818–19.
31. Emil G. Hirsch et al, "Urim and Thummim," http://www.jewishencyclopedia.com.
32. Driscoll, James F, "Urim and Thummim," T*he Catholic Encyclopedia.* Vol. 15 (New York: Robert Appleton Company, 1912), <http://www.newadvent.org/cathen/15224a.htm>
33. To tap into current research regarding this primordial soup, I refer you to an article in the May 2006 issue of *Scientific American*, "The First Few Microseconds," by Michael Riordan and William A. Zajc, 34A.
34. McConkie, *Mormon Doctrine, 26–28.*
35. Michio Kaku, *Parallel Worlds*, 147–60.
36. Ibid., 160.
37. Richard Draper, *Opening the Seven Seals: The Visions of John the Revelator*, 247–48.
38. Bryson, *A Short History of Nearly Everything*, 145–46.
39. Kaku, *Parallel Worlds,* 177.
40. Bryson, *A Short History of Nearly Everything*, 145–46.
41. Hugh Nibley, *Temple and Cosmos*, xv.
42. Ibid., 15; bold added.
43. Draper, *Opening the Seven Seals*, 234.
44. Ibid., 236; bold added.
45. Bruce R. McConkie, *Doctrinal New Testament Commentary, vol. 3*, 588; bold added.
46. Brown, *The Gate of Heaven*, 73; bold added.
47. *Journal of Discourses*, 25:231.
48. McConkie, *Doctrinal New Testament Commentary*, 588.
49. Kaku, *Parallel Worlds*, 111.
50. For a more complete understanding of wormhole travel, refer to Brian Greene, *The Fabric of the Cosmos.*
51. Kaku, *Parallel Worlds*, 160.
52. Truman Madsen, *Joseph Smith the Prophet*, 103–104.

53. *History of the Church,* April 15, 1842, 4:597; bold added.
54. Greene, *The Fabric of the Cosmos,* 144–45; bold added.
55. Kaku, *Parallel Worlds,* 128.
56. Greene, *The Fabric of the Cosmos,* 178.
57. Kaku, *Parallel Worlds,* 130.
58. Julian Barbour, *The End of Time: The Next Revolution in Physics,* 14.
59. Greene, *The Fabric of the Cosmos,* 510.
60. Ibid., 335.
61. Joseph Smith, April 15, 1842, *History of the Church,* 4:597.
62. Barbour, *The End of Time,* 14.
63. See Kaku, *Parallel Worlds,* 132–33.
64. Brigham Young, *Journal of Discourses,* 14:231.
65. Rodney Turner, *This Eternal Earth,* 163.
66. Eric N. Skousen, *Earth: In the Beginning,* 327
67. Turner, *This Eternal Earth,* 165.
68. Hugh Nibley, *Enoch the Prophet,* 178.
69. Ibid., 73–77, 178–80.
70. Gerald L. Schroeder, *The Science of God,* 206.
71. Ibid., 206)
72. Parley Pratt, *Journal of Discourses,* 1:331.
73. Schroeder, *The Science of God,* 202.
74. Henry Eyring, *Reflections of a Scientist,* 53–62.
75. Galileo Galilei, *The Assayer.*
76. Eyring, *Reflections of a Scientist,* 53-62.
77. Ibid., 53–62.
78. C. Folsome, "Life: Origin and Evolution," *Scientific American* Special Publication, 1979.
79. *Scientific American* printed a follow-up article written by John Horgan in 1991.
80. Eyring, *Reflections of a Scientist,* 53–62.
81. Saint Augustine, *The Literal Meaning of Genesis,* translated and annotated by John Hammond Taylor, S.J., 1:41.
82. Schroeder, *The Science of God,* 88–89.
83. Ibid., 93.
84. Eyring, *Reflections of a Scientist,* 53–62.
85. Francis Collins, *The Language of God,* 3.
86. Collins, *The Language of God,* 141.
87. Eyring, *Reflections of a Scientist,* 53–62.
88. Lewis, *The Problem of Pain,* 68–71.
89. Collins, *The Language of God,* 58.
90. William Wordsworth, "Ode: Intimations of Immortality, from Recol-

lections of Early Childhood."

91. Hugh Nibley, *Nibley: On the Timely and Timeless*, 79.
92. *Nibley: On the Timely and Timeless*, 80.
93. Collins, *The Language of God*, 58.
94. *Nibley: on the Timely and Timeless*, 86.
95. Greene, *The Fabric of the Cosmos*, 45.
96. Ibid., 47.
97. *Nibley: On the Timely and the Timeless*, 82–83.
98. Ibid., 86.
99. Greene, *The Elegant Universe*, 114.
100. Parley P. Pratt, *Key to the Science of Theology: A Voice of Warning*, 47.
101. Bruce R. McConkie, *New Witnesses for the Articles of Faith*, 70.
102. Joseph Smith, April 15, 1842, *History of the Church*, 4:597.
103. *Teachings of the Presidents of the Church—Joseph Smith*, 211.
104. *The Words of Joseph Smith*, comp. Andrew F. Ehat and Lyndon W. Cook (Salt Lake City: Bookcraft, 1980), 62.
105. Ibid., 208.
106. Ibid., 60.
107. Robert Millet, *Studies in Scripture, Volume One: The Doctrine and Covenants* (Randall Book, 1984), 558.
108. John A. Widstoe, *Discourses of Brigham Young*, 576.
109. Daniel H. Ludlow, *Latter-day Prophets Speak*, 26.
110. Harold B. Lee, BYU Devotional, October 15, 1952.
111. Parley Pratt, *Key to the Science of Theology*, 80.
112. *History of the Church*, 6:52.
113. Joseph F. Smith, *Gospel Doctrine*, 455.
114. McConkie, *Mormon Doctrine*, 402.
115. Ludlow, *Latter-day Prophets Speak*, 35.
116. *Manuscript History of Brigham Young: 1846-47*, Historical Dept., The Church of Jesus Christ of Latter-day Saints, 528–31.
117. *Journal of Discourses*, 4:136.
118. Ibid., 3:230.
119. Ludlow, *Latter-day Prophets Speak*, 26.
120. Greene, *The Fabric of Space*, 386–88.
121. Ibid., 393.
122. *Journal of Discourses*, 9:317.
123. Joseph Fielding Smith, *Doctrines of Salvation*, comp. Bruce R. McConkie, 3 vols., 2:120.
124. Andrus, *They Knew the Prophet*, 61.
125. Brigham Young, *Journal of Discourses*, 14:231.
126. C. S. Lewis, *The Great Divorce*, 122.

127. Paul Davies, *Cosmic Jackpot*, 81.

128. *History of the Church*, 6:303–305, 308.

129. Kaku, *Parallel Worlds*, 240.

130. Ibid., 283.

131. Schroeder, *The Science of God*, 85.

132. *Scientific American*, Feb. 2008, 30.

133. Davies, *Cosmic Jackpot*, 167.

134. *Teachings of the Prophet,* comp. Joseph Fielding Smith, 181.

135. *Journal of Discourses*, 9:317.

CHAPTER 4

The Character of God: His Nature and Intelligence

With much trepidation, I will endeavor to provide some evidence from the scriptures and other sources as to God's character, nature, and intelligence.

For one of its definitions, the Merriam-Webster Online Dictionary describes the word *character* as follows: "Character: . . . the complex of mental and ethical traits marking and often individualizing a person."

What are the ethical (moral) and mental traits that individualize God?

Let's start with the mental traits. In chapter three, verse 18, of the Book of Abraham, the prophet Abraham is told something about all mankind that helps us understand God's intelligence and mental capacity. Speaking of all the spirits and beings in the universe, Abraham says: "[They] . . . have no beginning; they existed before, they shall have no end, they shall exist after, for they are gnolaum, or eternal" (Abraham 3:18).

Joseph Smith also taught: "The intelligence of spirits had no beginning neither will it have an end. . . . Intelligence is eternal and exists upon a self-existent principle. It is a spirit from age to age and there is no creation about it."[1]

In addition to the idea that our spirits or intelligences have enjoyed an infinite or eternal existence, at the beginning of verse 18 in Abraham chapter three, we read that the amount or quality of intelligence of these spirits varies—that there is always one more intelligent than another. Then in verse 19 Abraham teaches: "And the Lord said unto me: These two facts do exist, that there are two spirits, one being more intelligent than the other; there shall be another more intelligent than they; **I am the Lord thy God, I am more intelligent than [them] all**" (bold added).

The Lord goes on to say that when the priest of Elkenah had sought to sacrifice Abraham on the altar, He sent an angel to Abraham to deliver him. Then in verse 21 God talks about those angels and His relationship to them: "I dwell in the midst of them all [the angels]; I now, therefore, have come down unto thee to declare unto thee the works which my hands have made, **wherein my wisdom excelleth them all,** for I rule in the heavens above, and in the earth beneath, in all **wisdom** and **prudence,** over all the intelligences thine eyes have seen from the beginning" (bold added).

So, let's take a moment to dissect these verses and pull the meaning and truth out of them:

1. Verse 18 teaches that all spirits have existed and will forever exist.
2. Spirits/intelligences had no beginning and will have no end. That should be interesting because you and I are one of those spirits, as is God.
3. In verse 19 Abraham is told that the intelligence of these spirits differs widely and that God is the most intelligent of them all.
4. Then in the last quoted verse (21) God reveals the following: He lives with the angels, His wisdom is greater than all of them, and He rules over them and all things in wisdom and prudence.

A couple of words intrigued me as I read this last phrase. Even the word order is intriguing. First, He rules in *wisdom,* and second, in *prudence.* Let's take the word wisdom. In a dictionary that was written in Joseph Smith's time, Noah Webster's *American Dictionary of the English Language,* the word is linked to "wise" and provides the following definition: "Properly having knowledge; hence, having the power of discerning and judging correctly or of discriminating between what is true and what is false; between what is fit and proper, and what is improper."

These are certainly characteristics of the Lord. He rules his kingdom(s) in wisdom. He has all knowledge, knowing what it true and what is false, what is fit and proper.

The other key word in that scripture is *prudence.* Abraham was shown that God rules all his creations in wisdom and *prudence*. What does that mean? In the same 1828 dictionary, "prudence" yields this definition:

Wisdom applied to practice. Prudence implies caution in deliberating and consulting . . . Prudence differs from wisdom in this . . . prudence implies more caution and reserve than wisdom . . . A prudent person is 'Cautious; circumspect, practically wise; careful of the consequences.' "

What an interesting combination of adjectives *wisdom* and *prudence* are when used together. Wisdom means doing things right and prudence means being cautious and careful in exercising that wisdom. We should be forever grateful for a Heavenly Father who rules and judges in righteousness and does so *carefully* and *cautiously* with respect to what the short- and long-term consequences might be.

Perhaps I can provide an example of someone exercising wisdom with prudence. While on his mission, one of my sons had a senior companion who simply wouldn't work. Instead of getting out on the streets to talk with people about the restored gospel, he chose to stay inside playing video games most of the day. Then, worse yet, this missionary berated my son for wanting to work and made fun of him in front of other disobedient elders. Finally, after a month of this and getting nowhere, our son contacted the mission president about the situation. The president immediately transferred my son, but wasn't quite sure how to handle things or where to place the blame. Making matters even more complicated, the disobedient elder lied to the mission president, telling him that it was my son who was at fault. This elder then went on to do his best to spread those lies throughout the mission. Compounding the problem even more, one of the assistants to the mission president was from the same area as this elder and they were good friends having attended the same high school. This assistant apparently believed the lies. So the mission president was influenced by what he was told by my son's companion and by his assistant.

To make a long story short, because of this situation the mission president left my son as a junior companion for a long time, even though he was known by his fellow missionaries as a good, extremely hardworking missionary. A couple of months after this frustrating period, my son received a new companion who had also served with the same elder—and who had experienced the same thing but had not reported the problem to the mission president.

About the time all of this was happening, I became fed up with it. I was on my way out the door to talk to the stake president, a letter in hand to mail along the way. I was going to read that mission president the riot act for how he had handled things. In the letter I explained that I had dealt with sociopathic personalities in my personal life and in business, and warned him that this missionary certainly exhibited those characteristics, posing a danger to all the missionaries and possibly to the mission president himself.

Prior to leaving the house, I knelt in prayer and asked the Lord if I should send the letter and talk to the stake president. I immediately received the distinct feeling that I should just leave things alone. I obeyed the impression and didn't mail the letter or visit with the stake president. I did just what I had been told: nothing.

Our son was greatly blessed during the course of his mission, baptizing many in nearly every area in which he served. He worked hard and was happy. He loved serving the Lord in any capacity. This good son learned some hard lessons in humility and obedience, inasmuch as his three older brothers had, early on, been made senior companions and served as zone leaders and assistants to their mission presidents. Eventually my son became a senior companion and even served as a successful district and zone leader. I have since learned that the mission president came to know the truth about the missionary who had caused so many problems. The president worked hard to give that elder every opportunity to succeed and return home with honor.

Is it possible the Lord wanted this young man to have all the opportunities he could to successfully finish his mission? What might have happened if my letter to the mission president and my stake president visit had forced the issue and caused the disobedient missionary to be sent home before he had plenty of opportunity to change? His soul, not my son's, was in the balance.

Looking back, maybe this young man had strayed so far from the truth that he could no longer respond to the Holy Ghost's whisperings. Maybe he just needed another chance. This is somewhat reminiscent of Alma the younger when he and his friends were doing their best to destroy the church. As you may know, they too were miraculously given another chance to change and follow the Lord.

During my son's mission, I too learned some lessons about humility and submissiveness, about the importance of doing something the

Lord's way rather than my own. Here truly is an instance of where the Lord acted not only with wisdom, but also with prudence. Careful and slow to act, He considered the long term consequences of each of the lives involved. We should ever be grateful for a loving Father who rules in this fashion. I am sure that in each of our lives the Lord has repeatedly exercised cautious wisdom. Every one of us has been given countless chances to learn, improve, and repent . . . most likely, more chances than we realize or deserve. As I look back on my life, I am so grateful for a Heavenly Father who has been willing to work with me and cautiously guide me through life's lessons.

Mercy not vengeance seems to rule God's character. Even when angels have begged Him to allow them to unleash the forces of nature against the human race, He holds them back as long as possible. In the Book of Revelation, upon the opening of the sixth seal (which represents the time we live in), John states: "And after these things I saw four angels standing on the four corners of the earth, holding the four winds of the earth . . . And I saw another angel ascending from the east, having the seal of the living God: and he cried with a loud voice to the four angels, to whom it was given to hurt the earth and the sea, Saying, Hurt not the earth, neither the sea, nor the trees, till we have sealed the servants of our God . . ." (Revelation 7:1–3)

Reading farther down in that chapter, verse nine states that the multitude of those that were sealed was so great during this period that it could not be counted by man, a numberless throng that included people from all nations, kindreds, and tongues. So, it appears that God postpones the destruction of the wicked as long as He can so that he can gather His faithful and give the ungodly an opportunity to repent and come unto Him.

In similar fashion, during Enoch's time when angels were pleading with God to release the floodwaters and wipe out the human race, we witness a compassionate and long-suffering God, exercising wisdom with a layer of prudence over all:

> When angels beg God to get on with the work and wipe out the unworthy human race, he replies in a Hebrew Enoch fragment, "I have made and I remove, and I am long-suffering, and I rescue!" Further, "[Enoch] showed me the angels of punishment who are prepared to come and let loose all the powers of the waters . . . to bring judgment and destruction on all who dwell on the earth. And the Lord of Spir-

its gave commandment to the angels who were going forth, that they should not cause the waters to rise, but should hold them in check; for those angels were over the power of the waters."[2]

As one pauses to consider our God and His wonderful character, what is found? Do the following adjectives pertain to the Lord: merciful, honorable, faithful, true, virtuous, patient, long suffering, kind, loving, diligent, charitable, temperate, and thankful? What about these adjectives: judgmental, angry, and vengeful? Yes, these too have their place.

Suffice it to say, many traits are necessary character attributes of God. Let's list as many as we can, in no specific order.

• Wise	• Loving
• Prudent	• Caring
• Good	• Joyful
• Honorable	• Diligent
• Faithful	• Charitable
• True	• Temperate
• Virtuous	• Thankful
• Forgiving	• Passionate
• Patient	• Creative
• Long-suffering	• Sorrowful
• Merciful	• Judgmental
• Kind	• Angry
• Pitying	• Vengeful

I expect you can come up with some characteristics that I missed. At the same time, there are some you might take issue with. However, I do believe that God exercises a measure of wisdom and prudence before He does anything. Because of this, the traits of anger and vengeance are only used as a last resort, when there is no other option, no hope of change.

Here again, Hugh Nibley describes how kind and forgiving and loving God is by showing what He did for the terribly wicked people of Enoch's day:

> The ultimate vindication of God's goodness in Enoch is the final disposal of the issue. The fallen angels and their followers were to be cast into a special prison (cf. Moses 7:38) and kept in chains of dark-

ness, but only for a certain set period of time, after which they were to be given another chance to repent (cf. Moses 7:39) and then stand a fair trial. Repentance would receive forgiveness through the power of the atonement. . . . "For Christ also hath once suffered for sins, the just for the unjust . . . quickened by the Spirit: By which also he went and preached unto the spirits in prison; Which sometime were disobedient, when once the longsuffering of God waited in the days of Noah . . . " (1 Peter 3:18–20).[3]

God, in His kindness and mercy, created a spirit prison where the disobedient can go and continue to work out their salvation. The Atonement applies in mortality and continues to apply in the spirit world.

The Doctrine and Covenants is filled with scriptures describing God's and Christ's greatness of character. In particular, Section 133 offers a good view of Christ's personality: "And now the year of my redeemed is come; and they shall mention the **loving kindness** of their Lord, and all that he has bestowed upon them according to his **goodness**, and according to his loving kindness, forever and ever. In all their afflictions he was afflicted. And the angel of his presence saved them; and in his **love**, and in his **pity**, he redeemed them, and bore them, and carried them all the days of old" (D&C 133:52–53; bold added)

Here we see God giving us a glimpse into the future as He tells us that Christ's second coming is upon us: "And now the year of my redeemed is come . . ." At the same time, he briefly describes what his Beloved Son, our Savior, did for us: "In all their afflictions he was afflicted . . . in his love, and in his pity, he redeemed them, and bore them, and carried them." As one considers this, it is easy to see that Christ, through His goodness, kindness, pity, and love, has bestowed and will bestow upon us marvelous gifts. He suffered greatly for our sins. He redeemed us from death and sin. And, in all of our afflictions, he was afflicted and sent an angel(s) to save us and to carry us, as in all the days of old.

As we review the character traits listed earlier, it's difficult to pick one that Christ did not exhibit while fulfilling His divine earthly mission or will not exhibit as he fulfills his role as the God of heaven and earth, the great Jehovah. Even those of "anger" and "vengeance" are necessary Godly traits (see D&C 133:46–51).

The wonderful thing is that God's character embraces all of His traits in perfect proportion—all exercised prudently, with great wisdom. Never does God judge imperfectly. We are His passion; as His children,

He is willing to do almost anything to help us become more like Him. He knows that as we are obedient and become one with Him and His Son, we will experience a fullness of joy.

C. S. Lewis wrote the following about God's passion for us: "We are a Divine work . . . something that God is making, and therefore something with which He will not be satisfied until it has a certain character."

In this regard, Lewis goes on to say: "It is natural for us to wish that God had designed for us a less glorious and less arduous destiny; but then we are wishing not for more love but for less. . . . To ask that God's love should be content with us as we are is to ask that God should cease to be God: because He is what He is, His love must, in the nature of things, be impeded and repelled by certain stains in our present character, and because He already loves us, He must labor to make us loveable . . ."

And finally: "We are bidden to 'put on Christ,' to become like God. That is, whether we like it or not, God intends to give us what we need, not what we now think we want. . . . He gives us the happiness that there is. . . . To be God—to be like God and to share His goodness . . . these are the only . . . alternatives. If we will not learn to eat the only food that the universe [God] grows . . . then we must starve eternally."[4]

God broods over us. Because of us, He experiences much joy; also because of us, He suffers much. We are His children. Because of the love He has for us and His high hopes for us, He patiently submits to ongoing sorrow as we act contrary to His "good" will.

As part of the burden of the Atonement and Crucifixion, God and Christ continue to suffer! Their sorrow is truly that which only gods can endure. There are times when, as they lose a child to sin and transgression, their great hearts all but break. And, alternatively, there are times when they experience incalculable joy as a son or a daughter repents and returns to their safe fold.

Loving His children as he does, God's amazing plan and creation is for them, and includes all the angels, beings, spirits, and intelligences that follow him and accept His great plan. The Atonement is for us! He gave us His son so we could have the opportunity and make the effort to return to Him. In this finite existence, we can only capture a glimmer of His greatness. But as you can see from reading this book on science and scripture, there is a much to be learned about God.

The *Lectures on Faith* states: "Let us here observe, that after any portion of the human family are made acquainted with the important fact that there is a God, who has created and does uphold all things, the extent of their knowledge respecting his character and glory will depend upon their diligence and faithfulness in seeking after him."[5]

So do it! Seek after Him. Seek to know Him. Work at it! As you do so, you will become friends with Him—and your faith will grow. You will be better and blessed for doing it.

NOTES

1. *Teachings of the Presidents of the Church—Joseph Smith*, 210.
2. Nibley, *Enoch the Prophet*, 70.
3. Ibid., 84.
4. Lewis, *The Problem of Pain*, 34–47.
5. Joseph Smith, *Lectures on Faith* (Salt Lake City: Deseret Book, 1985).

CONCLUSION

"The test of a first-rate intelligence is the ability to hold two opposed ideas in the mind at the same time, and still retain the ability to function."[1]

The past has surely taught us that concepts found in science and religion can be diametrically opposed. The key is to not give up on one or the other. We have been blessed to live in a day when much truth in both religion and science has been and continues to be revealed. Each of us needs to be reminded that truth is the same, whatever its source. We should not choose to shoot the messenger because we don't like his looks or upbringing.

We could progress faster and be more at peace with ourselves and those around us if we would adopt the faith and attitude of scientist Henry Eyring:

> He had no difficulty with apparently contradictory ideas, so long as both were founded in truth. Most of us don't like trying to do that; we prefer to simplify the world. When two ideas seem opposed, we ultimately choose one or the other, even if both may be true. . . . Henry, though, was content with this kind of ambiguity . . . In his mind . . . science and religion weren't fundamentally at odds with one another; they just weren't fully reconciled yet. Henry reasoned that God knows all the answers and will ultimately reveal them and show how everything fits together. Rather than being irritated by the missing pieces of the puzzle and the apparent contradictions between science and religious doctrine, Henry was intrigued . . . the so-called contradictions were just paradoxes—truths seemingly in opposition but true nonetheless.[2]

219

One of the purposes of this book has been to demonstrate that science reveals the both grandeur and the complexity of God's handiwork, His marvelous creations.

The questions that should be asked by all of us are: How do we find God? Where is He? Who is He?

The Noah Webster Dictionary of 1828 provides us a description: "God: Any person or thing exalted . . . in estimation, or deified and honored as the chief good."

The question that immediately comes to mind is: What is it or who is it that mankind deifies, honors, and worships as the "chief good"? When each of us honestly reflects on this question, what responses are elicited? Does a person not worship that which he pursues with his heart, might, mind, and strength? This being the case, each of us needs to decide whether we worship the true God, our Eternal Father, the Creator and Overseer of the universe; or in reality, do we seek after and worship something else, things such as position, power, wealth, popularity, beauty, immorality, drugs, sports, television, the Internet, drugs, pornography, or some other versions of false and degenerate gods that corrupt and enslave us? Each of us ought to honestly be able to see that, to a lesser or greater degree, we worship those things we most desire.

C. S. Lewis instructs us in our need to choose God over our selfish appetites: "The 'fall of Adam and Eve' exists in all of us. From the moment one becomes aware of God, the terrible alternative of choosing God over self is opened to us. The sin of choosing self is committed daily by both youth and ignorant or sophisticated adults. Thus the 'fall' occurs daily in every individual's life. Selfishness is the first sin behind all others. You and I are either committing it, or about to commit it, or repenting of it."[3]

Every man has been blessed with a conscience, "the light of Christ." We are all aware that our conscience helps us to know the difference between right and wrong, good and evil. So, when a person's life gets out of kilter, when one deifies something other than God, it is a wonderful blessing to have a conscience. It is at these times that a person feels guilt, experiences pain, and is uncomfortable with his behavior. This feeling may not last long as most of us don't like feeling pain and do our best to avoid, resolve, or ignore it.

When we strive to be somewhat in tune with and obedient to our knowledge of what is right and good, the Spirit prompts us to shake off the shackles of this world. In those times, God Himself blesses us with a desire to draw nearer to Him, to put our lives in order, to put ourselves in His capable hands. Is it as simple as He says, "Draw near unto me and I will draw near unto you; seek me diligently and ye shall find me . . . ?"

God is amazing! He wants us to become like Him, be with Him, and have all that He has. We should not disappoint Him—or ourselves!

As a final testament to God, Christ, and their countless amazing creations, we should consider the words of the prophet Moroni:

> Behold, I will show unto you a God of miracles, even the God of Abraham, and the God of Isaac, and the God of Jacob; and it is that same God who created the heavens and the earth, and all things that in them are. . . . O all ye that have imagined up unto yourselves a god who can do no miracles. . . . Behold I say unto you . . . God has not ceased to be a God of miracles. Behold, are not the things that God hath wrought marvelous . . . ? Yea, and who can comprehend the marvelous works of God? Who shall say that it was not a miracle that by his word the heaven and the earth should be; and by the power of his word man was created of the dust of the earth; and by the power of his word have miracles been wrought? (Mormon 9:11,15-17)

Together, science, the scriptures, the prophets, and personal revelation testify of God, His great power, and His amazing creations. We are so very fortunate to live in this age when so much has been and continues to be revealed. May the Lord bless each of us as we continue to study and seek truth!

The following concluding counsel is from our beloved Prophet Joseph Smith:

> O ye Twelve! and all Saints! profit by this important Key—that in all your trials, troubles, temptations, afflictions, bonds, imprisonments and death, see to it, that you do not betray heaven; that you do not betray Jesus Christ; that you do not betray the brethren; that you do not betray the revelations of God, whether in the Bible, Book of Mormon, or Doctrine and Covenants, or any other that was or ever will be given and revealed unto man in this world or that which is to come.[4]

Indeed, let us not betray the revelations of God, from whatever source they may come.

NOTES

1. F. Scott Fitzgerald, *The Crack-Up*, 69.
2. Eyring, *Mormon Scientist,* 164–65.
3. Lewis, *The Problem of Pain*, 70.
4. *History of the Church*, 3:385; from a discourse given by Joseph Smith on July 2, 1839, in Montrose, Iowa; reported by Wilford Woodruff and Willard Richards.

APPENDIX

Light and Special Relativity

The brightness of light is a factor of the combined number of photons; and the color of light is a function of the amount of energy contained in each photon.

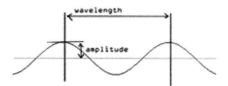

In the "wave" view of light, waves are a combination of changing electric and magnetic fields, which propagate through space, forming an electromagnetic wave. This wave has both amplitude, which specifies the brightness of the light, and wavelength, which determines the color of light.

It is most important to remember that light simultaneously exhibits properties of both waves and particles.

Light is eternal; it never diminishes. The light that comes from distant parts of the universe is 14 billion years old when it reaches us. Each particle of light we see is as strong and bright as it was moments after it left those ancient, remote galaxies.

The following is something that was presented earlier in the section on time; but, it is so pertinent to light that it needs to be repeated. It helps to understand why light doesn't age, diminish, or slow down.

Einstein's theory of special relativity of declares: "The combined speed of any object's motion through space and its motion through time is always precisely equal to the speed of light."

A simple calculation for this is $X + Y =$ Speed of Light, where X is the speed at which an object is traveling and Y is its motion through time. If you increase an object's speed, time will, in turn, slow down for that object. If you decrease the object's speed, time will speed up.

Having a sense for this speed-time relationship is critical. Einstein discovered that the motion of time and the motion of an object through space are inherently related. When you watch a jet take off and fly away from you, you are really seeing that a slight amount of the airliner's motion through time is being diverted to motion through space. Thus, the speed of the jet and its movement through time keep their combined total (speed of light) unchanged. Clocks on a jetliner actually run minutely slower than those on the ground for two reasons. One is because the motion of the clock on the jetliner relative to clocks on the ground and the other is because a clock on a jetliner it is farther away from the mass of the earth than clocks on the ground.

A relevant question is: Why does time stop for an object when it travels at the speed of light? It is because all of the object's motion through time has been taken over by its motion through space. To reiterate: *The combined speed of any object's motion through space and its motion through time is always precisely equal to the speed of light.*

Nothing ages that travels at the speed of light because all of the objects' motion through time has been assumed by its motion through space. So, even though we haven't discovered the fountain of youth that Ponce de Leon and so many of us have been seeking after, we can see that light has. It doesn't age, grow dim, or diminish in speed!

In his research, church scholar Hugh Nibley found ancient documents that, if authentic, indicate how very important this "never aging, never diminishing" light is to God. He never lets it go to waste. According to these documents, God has even assigned angels to go around and collect it. The idea of "waste not, want not" seems to be a heavenly dictum, not just an earthly one. "God's assistants . . . the faithful servants . . . rescue and preserve the light particles lest any be lost in space . . . It is like a tiny bit of God himself."[1]

Light doesn't diminish, neither does it slow down. The light, which we detect through the Hubble Telescope, is still traveling at the same speed it was the moment it was generated by the stars in that remote part of the universe. What's more, each particle still has the same amplitude (brightness) and wave length (color) that it had billions of years earlier.

One of the more special characteristics of light is that it is an "individual phenomenon." What do we mean by this? We mean that it always travels at the same speed towards or away from an individual, no matter the direction or speed that the person moves. The speed of light, Einstein declared, is 186,282 miles per second *relative to anything and everything.* In other words, you can't catch up to light no matter how fast rocket through space.

Well, this is certainly a simple statement . . . The problem is that it also seems crazy. If you run after a departing beam of light, common sense dictates that from your perspective the speed of departing light has to be less than 670 million miles per hour [186,282 miles per second]. If you run toward an approaching beam of light, common sense dictates that from your perspective the speed of the approaching light will be greater than 670 million miles per hour. Throughout his life, Einstein challenged common sense. In this case, he forcefully argued that regardless of how fast you move toward or away from a beam of light, you will always measure its speed to be 670 million miles per hour—not a bit faster, not a bit slower, no matter what.[2]

If you were to chase after light at incredible speeds, it still would move away from you at the same speed as if you were standing still—670 million miles per hour. If you were to fly at an incredibly high speed toward a beam of light coming directly at you, you would find that it is still coming at you at the same speed (before you began to fly towards it). The rate of speed of the light coming at you is still 670 million miles per hour.

To better understand this, consider the following example. Suppose that two spaceships, A and B, pass one another traveling at 93,141 miles per second, or half the speed of light. Now let's suppose that both spaceships are just passing Mars, with ship A heading directly toward planet earth and B going in the opposite direction, moving away from the earth. Suddenly someone on earth sends up a super-sized flare that both ships can see. Those on the earth rightly observe that light from the super flare will reach the spacecraft heading toward the earth in half the time it would if the craft were standing still relative to earth. They will also correctly observe that it takes twice as long for light to reach the spacecraft that is speeding away from them.

The spaceship passengers, however, observe a totally different thing. The light traveling towards both ships is seen as moving at exactly the speed of light, not faster or slower. It is as if the speed of the crafts moving away from or toward the light doesn't matter at all. To the observers on the spaceships, the light moving towards their individual crafts is exactly moving at 186,282 miles per second, the speed of light. No matter how fast they fly, away from or towards the light, they will not gain on it. Both sets of passengers and those on earth correctly observe that light is an individual phenomenon. For us, it always travels at the same speed no matter how fast we might be moving relative to it.

You may ask, "How can this be?" Einstein realized that experimenters who are moving relative to one another, such as those living on the earth and those aboard spaceships, will not find identical values for measurements of distances and durations. When moving relative to one another, their perceptions of space and time are different.

We conclude that **space and time is in the eye of the beholder**. Each of us carries our own clock, our own monitor of the passage of time. Each clock is equally precise, yet when we move relative to one another, these clocks do not agree. They fall out of synchronization; they measure different amounts of elapsed time between two chosen events. The same is true for distance. Each of us carries our own yardstick, our own monitor of distance in space. Each yardstick is equally precise, yet when we move relative to one another, these yardsticks do not agree; they measure different distances between the locations of two specified events . . . [Einstein] was able to show precisely how one person's measurements of distances and durations must differ from those of another in order to ensure that each measures an identical value for the speed of light.[3]

If you measure the length of an airplane sitting on the runway, it will be one length. When you then observe the airplane speeding past you at a high speed, you will find the length of the airplane to be shorter than when on the runway. Of course, to the airplane's pilot it will not have changed at all; it will appear to be the same length as when stationary.

The same is true for time. You will find that an airplane passenger's clock is running slower than your own. However, he will think his clock is correct and that yours is running fast.

Somehow, space and time adjust themselves perfectly for each individual, regardless of how fast or slow observers are traveling. That is, their individual observations of light's speed yield the same result. Another way of saying this is that light is perfectly tailored to fit each individual. We can't do anything to change the way light interacts with us.

The Uncertainty Principle

The following is a reiteration of the Uncertainty Principle, which may be a vital concept to understand if one is to gain a more correct knowledge of God.

Basic to quantum theory is the idea that there exists a probability that all possible events *might* occur, no matter how wild or crazy they might be. You should consider the last sentence again, because it is an important aspect of the foundation for modern physics.

Niels Bohr, one of the all-time giants of physics, was instrumental in defining quantum mechanics. Bohr championed the following notion: *Before one measures an electron's position, there is no sense in even asking where it is.* An electron does not have a definite position. There is a great likelihood that the electron, when properly examined, will be found here, there or anywhere, or even everywhere. The electron simply doesn't have a definite location until a measurement is done. *The act of measuring the electron somehow helps create our reality.* Until the electron is viewed or measured, it is here, there, and possibly everywhere at the same time. Our definition of the reality of the location of the electron does not occur until the electron is *measured or viewed.*

In regards to this uncertainty principle, Werner Heisenberg, in 1927, postulated the following: "A particle, according to quantum theory, cannot have a definite position and a definite velocity; a particle cannot have a definite spin (clockwise or counterclockwise) about more than one axis; a particle cannot simultaneously have definite attributes for things that lie on opposite sides of the uncertainty divide." In effect, what Heisenberg is saying is that particles hover in quantum limbo, in a fuzzy, probabilistic mixture of all possibilities; and only when a particle is measured is a definite outcome selected from an infinitely many.

If this mystical capability didn't exist at the quantum level, our world as we know it would collapse. For instance, if atoms obeyed Newton's laws, they would disintegrate whenever they bumped into one another. What keeps two atoms locked in a stable molecular state is the reality that electrons can be in many places at the same time. Electrons form "electron clouds," which bind atoms together—and which then act like force fields to protect atom's nucleuses, keeping them from bumping into one another. Hence, the reason molecules are stable and the reason the universe doesn't disintegrate, is because electrons can exist simultaneously in many places.

Becoming One with God, Becoming Like God

Since the universe is expanding and galaxies are rushing away from each other, does it appear that there constantly exists abundant room for the creation of more galaxies and clusters of galaxies? The answer is an obvious "yes." If this is true, then there must be room in the universe for us, under God's gentle and generous tutelage, to one day create our own kingdoms as we become God's ourselves.

Do we know of any mortal beings who have become exalted beings like God and Christ? In D&C 132: 37 it states: "Abraham . . . Isaac . . . and Jacob did none other things than that which they were commanded; and because they did none other things than that which they were commanded, they have entered into their exaltation, according to the promises, and sit upon thrones, and are not angels but are gods."

Are Abraham, Isaac and Jacob now acting as gods over their own galaxies or universes? Physics says that it is possible. This book's section on parallel universes delves more deeply into this subject.

Doctrine and Covenants 84:36–39 records this wonderful promise from the Lord: "For he that receiveth my servants receiveth me; And he that receiveth me receiveth my Father; And he that receiveth my Father receiveth my Father's kingdom; therefore all that my Father hath shall be given unto him. And this is according to the oath and covenant which belongeth to the priesthood."

A similar pledge from our Savior is found in Doctrine and Covenants 93:20: "If you keep my commandments you shall receive of his fullness, and be glorified in me as I am in the Father."

To paraphrase, if we keep God's commandments, we shall receive all that He has! We will be glorified in Christ as He is in the Father.

As we here consider a few of the things God and Christ have done, it is remarkable and wonderful to consider that we are simply asked to bend our will to theirs, to be obedient, and, in turn, they are willing to share with us all they have.

So, who is God?

1. He directed the creation of the Heavens and all kingdoms, large and small, including our own earth.
2. He is the law by which all kingdoms are governed.
3. He created our physical bodies.
4. He offered His Beloved, only begotten Son as a sacrifice for each of us.

And who is Christ?

1. He is the person by whom God made the Heavens and the earth.
2. He administers the law; following our resurrection, He will serve as our Judge.
3. In the Grand Council, He agreed to God's plan and willingly carried it out, offering Himself as a sacrifice for each of us.
4. In mortality He was born in the most humble of circumstances and lived a humble life.
5. He set the example for each of us.
6. He suffered horribly in Gethsemane and on Calvary—bled and died for each of us so that we could be forgiven of our sins.
7. He was resurrected for us and all creatures. (For a reference about the resurrection of creatures, see 1 Corinthians 15:34–40.) Christ was the first fruits of the dead. We will all be resurrected because of Him.

Let's take a moment to think about Christ and His life. Before he was crucified, He, in the presence of His Apostles, offered a wonderful prayer, often called the Great Intercessory Prayer or High Priestly Prayer found in John 17:5, 6, 9, 11, 14, 15, 17, 20–23:

And now, O Father, glorify thou me with thine own self with the glory which I had with the before the world was. I have manifested thy name unto the men which thou gavest me out of the world . . . I pray for them: I pray not for the world, but for them which thou has given me; for they are thine. . . . Holy Father, keep through thine own name those whom thou has given me, that they may be one, as we are one. I have given them thy word; and the world hath hated them, because they are not of the world, even as I am not of the world. I pray not that thou shouldest take them out of the world, but that thou shouldest keep them from the world. Sanctify them through thy truth. . . . **Neither pray I for these alone, but for them also which shall believe on me through their word; That they all may be one; as thou, Father, art in me, and I in thee, that they also may be one in us:** that the world may believe that thou hast sent me. And the glory which thou gavest me I have given them; that they may be one, even as we are one: I in them, and thou in me, that they may be made perfect in one. . . . (bold added)

Clearly, Christ and God want us to become one with them. As we learn to obey and become one with them, will we not have we become like them?

The enlightened author C. S. Lewis affirmed this truth when he said, "We are bidden to 'put on Christ', to become like God."[4]

Most of us don't make it easy. Each of us wants a life on our terms, of our own choosing, usually one of peace, happiness and ease. Even so, "Whether we like it or not, God intends to give us what we need, not what we now think we want."[5] So, instead of a life that is just of our choosing, we get trials, tribulations, hard work, failures, and lots of "tough" love, all of which helps us to improve and become like Him and one with Him.

Renaissance

We live in a remarkable age of enlightenment. From the time of Noah until now, there has never been more truth and knowledge available to mankind. However, not too long ago, there was a dark, thousand year period when it was pretty awful to live on planet earth. These bleak, dark centuries followed shortly on the heels of the Savior's life; a time we commonly refer to as the Dark Ages. About 150 years following Christ's birth, the world was plunged into spiritual and intellectual darkness, the like of which was never seen before and hopefully will never be seen again. It was a millennium of famine, cruelty, and intellectual and spiritual darkness.

Prior to the Dark Ages, many ancient prophets were privileged to see and prophesy about our day. Among these greats was Ezekiel, who was carried away captive by the Babylonian King Nebuchadnezzar. Ezekiel was also somewhat contemporary with other great prophets such as Lehi, Nephi, Daniel, and Jeremiah.

One of Ezekiel's most notable prophesies was that one day the stick of Judah (Bible) and the stick of Ephraim (the Book of Mormon) would be joined together (Ezekiel 37:16–17). He saw in vision the exterior and interior of a great temple that would one day be built, the restoration of Israel in our day, and much about the glory of the millennial reign of the Lord. He even witnessed the Resurrection. As Ezekiel and other prophets peered into the future, it must have been difficult for them to fathom our modern world of science and technology.

The prophet Isaiah saw even more, going so far to explain as best he could modern day conveyances such as trains and airplanes: "and, behold, they shall come with speed swiftly; None shall be weary nor stumble among them . . . and their horses' hoofs shall be counted like flint, and their wheels like a whirlwind: Their roaring shall be like a lion" (Isaiah 5:26–29, also 2 Nephi 15:26–29)

Another prophet, John the Beloved (John the Revelator), from Christ's time, also saw in vision much of our day. In the Book of Revelation, John recorded many of our contemporary implements of war. In chapter 9 verses 7 and 10 he describes what could be jet aircraft or helicopters: "And the shapes of the locusts were like unto horses prepared unto battle . . . and their faces were as the faces of men. And they had breastplates . . . of iron; and the sound of their wings was as the sound of chariots of many horses running to battle. And they had tails like unto scorpions, and there were stings in their tails."

Then in the same chapter verses 17 and 19, a description appears of what looks to be tanks: "And thus I saw the horses in the vision, and them that sat on them, having breastplates of fire, and of jacinth, and brimstone: and the heads of the horses were as the heads of lions; and out of their mouths issued fire and smoke and brimstone. . . . For their power is in their mouth, and in their tails: for their tails were like unto serpents, and . . . with them they do hurt."

In John's marvelous Book of Revelation, he saw the entire history of the earth, past and future. Seven seals are opened in the course of his vision, each of which depicts different thousand-year periods. Tellingly, John saw that only Christ was given the power to open each of the seven seals. The first of those seals deals with the time when the prophet Enoch lived, another when Abraham lived, yet another when Christ Himself lived, and so on. The sixth seal, opened by Christ, represents the time period in which we live. The opening of this seal likely occurred around AD 1100.

Now, a lot has happened in the past thousand years. We have witnessed a remarkable enlightening of mankind. The dark ages drew to a close and a reawakening, a renaissance, took hold. Huge advancements have been made in art, literature, music, religion, and science. And the tribe of Judah was even restored to its homeland.

This last dispensation has seen courageous seen reformers such as Martin Luther, John Calvin, John Wycliff, and William Tyndale fight for truth and religious freedom. Joseph Smith became even more than a reformer; he was a restorer, a revelator, a modern-day prophet. Joseph Smith and many of the reformers gave their lives for the work to which they were each ordained. Most of the freedoms we enjoy today were won through the sacrifices of these great men. We even owe much of the English language to one of these reformers, William Tyndale, the author of about 80 percent of the King James Bible. Nearly all literacy in England came about through the in-home study of his translation of the scriptures. The reformers gave everything they had, including their lives, to bring forth the truth and to prepare for and accomplish the restoration.

Remarkable scientific advancements took place during the Renaissance:

- Nicolaus Copernicus ultimately convinced the world that the earth and its companion planets rotate around the sun.
- Johannes Kepler discovered that the planets move in elliptical orbits around the sun.
- Galileo Galilei, founder of theoretical and experimental mechanics, discovered, among other things, the moons of Jupiter. He also learned a great deal about gravity discovering that objects of different sizes fall to the earth at the same speed, and that the speed of falling objects increases at a constant rate.
- Isaac Newton almost single-handedly discovered the law of gravity, created optics, and laid the groundwork for mechanics and calculus.
- Leonhard Euler, perhaps the most prolific mathematician of all

time, was responsible for large parts of the application of calculus to mathematical physics.

- Joseph-Luis Lagrange worked with sound waves and helped create a comprehensive, successful theory for acoustics. He also capitalized on work done by Euler, discovering the principle of conservation of energy, which recognizes two forms of energy, potential and kinetic. Potential energy is the energy an object has by virtue of its position (a body on top of a hill has more potential energy than one down in a valley), while kinetic energy is the energy a body has by virtue of its speed (it is more difficult to slow down a body that has rolled off a cliff than to stop one that is slowly rolling down a hill). During motion, and in the absence of friction, these two forms of energy can be converted into each other.

- Albert Einstein gave us the laws that governed physics in the twentieth century: special and general relativity. From that, the power of the atom was unleashed, black holes were discovered, parallel universes were hypothesized, the ever-expanding universe was discovered, and much, much more.

- Niels Bohr gave us many of the postulates that govern quantum theory.

These and many, many other inspired men and women revealed a vast and astonishing foundation for today's technological advancements. Because of their efforts, we enjoy the benefits of telescopes, trains, radios, television, electronics, x-ray machines, atomic power, automobiles, telephones, radar, airplanes, jet planes, rockets, digital watches, computers, vacuum cleaners, washing machines, microwave ovens, cellular telephones, suspension bridges, and communications satellites. We also suffer the terrible consequences of inventions such as tanks, cruise missiles, machine guns, nuclear warheads, pollution, and even global warming.

Why do we live in a world of such remarkable and sometimes dreadful discovery and understanding? I believe it is because we live in the fullness of times, a time when truth and priesthood have been restored to the earth, a time when God is sending the restored knowledge of the gospel to all on the earth. It is also a time when God is preparing the earth and its people for the Millennium, when Christ will return to personally rule and reign.

NOTES

1. *Nibley: On the Timely and Timeless,* 86.
2. Greene, *The Fabric of the Cosmos,* 45.
3. Ibid., 47; bold added.
4. Lewis, *The Problem of Pain,* 46.
5. Ibid., 46–47.

BIBLIOGRAPHY

Andrus, Hyrum L. and Helen Mae. *They Knew the Prophet*. Salt Lake City: Bookcraft, 1974.

Barbour, Julian. *The End of Time: The Next Revolution in Physics*. New York: Oxford University Press, 1999.

Brown, Matthew B. *The Gate of Heaven*. American Fork, Utah: Covenant Communications, Inc., 1999.

Bryson, Bill. *A Short History of Nearly Everything*. New York: Broadway Books, 2003.

Collins, Francis S. *The Language of God*. New York: Free Press, A Division of Simon & Schuster, Inc., 2007.

Davies, Paul. *Cosmic Jackpot*. New York: Houghton Mifflin Company, 2007.

Draper, Richard D. *Opening the Seven Seals: The Visions of John The Revelator*. Salt Lake City: Deseret Book Company, 1991.

Eyring, Henry. *Reflections of a Scientist*. Salt Lake City: Deseret Book Company, 1983.

Eyring, Henry J. *Mormon Scientist: The Life and Faith of Henry Eyring*. Salt Lake City: Deseret Book Company, 2007.

Fitzgerald, F. Scott. *The Crack-Up*. New York: New Directions Publishing, 1993.

Greene, Brian. *The Elegant Universe*. New York: Vintage Books, 2000.

Greene, Brian. *The Fabric of the Cosmos.* New York: Vintage Books, 2005.

Hawking, Stephen. *A Brief History of Time.* New York: Bantam Books, 1988.

Journal of Discourses. 26 vols. London: Latter-day Saints' Book Depot, 1854–86.

Kaku, Michio. *Parallel Worlds.* New York, Auckland: Doubleday, 2005.

Lewis, C. S. *Mere Christianity.* New York: HarperCollins, 2001.

———. *The Great Divorce.* New York: Collier Books, McMillan Publishing Company, 1946.

———. *The Problem of Pain.* New York: HarperCollins, 2001.

Ludlow, Daniel H. *Latter-Day Prophets Speak.* Salt Lake City: Bookcraft, 1967.

McConkie, Bruce R. *Doctrinal New Testament Commentary, Volume III.* Salt lake City: Bookcraft, 1973.

McConkie, Bruce R. *Mormon Doctrine.* Salt Lake City: Bookcraft, 1966.

Morgan, Stephen G. *Hidden Treasures of Knowledge.* Salt Lake City: Deseret Book Company, 2006.

Nibley, Hugh. *Enoch the Prophet.* Salt Lake City: Deseret Book Company, 1989.

———. *Nibley: On the Timely and the Timeless.* Provo, Utah: Religious Studies Center, 2004.

———. *Temple and Cosmos.* Salt Lake City: Deseret Book Company, 1992.

Pratt, David. *The Impossible Takes Longer.* New York: Walker and Company, 2007.

Pratt, Parley P. *Key to the Science of Theology: A Voice of Warning.* Salt Lake City: Deseret Book Company, 1978.

Schroeder, Gerald. *The Science of God.* New York: Broadway Books, 1998.

Skousen, Eric N. *Earth: In the Beginning.* Orem, Utah: Verity Publishing, 2006.

Joseph Smith. *History of The Church of Jesus Christ of Latter-day Saints.* Edited by B. H. Roberts. 2d ed. rev., 7 vols. Salt lake City: Deseret Book Company, 1932–51.

Joseph Smith. *Lectures on Faith.* American Fork, UT: Covenant Communications, Inc., 2000.

Stewart, Ian. *Does God Play Dice?* Malden, MA: Blackwell Publishing, 2004.

Teachings of the Presidents of the Church—Joseph Smith. Salt Lake City: The Church of Jesus Christ of Latter-day Saints, 2007.

Teachings of the Prophet Joseph Smith. Compiled by Joseph Fielding Smith. Salt lake City: Deseret Book Company, 1969.

The Words of Joseph Smith. Compiled by Andrew F. Ehat and Lyndon W. Cook. Salt Lake City: Bookcraft, 1980.

Turner, Rodney. *This Eternal Earth.* Orem, Utah: Granite Publishing and Distribution, L.L.C., 2000.

Widtsoe, John A. *Evidences and Reconciliations.* Arranged by G. Homer Durham. Salt Lake City: Bookcraft, 1987.

Widtsoe, John A. *Joseph Smith as a Scientist.* The General Board Young Men's Mutual Improvement Association. Salt Lake City, Utah, 1908, and published by Eborn Books, 1990.

About the Author

Dan graduated from the University of Utah with a master of science degree in business and from Brigham Young University with a bachelor of science degree in sociology.

From July 1997 until November 2006 he was president and owner of iTera, Inc., an international software development company. iTera focused on the development of software solutions for high availability and disaster recovery. A large number of iTera's customers are Fortune 500 and Fortune 1000 companies. The following businesses are examples of iTera's clientele: Target, Electrolux, Wal-Mart, SYSCO Foods, Intermountain Health Care, Sinclair Oil, Time Warner, Harley Davidson, Polaris, Newsweek, Swift Transportation, The Church of Jesus Christ of Latter-day Saints' Distribution Center, Comcast Cable, and more.

Currently, Dan is the CEO and owner of iSYS Global Solutions, a software developer that is working to improve the power of video for healthcare, education, entertainment, and business in general.

Dan served a full-time mission in Argentina for The Church of Jesus Christ of Latter-day Saints. He has had many callings since then that include elders quorum president, high priests group leader, counselor in a bishopric, Sunday School teacher, Sunday School president, Young Men advisor, ward mission leader, and high priests group instructor. He also taught high school seminary at Woods Cross High School. As of this writing, Dan and his wife, Janine, are currently serving as Sunday School teachers in the Fruit Heights Fifth Ward, and they work as ordinance workers in the Bountiful Temple.

He and his wife are the parents of five children and nine grandchildren.